Zoot Suit

Zoot Suit

THE ENIGMATIC CAREER
OF AN EXTREME STYLE

KATHY PEISS

PENN

UNIVERSITY OF PENNSYLVANIA PRESS

PHILADELPHIA

Published by
University of Pennsylvania Press
Philadelphia, Pennsylvania 19104-4112
www.upenn.edu/pennpress

Printed in the United States of America
on acid-free paper

1 3 5 7 9 10 8 6 4 2

Library of Congress Cataloging-in-Publication Data

Peiss, Kathy.
Zoot suit : the enigmatic career of an extreme style / Kathy Peiss.
p.   cm.
Includes bibliographical references and index.
ISBN: 978-0-8122-4337-6 (hardcover : alk. paper)
1. Clothing and dress—Social aspects—United States.   2. Fashion—United
States—History—20th century.   3. Minority youth—United States—Social life
and customs—20th century.   I. Title.
GT525 .P45   2011
391'.10973—dc22   2011010284

In Memory of Susan Porter Benson

As soon as this man caught sight of her, he began to look himself over. Starting at the bottom with his pointed shoes, he began to look up, lifting his peg-top pants the higher to see fully his bright socks. His coat, long and wide and leaf-green, he opened like doors to see his high-up tawny pants, and his pants he smoothed downward from the points of his collar, and he wore a luminous baby-pink satin shirt. At the end, he reached gently above his wide platter-shaped round hat, the color of a plum, and one finger touched at the feather, emerald green, blowing in the spring winds.

    EUDORA WELTY, "LIVVIE IS BACK," 1942

We were unable to find any one thing that started this rage or where it originated.

    FRANK WALTON, *THREAD OF VICTORY*, 1945

Perhaps the zoot suit conceals profound political meaning, perhaps the symmetrical frenzy of the Lindy Hop conceals clues to great potential power—if only Negro leaders would solve this riddle.

    RALPH ELLISON, *NEGRO QUARTERLY*, 1943

A key chain six times too long is just long enough to hold NO keys.

    LANGSTON HUGHES, *CHICAGO DEFENDER*, 1943

It is a symptom of profound weakness in our American civilization.

    AGNES E. MEYER, *WASHINGTON POST*, 1943

ZOOT (adj.): exaggerated.
ZOOT SUIT (n.): the ultimate in clothes. The only totally and truly American civilian suit.

    CAB CALLOWAY, *THE HEPSTER'S DICTIONARY*, 1944

CONTENTS

INTRODUCTION

I n June 1943, in the midst of World War II, the city of Los Angeles erupted in violence. White sailors and soldiers, egged on by Anglo civilians, stopped streetcars and invaded movie theaters in search of young Mexican American men—known as *pachucos*—beating them, tearing their jackets, and stripping them of their trousers. With newspapers and radio adding fuel to the fire, the mayhem continued for more than a week. As some Mexican American youths fought back, the navy finally put the city off limits for shore leave, and the police appeared in force—arresting these young people as troublemakers, delinquents, and rioters. No one was killed, but more than a hundred individuals landed in the hospital with serious injuries. When the riot ended, investigators and journalists spun out numerous explanations for what had occurred. Many Anglos asserted that Hispanic youth were inherently violent and criminal, while liberal voices and the African American press charged racial discrimination, magnified by wartime tensions over inadequate housing, the lack of jobs, and segregated recreational facilities. Some saw the influence of Communism guiding the riot, and others perceived the frightening presence of a fascist Fifth Column.

In the weeks and months after the Los Angeles riot, racial conflict and urban conflagration swept across the American home front, in such places as Beaumont, Texas, New York City, and Detroit, leaving death, destruction, and heightened enmity in their wake. Only in Los Angeles, however, did a style of dress become the focal point of unrest or figure prominently in the response. Most participants and observers did not refer to it as a race riot, and even fewer saw it as servicemen's vigilantism. Rather, the unrest became enshrined as the "zoot suit riot," perhaps the only time in American history that fashion was believed to be the cause of widespread civil unrest.

"Zoot," says Cab Calloway's *Hepster's Dictionary*, means something done or worn in an exaggerated style: the long killer-diller coat with a drape shape and wide shoulders; pants with reet-pleats, billowing out at the knees, tightly tapered and pegged at the ankles; a porkpie or wide-brimmed hat; pointed or thick-soled shoes; and a long, dangling key-chain. This was a striking urban look of the 1940s—a street style created by African Americans that extended conventional menswear to the point of caricature. The zoot suit was associated with racial and ethnic minorities and working-class youth, celebrated in the world of jitterbug, jive, and swing, and condemned by government authorities seeking to conserve precious textiles for the war effort. It was a style that sparked the imagination, whether as an object of fear or admiration. Where had it come from? What did it mean? Why did it evoke such visceral reactions? In the wake of the riot, journalists, social workers, psychiatrists, and police officers scrambled to comprehend the phenomenon, trying to fix its meaning within recognizable frameworks of social science, psychology, and common sense.

Despite these efforts, the zoot suit, and the circumstances in which it was worn, had a bewildering strangeness that no one could quite explain. Frank Walton, who directed the government's wartime effort to conserve textiles and clothing, simply shook his head: "Many attempts have been made to analyze the idea and to see just what caused it and what was behind it but so far there is no good answer." Months before the Los Angeles riot, Ralph Ellison pointed to the zoot suit as one of many "myths and symbols which abound among the Negro masses" and offered clues to the state of black America, a puzzle the political class needed to decipher. Living in Los Angeles during the war, writer Octavio Paz pondered the style of Mexican American youth in the United States, whose "whole being is sheer negative impulse, a tangle of contradictions, an enigma. Even his very name is enigmatic: *pachuco*, a word of uncertain derivation, saying nothing and saying everything."[1]

Over the years, the extreme style of the zoot suit has continued to resonate. It inspired the "swing youth" in 1940s Europe, attracted to the unusual dress, jazz music, and jitterbug dancing associated with American popular culture; French *zazous* wore elements of the style in defiance of the German Occupation. After the war, the zoot suit became a hallmark of black South African youths known as *tsotsis*, who integrated it into their gang and street life. Young men in Russia called *stiliagi* adopted the style to distance themselves from the psychological and sartorial regimentation of the Soviet Union. Counterparts emerged throughout the Eastern bloc, from Hungarian *jampec* to the Polish *bikiniarze* or "bikini boys." In the 1960s and 1970s, the zoot suit became a powerful touchstone of Chicano politics and culture. Luis Valdez's 1978 play *Zoot Suit*, made into a film in 1981, revived the popular Mexican American youth style and recalled the wartime incident for a wider public and new generations. Inviting us to "put on a zoot suit and play the myth," Valdez exalted the *pachuco* as a legendary hero who stood against white Americans' prejudice and discriminatory practices.[2]

Since the mid-1980s, the zoot suit has also captivated scholars of American ethnicity and race. African American historians place zoot suiters within a longstanding tradition of black style and performance, but also consider them in relation to the resurgent civil rights activism of the war years.[3] An even greater number of books, articles, and dissertations have focused on Mexican American youth culture and civil unrest in wartime Los Angeles: They document the lives of *pachucos* and *pachucas*; explore gender, family, and community; trace patterns of discriminatory employment, schooling, and policing; and rediscover a nascent political movement. The zoot suit riot is now understood as a formative event in Mexican American history.[4] Whatever the specific emphases of these studies, they share an intellectual framework that attributes to style, dress, and gesture significant political behavior by those who had little formal power or ability to represent themselves through speech or texts. In this view, style offers the powerless a potent means to communicate resistance to or alienation from the dominant social order. Scholars thus see the zoot suit as an early and particularly effective form of such "style warfare," challenging the dominant social order to such an extent that it sparked a repressive and violent response.

This book also focuses on the zoot suit, but with a different aim in mind. It takes as its starting point the enduring interest in an odd style of clothing created not by social elites and fashion designers but primarily by poor black youths and marginal tailors. It explores the proliferation of meanings and values attached to this style, and the social, cultural, and political processes that generated them. It does so to challenge and contest the mode of cultural understanding that reflexively reads the aesthetic as politics by other means. This is not to say that style has nothing to do with struggles for power. There have been many moments in history when dress did, in fact, clearly signal a political position—the Phrygian cap of liberty in the French Revolution, the bloomer costume of nineteenth-century feminists, the dashiki in the Black Power movement of the 1960s. Unlike these instances, the zoot suit represented a more polyvalent style to those who wore it and those who observed it. This study does not call for a return to an idea of culture as a discrete realm but is rather an effort to examine more closely the circumstances in which a cultural style may or may not be in fact political. It seeks to put the political in its place—not outside culture but occupying less of the cultural domain than contemporary scholarship bestows. In this way, we might begin to use more precisely defined concepts of politics, resistance, subculture, and identity, and trace more rigorously the meaning of style.[5]

*   *   *

Going back to the early twentieth century, social investigators and academics have been interested in the culture and style of disadvantaged youth in an urban, industrial environment. The Chicago School of sociology led the way, with such studies as Frederick Thrasher's *The Gang*, which examined young men's petty criminality in relation to neighborhood identity and peer solidarity, and Harvey Zorbaugh's *The Gold*

Coast and the Slum, which followed Filipinos as "marginal men" who sought compensatory pleasures by paying women to dance with them. Questions about the socialization of youth into appropriate adult roles became more pressing as the motion pictures and other forms of mass culture depicted fantasy worlds of luxury, sexuality, crime, and consumption. National mobilization during World War II only heightened concerns over juvenile delinquency, even as the fads and foibles of the young were a subject of endless speculation.[6]

By mid-century social scientists had delineated the concept of subculture to describe distinctive social worlds within the overall society, with a particular interest in subsets of youth within and among specific racial, ethnic, and economic groups. Emerging at the same time that the concept of mass culture had become commonplace, the term *subculture* conveyed a sense of marginality and deviance from a normative, cohesive culture, even as it explained the cultural rituals, beliefs, and styles that created particular group identities and affiliations.[7] Indeed, the experts' response to the zoot suit after the 1943 riot helped forge the view that certain styles, tastes, and cultural practices might constitute a subculture outside of or even in opposition to the mainstream.

By the 1960s, some students of subcultures had begun to turn the earlier focus on deviance and alienation on its head. Influenced by the expansion of postwar youth cultures and the rise of a teen market, they began to see style as a critical mode of social communication. The most influential rethinking of youth culture occurred at the Centre for Contemporary Cultural Studies at the University of Birmingham in England. Strongly influenced by postwar British Marxism, which gave fresh attention to everyday life, cultural practices, and the subjectivity of the working class, scholars and activists affiliated with the Birmingham School were also newly cognizant of the way consumerism, mass media, and the welfare state were reshaping what it meant to be working class. Young men, breaking away from traditional working-class mores and commitments, embraced a congeries of styles and tastes that drew on mass culture only to parody and undermine its dominant messages. Viewed as more than simply youthful fads, teddy boys, mods, rockers, and punks could offer insight into profound changes in British culture and class relations from the 1950s through the 1970s. The Birmingham cultural analysts sought to explain youths' embrace of extreme fashion, new music, and spirited pleasure-seeking in political terms, even as they moved beyond an understanding of politics as formal, deliberate, and collective behavior to consider what Ralph Ellison decades earlier had called "incipient forms of action."[8]

Dick Hebdige's *Subculture: The Meaning of Style* (1979) was an especially compelling exposition of this view, with its attention to youth self-fashioning in the context of socioeconomic and political transformations. Citing British punks as an example, Hebdige argued that subcultural groups appropriated and refashioned the objects of consumer culture into distinctive ensembles. This mixture of aesthetic elements, typically spectacular in style and visibility, carried "'secret' meanings [that] express, in code, a form of resistance to the order which guarantees their continued subordination." Strong assertions of style reinforced group identity—as earlier analysts claimed—but did even more: Song lyrics, dance steps, and clothing styles expressed the questioning and rejection of a social order that had placed unemployed and disadvantaged youths at the margins. Even so, this inchoate resistance was less likely to lead to a deepened political consciousness than to reinforce subordination. Hebdige pointed to the ways that music and fashion originating among lower-class youths were easily domesticated and profitably commodified in a consumer society. At the same time, authorities moved to label these phenomena as deviant or abnormal, as a way to contain them. "The cycle leading from opposition to defusion, from resistance to incorporation encloses each successive subculture," he concluded.[9]

The object of such cultural analysis was a more sophisticated understanding of socioeconomic class in late capitalism. Critical extensions of this perspective came quickly, with studies that underscored the importance of gender, sexuality, race, and ethnicity in comprehending young people's subcultures and the conditions of social marginality and discrimination. These offered important correctives to approaches that tended to romanticize white male subcultures and spotlight class analysis to the exclusion of feminist and critical race perspectives.[10] As the ideas and interests of the Birmingham School spread and became codified into the field of cultural studies, however, this broad social analysis frequently became merely prelude to the exploration of style, music, and consumer culture as a form of agency and a means of resistance. These subjects would become central areas of inquiry in the humanities and qualitative social sciences in the late twentieth century.

Remarkably, the Birmingham School's approach to the politics of style, formulated in the 1970s, continues to have a durable grip on the work of contemporary American historians and other scholars, who understand twentieth-century fashion, music, and dance as markers of an oppositional social identity among youth rooted in class and racial experience. This is readily apparent in studies of the zoot suit riot. An instructive contrast may be drawn between the first two published works on this subject. Mauricio Mazón's 1984 book, *The Zoot-Suit Riots: The Psychology of Symbolic Annihilation*, stressed the psychodynamics of the riot; his analysis, however well respected, did not become a model for later historical work. In the same year, Stuart Cosgrove's "The Zoot-Suit and Style Warfare" (1984) applied Hebdige's framework to what seemed a perfect historical antecedent. Calling the zoot suit "a subcultural gesture that refused to concede to the manners of subservience," Cosgrove viewed the Los Angeles unrest in 1943 not as "political riots in the strictest sense" but rather as an "entry into the language of politics, an inarticulate rejection of the 'straight world' and its organization." On a political spectrum from acquiescence to collective action, Mexican American zoot suiters occupied an amorphous middle ground, where they acted out their defiance in a symbolic if not a strategic way.[11]

These ideas about style politics and resistance dominate subsequent historical accounts of the zoot suit. To George Lipsitz, the zoot suit "conveyed a bold sense of self-assertion that reflected the social struggles waged for equal rights and fair employment practices." Black zoot suiters were " 'race rebels' of sorts," argues Robin Kelley, "challenging middle-class ethics and expectations, carving out a distinct generational and ethnic identity, and refusing to be good proletarians." "The struggle for dignity by zoot suiters was thus a politics of refusal," observes Luis Alvarez, whose work aims to show "how the zoot functioned as a form of opposition at the same time that it reinforced wartime hierarchies of race, gender and class power."[12] Although cognizant of formal organizations and self-conscious political actors, these works place greater weight on the bundle of everyday cultural rituals and symbols, including styles of clothing, that enable political or quasi-political expression.

Notwithstanding the significant contributions of these and other scholars to our understanding of the war years, these statements are symptomatic of the enduringly problematic practice of reading aesthetic forms as politics. Certainly the history of many disadvantaged and marginalized groups is filled with examples of resistance that do not operate at the level of collective or intentional political action. We can recognize the many ways that style, music, and dance articulate and foster a sense of group identity and collective behavior that may challenge cultural norms and offer political commentary. This is especially the case among African Americans, whose traditions of "styling," lampooning performances, and subterranean codes of communication have been thoroughly documented by historians, anthropologists, folklorists, and literary critics. Without the same degree of continuity, American women, working-class peoples, immigrants, and various ethnic groups have on many occasions interpreted and deployed appearance to make such points. In the words of anthropologist James C. Scott, the cultural domain provides certain "weapons" to the weak; the "hidden transcripts" of their deployment may be read not only by those using them, but also by discerning scholars.[13]

For many students of popular culture, however, the idea that the aesthetic realm is subsumed within the political is simply a given, and crucial questions about the relationship between these domains are left unexplored. Is there an enduring relationship between fashion and social action? When should aesthetic and cultural forms be seen as political, and how will we know it? Is simply donning a zoot suit sufficient evidence of a politics? What intentions must lie behind it to qualify? Appearance, gesture, and style articulate a range of social meanings, including at times a rejection of perceived cultural norms. But historians have moved too easily to assimilate the zoot suit style to wartime politics, and to claim this aesthetic as a kind of resistance to political authority, stamping a template over the zoot suit beyond what the evidence can bear, and aggregating categories and considerations that should be kept analytically distinct.

Several problems arise in interpretations of the zoot suit and other extreme youth styles as political gestures of refusal. One is the dilemma of evidence. Zoot suiters did not leave diaries and letters explaining why they embraced the style and what it meant to them. Scholars have often relied on a small set of examples and documents to examine the meaning of the zoot suit for Mexican American and African American youth, and have done little to consider young white men of different ethnic backgrounds who also wore the style. Cosgrove's article, frequently reprinted and cited, has had extended influence since its publication in 1984, despite its use of only a small number of printed sources, mainly from the *New York Times* and other newspapers. More recently, a new generation of scholars has explored archival sources in Los Angeles and begun to collect oral histories of Mexican American and African American youth to gain insight into the daily lives of surviving participants. Such interviews offer a significant counterweight to the representations of racial minorities that recur in the written record of the time.[14] Still, memory has been filtered through the decades after World War II, a period marked by strengthened commitment to civil rights and an assertive Latino identity which now shapes the viewpoint of those looking back on their earlier experiences. Analysis of historical evidence often reveals a conceptual confusion between the individuals who understand their *own* cultural practices and beliefs as a subculture and those who conceptualize subcultures, as sociologist Chris Jenks puts it, "for specific rhetorical, political, or moral purposes."[15] Inevitably we know much more about public attitudes toward the zoot suit—from journalists, commentators, experts, and government officials—than we do the contemporary views of those who wore the style.

And how do we read the evidence of fashion and style? Scholars have adopted a semiotic approach to dress and other aesthetic forms, but this method may be highly subjective if not corroborated by ethnographic or historical accounts that reveal the viewpoints of those who actually wore the garments. The plausibility of such readings may seem self-evident, but that may be due more to our contemporary attitudes toward cultural politics than to the preponderance of evidence from the past. Zoot suiters themselves spoke largely through their appearance—clothing, gestures, and personas—and these are treacherous signals to read. When they vocally addressed the meaning of their clothes at the time or in retrospect, it was most often to comment on the beauty and peculiarities of the style, its connection to dance and leisure, their arguments with parents over clothes, and local fights. There is much evidence of youths' confrontations with police and the military, as well as the discriminatory treatment they faced, but finding precise connections between the extreme style and an individual or collective sense of opposition is difficult, if not impossible.

Indeed, historians repeatedly highlight a handful of individuals to represent the politicized views of zoot suiters. Caught in a police roundup and harangued in court about his looks, Alfred Barela was one of the few Mexican American youths to leave a statement that explicitly linked his civil rights to the right to dress as he pleased. Beyond this exchange with the judge, we know little about him, yet he has come to embody the political perspectives of wartime *pachucos*.[16] Malcolm X produced a riveting account of his early life as Malcolm Little, a young black man in Boston and New York, where he embraced the world of zoot suiters and street hustlers, jive talk and jitterbug. Recalling those days twenty years later, he saw these urban pleasures as signs of his spiraling degradation as a black man; the son of a Garveyite and radicalized in the Nation of Islam, he understood the complexities of African

American politics, but he did not portray street life as a world of political meaning. Yet Malcolm X is widely accepted as evidence of the zoot suiter as a figure of resistance. In a prevailing interpretation, Robin Kelley reads *The Autobiography of Malcolm X* against the grain of the author's intentions, calling the style of the street an "essential element of his radicalization" and a way to "negotiate an identity that resisted the hegemonic culture." Kelley uses a series of active verbs—*challenge, refuse, carve out*—that suggest a sense of purpose in Malcolm Little's world. "While the suit itself was not meant as a direct political statement," he writes, "the social context in which it was created and worn rendered it so."[17] This begs the question of *whose* context: the men Malcolm describes as hustlers and homeboys? The African American communities responding to such men? Black intellectuals and commentators like Ralph Ellison? White media and political institutions? The context may in fact be our contemporary politics and culture, particularly on the left—a romantic view of rebellion and pushback "from below," not through formal politics or organization but through quotidian culture.

Readings of style for their political meaning often bolster the boundaries between youth subcultures and a unified "mainstream" culture. Thus scholars see the zoot suit as a symbol of disloyalty and disaffection of minority youth, and typically contrast it to the soldier's uniform, which stands for a militarized white American culture. This flat interpretation of clothing's symbolism reinforces the perception of opposition and hostility on each side, an oversimplification that fails to register a much more complex set of reactions. The concept of subculture also separates groups of youth from one another, a tendency exacerbated by the elaboration of academic subfields. The early studies of the zoot suit divided African Americans from Mexican Americans, East Coast from West; the propensity in subcultural studies to examine a single ethnic/racial group in a specific locale meant that the national and international dimensions of this style were left unexamined.

Since 1990, scholars of contemporary youth subcultures have moved away from the direct correlation between cultural styles and practices, on the one hand, and traditional categories of social relations, on the other. Taking a postmodern approach, such cultural analysts as David Muggleton and Sarah Thornton argue that the global circulation of goods, images, and identities has meant that style can no longer be affixed to coherent groups or subcultures defined by class, race, or region. Ethnographies of music and dance scenes around the world document not only the growing importance of consumption and leisure but also the critical role of the media in labeling and popularizing new subcultures, often in ways that oversimplify the messiness of cultural and social encounters. Emphasizing the fluidity of youth styles and social identities, they also tend to confine the idea of resistance through style to the cultural arena rather than perceiving a political critique or protest.[18]

These postmodern perspectives on modern-day youth culture have had significant impact among historians, particularly the idea of hybrid social identities and affiliations that may cross lines of class, race, or gender. Some recent historians of the zoot suit and the Los Angeles riot now identify a "zoot culture" in which African Americans, Mexican Americans, Filipinos, and other young people of color, along with some working-class whites, shared an obsession with extreme style, favored leisure pursuits over labor, forged public interracial connections that "challenged the segregated sensibilities of 1940s America," and formed an "imagined community."[19] This effort is suggestive, yet it too easily reifies cultural style as the basis of the social and political relationships of youth. Interestingly, young men who wore zoot suits rarely called themselves "zoot suiters"; indeed, they often objected to that name, distinguishing themselves from others who were the "real" zoot suiters. It may be, Sarah Thornton argues, that "subcultures are best defined as social groups that have been labeled as such."[20]

★   ★   ★

The zoot suit certainly gained a political charge in June 1943, when, in the context of the Los Angeles riot, many understood it to be a style of refusal and opposition. But before that moment and after, the zoot suit broadcast other meanings to wearers and non-wearers alike. As with all forms of dress, it was a material object—cloth cut and stitched to cover the body, to allow movement and to constrain it—and a malleable symbolic form, a medium of nonverbal communication. The phenomenon was as bound up in the choreography of sexual attraction, the negotiation of gender identity, conflict between generations, and the pursuit of pleasure within a specific music and dance culture as much if not more than it was motivated by a politics of opposition. Although usually discussed as a key element of Mexican American or African American youth subcultures, the zoot suit appeared *across* the main fault lines of social difference in the United States—among Filipinos, Japanese Americans, men of Jewish and Italian descent, jitterbug-crazy middle-class boys, and even Mexican American women and working-class lesbians. Created initially in an unspoken collaboration among manufacturers, retailers, and young male consumers—mainly but not exclusively African American— the zoot suit migrated quickly from Harlem and other urban centers to small cities and towns around the country. This rapid circulation was abetted by a segment of the garment trade, specialists in clothing fashions and fads they intentionally promoted as "extreme." Even after the government moved to conserve fabric required for military and other uses, the zoot suit grew in popularity as it entered into public awareness through music, movies, and the press. The reet pleat and drape shape came to be meaningful in a web of immediate social interactions and cultural representations. On the home front, it simultaneously signaled racial-ethnic identity and a broader youth identity, although neither was wholly separated from the rest of American culture. Indeed, as it began to travel around the world, these connections became tightly intertwined—the zoot suit as an identifiably American style.

More than the young men who embraced this style, it was the police and governmental authorities that created the political meaning of the zoot suit, as they sought a threatening symbol to describe and encapsulate an array of behaviors and demeanors that to them made little sense. The conditions that rendered the style political came to a head chiefly in one locale, Los Angeles, where a peculiar mix of elements in the early 1940s—the war economy, multiethnic and racial tensions, mass media, and local politics—narrowly focused attention on the zoot suit. For months, Mexican American men wearing zoot suits had become targets. The death of a young man in what became known as the Sleepy Lagoon murder case, along with a high-profile trial of *pachucos* in 1942, intensified the labeling of zoot suiters as a public danger and spurred a politicized sense of the attire. These perceptions deepened in the L.A. riot, feeding the fervor of sailors and civilians out to "punish" zoot suiters, and simultaneously fostering a more assertive politics among Mexican Americans. Only much later, however, did the zoot suiter became a heroic figure of popular resistance, when he became assimilated into the historical mythologies and political imagination of Chicano activists and artists, black nationalists, scholars of cultural studies, and radical historians.

This book examines an extreme fashion and its enigmatic career during and after World War II, in search of the zoot suit's many meanings. Capturing the imagination of people across the United States and around the world, the style generated many interpretations, including a host of forceful political readings. For those who wore the zoot suit, however, everyday aesthetics was less an assertion of politics than "a device for living" and "practice of the self," as Ian Hunter puts it.[21] How was this aesthetic practice related to the social lives and experiences of youths of many different backgrounds and to the cultural and political landscape of wartime America? Why did this style continue to resonate, in so many places and over the decades? How might we take a truer measure of the zoot suit?

1

Making the Suit Zoot

When civil unrest and violence erupted in Los Angeles in June 1943, the zoot suit became a preoccupation of adult Americans across the country: What was the zoot suit and where had it come from? "Here's what all the excitement's about," explained the newspaper *PM*, which ran a photographic triptych of the garment and its accoutrements. Reporters interviewed young men in Harlem, photographers snapped pictures of the drape shape, and columnists gave their angle on the phenomenon. "Last week practically everybody with any pretensions to journalism was ferreting out the origins of the zoot suit," observed the *New Yorker*.[1]

As it turned out, there were many conflicting stories about the genesis of the style. Tailors from New York to Memphis claimed to have invented it, while an obscure busboy in Georgia insisted on bragging rights. However tall the tale or self-aggrandizing the teller, these origin stories open a window into the making of an extreme fashion, before the zoot suit became the object of public commentary. They reveal the unusual commercial and creative exchange among manufacturers, retailers, and consumers that transformed normal menswear into something spectacular. The men's garment industry and clothing styles had changed in the face of the Great Depression, and clothiers found a variety of ways

Here's What All the Excitement's About:

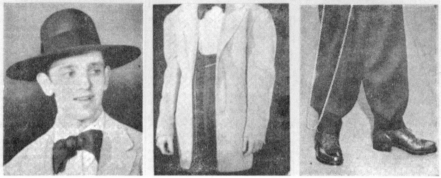

Figure 1. One newspaper's version of the zoot suit, the white model rendering it harmless. *PM*, June 13, 1943.

to respond to it, with some embracing novel fashions and fads. Among the young men who ordered and wore the zoot suit, a new aesthetic sensibility can also be discerned despite the disapproval of parents and tailors.

Most fashions run their course, but the zoot suit's path, perhaps uniquely in clothing history, was rerouted by the onset of World War II. Even as manufacturers and retailers promoted the style and young people embraced it, the government moved to clamp down on the wasteful use of textiles. If federal officials had their way, the zoot suit would have been a home-front casualty. Indeed, their efforts to prohibit the zoot suit and render it unpatriotic contributed greatly to the perception of the style, then and now, as a symbol of opposition to mainstream American values. The state's assertion of its regulatory role is a crucial aspect of the history of the zoot suit, affecting the manufacture, retailing, and marketing of this type of menswear. Although the intentions of such regulations were clear, their impact was far more ambiguous, fueling fascination with the very style the government sought to suppress.

*   *   *

The zoot suit was, in the first place, a *suit*, a garment made of cloth cut and sewn to cover and ornament the body. What made it "zoot" was the way it pulled out the lines and shape of the traditional suit to widen a man's shoulders, lengthen his torso, and loosen his limbs. The style itself varied from man to man and place to place, but however it was worn, it broadcast a self-conscious sense of difference from the conventional mode of respectable male appearance. Most Americans viewed the zoot suit as something new and peculiar, but those with a long memory recalled earlier periods when men put on similar outfits. Walter White, secretary of the NAACP, offered the perspective of a middle-aged man who had seen fashions come and go. "In the late 90's and early 00's long box back coats, full or peg-legged trousers, and flat felt or straw hats called boaters or pork pies, were worn on Fifth Avenue and Park Avenue as well as other places," he observed. "The modern zoot suits exaggerate but little the modes which will be remembered by many of us." The *Chicago Tribune* agreed, reminding readers what the well-dressed man of 1901 was wearing and recalling the fad for "Oxford Bags," voluminous pants worn by British university students, in the 1920s.[2]

These observers had a point: A practice of extreme styling had long been common in menswear. In the history of Western dress, the suit has enjoyed remarkable longevity. A banker in antebellum Boston would recognize his counterpart in today's global economy: matching jacket and trousers, simple lines, subdued colors, woven fabrics tailored to the body, lack of ornamentation except for a tie or cravat. Still, over its long history, the men's suit has varied in numerous if subtle ways, with styles deemed extreme or outré playing against the governing type. This dynamic may be seen in the emergence of the zoot suit amid broad changes in men's appearance.

The arrival of the men's suit is often termed the "great masculine renunciation," a fundamental shift in the way men looked and thought about their attire. Before the 1600s, elite men had worn rich textures, colors, and ornamentation, the pomp of their dress conveying their rank. According to clothing historians, the suit redefined the relationship between appearance and authority in an era of political, social, and cultural

transformation that challenged crown and church. The Protestant refor-
mation, the American and French revolutions, and the growth of trade
all reshaped attitudes toward the self, body, and clothing. Belief in equality and individualism made the showy display of wealth and rank increasingly suspect. Powdered hair, lace and ruffles, and ornate fabrics
were out. As they gained economic power, a bourgeois merchant and
manufacturing class set new norms of proper appearance. By the early
1800s, men's authority rested increasingly on the projection of character
and ability; thus inconspicuousness became the hallmark of the well-
dressed man. Ornamentation and display were left largely to women,
their fashions marking not a powerful rank but rather their status as
the weaker sex. Men—now self-reliant, self-motivated individuals—no
longer dressed their bodies to be the object of attention.[3]

Nevertheless, there were always some young men who tried to make
spectacles of themselves. Long before the arrival of the zoot suit, they
embraced vibrant colors and arresting silhouettes as a mark of distinction and fashion. In nineteenth-century cities, wealthy young men-
about-town and sporting men adopted modish looks for evening entertainment, the racetrack, and promenading. The dandy's attention to appearance was legendary. "A Man whose trade, office, and existence
consist in the wearing of Clothes," Thomas Carlyle pithily defined him:
"Others dress to live, he lives to dress."[4] Stylishness was also a point of
pride among working men of few means. Irish American mechanics and
firefighting "laddies" wore cheap clothing and castoffs that nevertheless
mixed colors, fabrics, and details in ways that demanded notice. Among
them, the Bowery Boy stood out: Parading lower Manhattan in a top
hat, fitted frock coat, bright vest, and plaid trousers, he became a social
type popularized on the stage in the years before the Civil War.

Similar clothes might be worn by African American men of the
1800s, for whom "styling" was an especially rich tradition bound up
with the cultural encounters of Africans and Europeans, the experience
of slavery, and the role of religion, festivals, and celebration in everyday
life. Dressing up breached class and racial codes of subservience. Those

Figure 2. Mose the Bowery Boy, a fashion-conscious "fire laddie" of New York's
East Side.

Gene Schermerhorn, *Letters to Phil, Memories of a New York Boyhood, 1848–1856* (New York: New York
Bound, 1982).

with few resources might use style to convey visually a sense of masculine
identity, stake out a public space, and demand that others acknowledge
their presence. Urban black men's flamboyant dress was so much in
evidence that it fueled the look of minstrelsy, even as minstrelsy turned
the desire to look fine into a racist stereotype. Thus the popular song
"Zip Coon," introduced by the white minstrel George Washington

Dixon in 1829, mocked the "natty scholar" for his pretensions; the image used on the sheet music prefigured the zoot suit, with its broad-shouldered frock coat, pleated trousers, watch fob, and glasses attached to a long chain.[5]

For some men, then, fashion had long punctuated ordinary life with extraordinary looks. Among African American freemen, Irish-born residents, and working-class youths, they embraced an aesthetic that played with high and low styles, and insisted above all on public visibility. Such styles served to make distinctions and even recalibrate social position, but they could also be used to craft larger points, a visual commentary with a political edge. Still, extreme style only worked in its relation to governing codes of appearance of a given time. Top hats, walking sticks, and vests were ripe for the picking by poor young men who wished to stand out, but these and other markers of Victorian formality and wealth would fade in a changing social and cultural climate.

The early twentieth century witnessed a gradual loosening of the form and style of menswear. The "sack" jacket, with straight lines and natural shoulders, appeared by 1900, initially long and loose, then somewhat shorter by World War I. A greater change occurred in the 1930s, when the "London cut" or "English drape" grew popular. Wanting to produce a body-conscious, masculine effect, London tailor Frederick Scholte designed a suit that looked like "a V resting on an attenuated column."[6] Jackets featured wide shoulders and chest, roomy armholes, and narrowed waist, and were worn with high-waisted, tapered pants. Perfect proportions were critical to Scholte, who made his suits for the carriage trade and refused requests for exaggerated shapes and details, which he associated with entertainers.

Nevertheless, the style created by a London bespoke tailor quickly came to epitomize the look of American men. In the midst of the Great Depression, when men's role as breadwinner and household head was on trial, the drape cut emphasized male athleticism and virility, the he-man and the man of action. The flow of the fabric eased men's stance, relaxed the way they inhabited their clothes, and swung with the body.

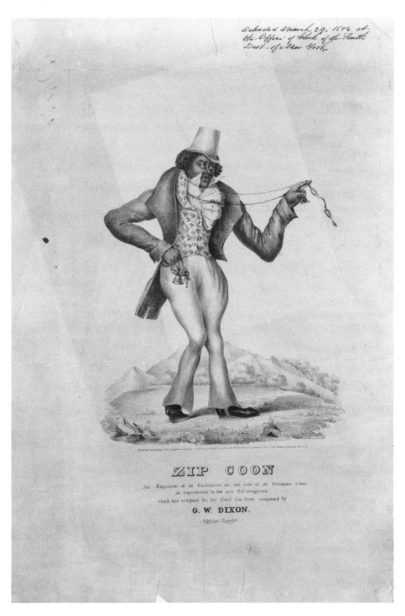

Figure 3. The minstrel figure Zip Coon caricatures the high style of urban African Americans.

Endicott & Swett sheet music, 1834, Library of Congress, Prints and Photographs Division, LC-USZ62-126131.

Hollywood embraced the drape cut in the mid-1930s, producing different versions to convey distinct character types. While such leading men
as Cary Grant and Clark Gable wore impeccable draped suits that were
integral to their screen personas, James Cagney and other movie gangsters wore more exaggerated broad-shouldered "breakaway" jackets that
cut in at the waist. Even period films had an influence on contemporary
fashion, especially the eye-catching frock coats and wide-brimmed hats
worn by Gable in *Gone with the Wind* (1939) and Errol Flynn in *Virginia
City* (1940).[7] By 1940 the drape style had become widely known as the
"American cut," and it would continue to define a national masculine
ideal through the 1950s.

   During these years, the menswear trade as a whole became a more
style-conscious industry. As the Great Depression deepened, Americans
cut back on clothing expenditures. With money tight, families carefully
weighed the decision to buy a new business suit for the male breadwinner, as it meant that wives would have to scrimp on new clothes and
refurbish old ones for themselves and their children. Looking for ways
to save money yet look presentable, men made a virtue of necessity,
going without hats and vests, and mixing jackets with mismatched trousers. In response, manufacturers tried everything from drastic price-cut-
ting to novelty styles in order to persuade consumers to buy. Some began
to adopt a new sales strategy focused on style promotion and marketing.
Arguing that price warfare was destroying business, journalist and editor
Arnold Gingrich urged manufacturers and retailers to foster greater fashion awareness and consumerism among American men, which would
lead them to pay a premium for stylish clothing. Toward this end, he
created the magazine *Apparel Arts* in 1931 for the men's clothing trade
and founded *Esquire* as a "magazine for men" two years later. Although
lagging behind women's fashions, menswear manufacturers and retailers
sought "tie-ins" with style-conscious celebrities, from Hollywood stars
to Edward, Duke of Windsor. "I was in fact 'produced' as a leader of
fashion, with the clothiers as my showmen and the world as my audience," observed the duke, who assiduously posed for photographs and

encouraged the British export trade with his signature style of soft dressing and touches of eccentricity.[8]

The 1930s also saw the takeoff of men's sportswear and casual clothing. Initially confined to athletic fields and the outdoors, sportswear crossed over into everyday street life. To many it seemed a style for hard times, as men limited their expenditures for clothing, especially suits. California had emerged as the center of American sportswear manufacture for both women and men, and the Golden State's relaxed lifestyle and sunlit ambiance led designers to create colorful, looser fitting, and casual clothes. This trend grew during World War II. When the government ordered the conservation of wool, many men swapped their business suits for assorted sports jackets and pants. Office workers who switched to higher-paying industrial jobs did not want to wear factory uniforms or overalls—a sign of blue-collar status—and put on a T-shirt and slacks instead. "A year ago this outfit might have been worn for a golf game," the *Men's Apparel Reporter* remarked. "Today it is a uniform for the war worker." The trade journal warned manufacturers to rid sportswear of its associations with idle wealth and effeminacy. "It just isn't funny any more to promote or display sports clothes that have a dash of lavender," it admonished. "This nation has got to get tough."[9]

The men's garment industry also turned to the youthful fads of the day, styles that adults would consider bizarre or outré. They began to cater to tastes for novelty through a manufacturing classification called "extremes," jackets and trousers with unusual colors, cuts, and styling. Style spotters for the industry went to the Yale Bowl, the Princeton campus, and the Belmont racetrack to search out new looks. By 1940 they were finding affluent young men sporting long, loose jackets and bold colors and plaids, styles they sold as "collegiate." Popular trends in music, dance, and film also inspired menswear. Even Sears, the benchmark of everyday, affordable clothes, offered "New Style Notes" for young men in its 1941 catalogue. Their models called "Swing Kings" and "Hollywood Styles" featured wide pant legs and enormous jacket lapels, with colors ranging from traditional brown and gray to teal blue and medium green. "Extreme styling makes this young men's style a smash hit wherever it is worn," Sears proclaimed.[10] These were not zoot suits, but contrasted sharply with the adult business attire the mail-order firm sold.

Thus the zoot suit was not a phenomenon that came out of nowhere, as so many observers at the time believed. For decades, some men had refused the style of invisibility that had been the hallmark of male appearance. Usually young, sometimes wealthy, but more typically from ethnic and racial minorities, they assumed styles to be noticed, to incite the reactions of passersby. The zoot suit followed in that tradition. It surfaced as other major changes in men's clothing were taking place: the popularity of the drape-cut suit, the growing influence of California manufacturers, the marketing of sportswear and casual clothes, and the broader emergence of a youth market. On the eve of World War II, wider shoulders, longer jackets, and pleated, looser pants had become generally popular. The zoot suit did not cast off those changes, but rather embellished and inflated them, until the suit lost its business function and became something else entirely.

*   *   *

As the newspaper *PM* admitted, "the origin of the zoot-suit is a mystery." Specific references to zoot suits appeared sporadically in newspaper stories and cartoons by early 1941. But the style commonly called "drapes" had begun to evolve in Harlem in the mid-1930s, as can be seen in clothing advertisements in the local African American newspaper, the *New York Amsterdam News*. In the early 1930s, they called men's suits "English drapes." A 1934 ad from Westin's clothing store, "Harlem's fashion originators," offered a cut similar to that sold by conventional clothiers—mid-length double-breasted jackets with broad shoulders, wide lapels, and breakaway waists, worn with conservative pleated pants. By 1936, the phrase "extreme English drapes" appeared in ads from J. C. Curtis; the look emphasized the loose flow of fabric over the body, with "extra wide shoulders, full peg pants, tapered as you like them." A year later this style had come to be called the "New York Drape" or "Harlem Drape," identified with the capital of American fashion and hub of black life. To underscore the change, Westin's ads were now filled with jive, assuring customers they were "catering to you solid." Another clothing store declared in 1938: "The new long drapes are here to stay." Ads for pegged pants—often called jitterbug pants or swing pants—also appeared by the mid-1930s, and wide-brimmed "drape hats" and oversized cowboy hats followed a few years later.[11] Photographs too reveal evidence of the extreme drape style in the late 1930s, in such places as Harlem's Savoy Ballroom, where the jitterbug craze took off. Certainly by 1940, it was widespread in African American communities and appeared among Mexican Americans, Filipinos, and other ethnic and racial groups.

A host of tailors claimed to have been the first to manufacture the zoot suit. In Harlem, it was said, clothier Charles Klein had teamed up with Vito Bagnato, the self-proclaimed "king designer of hot styles," and invented the zoot suit, which they promoted in Klein's Lenox Avenue store. Lew Eisenstein, owner of Lew's Pants Store on 125th Street, begged to differ. One day in 1934, when Eisenstein was out of town—so he told the *New Yorker*—his wife and a salesman took a batch of trousers that were not selling, tapered the bottoms, and soon they became the rage. Still another Harlem tailor, Charlie Kelly, claimed credit for the drape-shape coat. A young black man, confirming Kelly's version to a reporter, explained that "he had bought his first complete zoot suit from Charlie back in 1937, when peg-top pants had already been in vogue for several years."[12] Beyond Harlem, Harold Fox in Chicago, Louis Lettes in Memphis, and Nathan Elkus in Detroit all swore they had invented the style.

These men had much in common. They were white clothiers, predominantly Jewish, in keeping with the dominant ethnic makeup of the garment trade. Their stores were located in African American communities or working-class commercial districts with a racial and ethnic mix. Historically the relationship of these merchants to black consumers was fraught with misunderstanding and antagonism, if at times softened by familiarity. Through the 1930s African Americans accused white-owned stores in their neighborhoods of discriminatory prices and insulting treatment. Their "don't buy where you can't work" campaigns censured white-owned stores for refusing to hire black employees. Still, black consumers had little choice but to shop in these establishments, even as clothiers, struggling for sales in the Depression, searched for ways to move overstocked merchandise or come up with new stylistic elements to entice customers.[13]

Outside their storefronts on 125th Street in Harlem or Seventh Street in Washington, D.C., they watched the parade of street styles worn daily by young men going to work or hanging out on sidewalks, and sought inspiration in the costumes of entertainers and musicians performing at nearby theaters and nightclubs. Chicago tailor and trumpeter Harold Fox gained a clientele initially by designing band uniforms and entertainers' outfits, and then moved into custom-made zoot suits. His store on the Near West Side became a scene for jazz musicians, who enjoyed both his musical and clothing tastes. "On any given day you could run into people like Lionel Hampton, Stan Kenton, Dizzy Gillespie, Louis Jordan . . . EVERYONE," recalled drummer Marty Clausen. "It was very hip to have a Fox Brothers suit." Although Fox frequently was said to have invented the zoot suit, he acknowledged that it did not originate with him or the performers. "The zoot was not a costume or uniform from the world of entertainment," he recalled. "It came right off the street and out of the ghetto."[14]

The everyday interactions of tailors and clients produced an unusual alertness to consumer desires and rapidly changing tastes. In Memphis, for example, tailor Louis Lettes had a store near Beale Street with "a large patronage among the snappiest Negro dressers of the city." In the mid-1930s, his customers continually asked if "he could take the shine off the seats of their pants," so they would not have to invest in a new pair. Lettes's solution was to lengthen the coat to hide the worn cloth. To publicize the style, he dressed up a local high-school student named

Anderson Tate in the long-coated suit. Tate became a sensation among his classmates, who called on Lettes to make the same style for them.[15]

Clearly the zoot suit was not merely a creative means of extending the life of a man's wardrobe, although in the midst of the Depression, when women assiduously made over their dresses, darned socks, and repaired holes in pants, this purpose should not be underestimated. As Lettes's story suggests, the zoot suit's panache caught the eye. Tailors repeatedly told how young men came into their shops with measurements or a sketch of the suit they had in mind. "We didn't invent it," a Philadelphia tailor insisted. "They asked us to make coats longer, pants wider. They wanted coat pockets straight up and down, trousers pleated, knees baggy, cuffs skin tight. We wouldn't be caught dead the way they look."[16]

An example of such fashion initiative appears in the most widely circulated account of the zoot suit's origins, published in the *New York Times* at the end of the riot. Reporter Meyer Berger traced the outfit to Gainesville, Georgia, where a black busboy, Clyde Duncan, had ordered it from the Frierson McEver store in February 1940. Duncan wanted a coat thirty-seven inches in length, with two buttons, and asked for trousers with a twenty-six-inch circumference at the knees and fourteen inches at the ankles. Clothier A. C. McEver tried to persuade him that the measurements were all wrong. When Duncan insisted, McEver reluctantly sent them to the Globe Tailoring Company in Chicago, despite the fact that "he thought the idea ridiculous and he didn't hesitate to tell the customer and the tailoring company so." Duncan later recalled that "people laughed at him as he wore the suit around town two or three years before he joined the Army."[17]

The owners of many retail shops and wholesale garment factories initially resisted the style. When Louis Lettes sent the measurements for a fingertip-length jacket to a St. Louis garment manufacturing firm, the tailors there "thought he was either drunk or crazy." Similarly, Detroit retailer Nathan Elkus in 1939 marked up a regular suit pattern to create

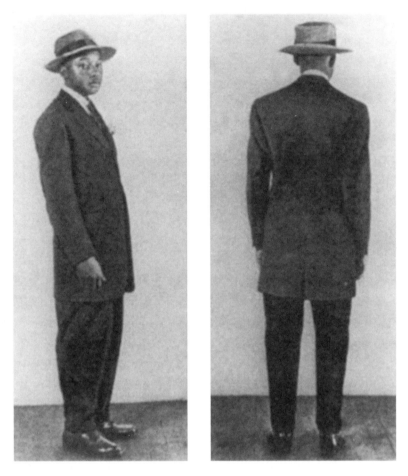

Figure 4. Clyde Duncan in an early zoot suit. *New York Times*, June 11, 1943.

the exaggerated effects of his "thunderbolt suit"—"a single-breasted model, fly front, slash pocket with a one-piece back, with peg legs having a 30-inch knee and 15-inch bottom"—and sent it to Blankson Clothes in New York City to produce a sample. At first manufacturer Irving Blank balked at the strange styling, telling Elkus "a dozen eggs won't guarantee a sponge cake will rise." He finally made the suit after Elkus

agreed to pay for one hundred of them up front. In the more sophisticated provinces of New York City and Chicago, however, the storeown-
ers learned to put on the cool demeanor of their young black clients. As
the *New Yorker* put it, "the tradesmen who cater to sharpies pride themselves on filling every order and being surprised at nothing."[18]

This unusual degree of consumer power over a clothing style occurred in large part because of the peculiar system of manufacturing and
retailing in the men's garment industry at this time, which combined
custom tailoring, ready-made clothes, and a third category known as
semi-custom tailoring. Custom tailors had always made suits to measure
and easily accommodated the desires of patrons for a style out of the
ordinary. Although many of these suits were expensive and designed for
a wealthier and stylistically more conservative clientele, informal custom
shops arose to serve the new zoot-suit trade. By 1940, black tailors in
Los Angeles had set up small workshops in their homes and garages,
sewing drapes in the evening after working in regular clothing stores by
day.[19]

Men also purchased ready-to-wear outfits from department stores or
neighborhood clothing shops that catered to their tastes and pocket-
books. Customers could have simple alterations done on trousers to create the desired "pegged" look, but there were also an array of stores that
specifically offered the drape style. In 1939, Kermisch's department store,
in the heart of the black commercial district of Baltimore, advertised
men's suits "at a depression price" and announced that "most trousers
ride high at the waist . . . with plenty of drape." One of its competitors
gave shoppers a choice of "conservative or drape," reminding them that
"we specialize in the drape style and ¾ length coat." When he went to
purchase his first zoot suit in such a store, Malcolm X vividly recalled,
the salesman measured him and then "picked off a rack a zoot suit that
was just wild: sky-blue pants thirty inches in the knee and angle-nar-
rowed down to twelve inches at the bottom, and a long coat that pinched
my waist and flared out below my knees." To match the suit, Malcolm

bought a blue hat, with a four-inch brim and feather. The salesman threw in a leather belt and long, gold-plated chain; the keychains were often given away as premiums.[20]

Most significant for the zoot suit was the practice of semi-custom tailoring. This was the system followed by McEver, Elkus, and Lettes, in which the retailer measured the customer and sent the order to a wholesale manufacturer, who made up the garment. The suit would be delivered to the client with no fittings or alterations. "A colored boy can, by paying a small deposit, order a suit with exact specifications as to material, length, drape, placing of pockets, and whatever else he can think of," reported the New Yorker. Semi-custom tailoring seems to have been especially common in sales to African Americans. For a fashion-conscious young man, these suits cost less than custom-made outfits but could be designed precisely as he desired. For the clothier, the extra work of fitting and alteration and, perhaps, the racial discomfort about fitting clothing to black bodies, made this a viable alternative. "We know what you want," Solomon's clothing store insisted to its Baltimore clientele, and "we will make your suit to suit you." Dry cleaners in small towns in the South also went into the zoot suit business, ordering them from Chicago and then pegging the pants.[21]

A number of clothing stores and manufacturers set up mail-order and door-to-door operations along similar lines. The National Clothing Company advertised frequently in the African American press, offering free catalogues of drape models and quick service; their ads also appeared in Spanish language newspapers in Los Angeles. Lew Eisenstein advertised his "jitterbug pants" for young men and women, making the "fine pegs from the store that made Harlem peg-conscious" available by mail order. The Chicago Defender and Pittsburgh Courier, among other black weekly newspapers, had a national circulation, and mail order was an especially important source of clothing in small towns, rural areas, and Southern cities, where African Americans were often barred from the dressing rooms of retail stores. Instead, they could dispatch measurements to firms in Chicago and New York and receive the finished garments in a few weeks. The catalogue of one Chicago manufacturing house, for example, made its way to Clearwater, Florida, in 1943, offering an array of zoot suits, from low-priced models named the "Sergeant" and "Marine" to the higher end "Diplomat" and "Ambassador."[22]

Prices for these clothes ranged widely. During World War II, Barney, the "bargain king" of Baltimore, sold Harlem-style zoot suits in gabardine from $14.75, while Lew's jitterbug pants started at $3.95. Prices for wool drape suits ran at least $20 and more typically $30 to $35, with some costing $85 and higher. During the Los Angeles riot, the press often remarked upon the high price of the zoot suit, underscoring their wearers' unseemly profligacy in a time of belt-tightening and sacrifice. Even the moderately priced suit would have been prohibitive for most young African Americans and working-class youths had retailers not offered installment plans. Malcolm X could not afford to buy his zoot suit outright, but his friend Shorty put him wise: "Homeboy, you never heard of credit?" Harold Fox allowed boys to pay off their zoot suits one dollar a week, with money earned on newspaper routes.[23]

At the same time, many found ways to adjust their clothes to mimic the look of drapes. The zoot suit, said *Newsweek,* was "making a lot of young men take in the bottom of their trousers in a way that would have seemed quite normal 30 years ago." An accommodating sister or relative could easily modify the silhouette of trousers, and many women had the sewing skills needed to let out a jacket. African American artist and writer Faith Ringgold remembers how her brother evaded their mother's disapproving eye: "Every day Andrew sewed his pants with big stitches at the ankles to make them appear pegged, but before he came into the house, he'd take out the stitches."[24]

Among the many origin stories of the zoot suit, one held that poor people and defense workers had started the fad by wearing old, oversized clothes. Frank Walton, director of the War Production Board's Textile, Clothing, and Leather Division, had heard two versions: one asserted that workmen in Western war plants "began working in combination outfits of old clothes and were not particularly careful as to whether the suits fitted or not"; the other observed that "an influx of people" to the Pacific Coast "began wearing old clothes which did not fit them." These tales fail to see the style in the zoot suit, what made it sharp and different. Existing photographs, however, do show quite a mix of looks, as men approximated an image with materials at hand. Like Louis Lettes's story—the zoot suit invented by the seat of the pants—the images do suggest how people with few resources could find a way to put on a stylish appearance. The zoot suit for them was a bargain struck between desire and necessity, an ideal fashioned from combinations of old clothes, hand-me-downs, and clothes bought a size or two too big.[25]

The shape and silhouette of men's suits has tended to change more slowly than women's dress, but the zoot suit was unusual in the rapid evolution of the style toward the extreme. The practice of semi-custom tailoring and mail order, with young men designing their own looks, speeded up the fashion cycle. The Gainesville clothier A. C. McEver found the zoot suit so peculiar that he photographed Clyde Duncan in 1940 and sent the pictures to the trade journal *Men's Apparel Reporter,* which ran it in early 1941 with the joking headline, "Exclusive Style Flash." Yet the front and side views reveal a restrained zoot suit, especially in its narrow shoulders and uniform fabric. Similarly, the photographs of Malcolm Little's zoot suit, probably taken in 1940, present a relatively moderate version. By 1942, many zoot suiters were seeking a more voluminous look, with baggy jacket and ballooning trousers. "The costumes are growing more and more fantastic, each designer striving to outdo his competitor," one African American newspaper reported. High-rise trousers reached higher, the length of jackets grew longer. The style's escalation may be seen in the widening difference between the width of the pants at the knees and at the ankles. For Duncan, this was only twelve inches, but, as *PM* reported, "the boys, trying to outdo one another, were soon wearing pegs that measured as much as 32 inches at the knee and 12 inches at the bottom," a twenty-inch difference. The most extreme version, called "superzoots," even had zippers at the ankle

Figure 5. Arthur Siegel's 1942 photograph, "back view of a Negro dressed in a zoot suit," captures an improvised style and the cowboy hat popular in Detroit.
Library of Congress, Prints and Photographs Division, FSA-OWI Collection, LC-USW3-016678-E DLC.

or calf so its wearer could pull his pants on over his shoes. "Superzoots" were not only worn by jazz musicians and Hollywood celebrities, but also prized by ordinary young men who, in their words, wanted their clothes to be "the end to end all ends."[26]

*   *   *

Government officials, putting a different interpretation on the phrase, simply wanted to end the zoot suit. It had begun to spread in 1939 and 1940 just as defense production and mobilization pulled the United States out of the Depression, and the style surfaced into public view in the months after the U.S. entered World War II. Thus its rise coincided with efforts by the federal government to conserve critical materials needed by the military, including textiles. In the context of total war, the zoot suit had become a problem.

Even before the Japanese attack on Pearl Harbor, plans were initiated to stockpile wool needed for military clothing, bedding, and other purposes. In early 1942, the War Production Board (WPB) met with leaders of the garment industry and clothing unions to determine how to limit civilian use of textiles for the duration. In March it issued restrictions on men's and women's apparel that curbed the use of fabric by requiring a slim silhouette, simplified decoration, and limited trimmings. Limitation Order L-73 (later renumbered L-224) ordered manufacturers to reduce the amount of wool in suits by 25 percent and remove cuffs, pleats, and pocket flaps. It also eliminated vests with double-breasted jackets and the second pair of trousers that traditionally came with suits.

The WPB decided against rationing clothing or prohibiting specific styles for either men or women, believing that controls on manufacturers' use of textiles and increased plant capacity would produce the needed material. The situation in the United States was less dire than in Great Britain, which imposed strict rationing and mandated "utility clothing" for civilians, or even in Canada, which issued "style-freezing" regulations. The foremost concern was to ensure sufficient resources for waging war, but American government planners also weighed the morale of civilians, sought to protect American businesses, and prepared for the postwar consumer market.[27]

Style was a consideration, even with respect to men's clothes. Some pooh-poohed the idea. "Do we need to be concerned about fashion in dressing men? Is it necessary for him to wear a full suit?" asked one manufacturer during a WPB meeting. "Most of us knew the days when it was only an odd trouser and serge coat." But most industry leaders and government officials opposed the regimentation of clothing. "Many years have been spent in building and creating style and fashions," argued one WPB administrator. "They should not be lightly tossed aside at a time of stress without giving considerable thought to the repercussions that will be created in a post-war economy." Even as the WPB ordered standard measurements to conserve fabric, it encouraged designers, manufacturers, and magazine editors to develop and promote attractive garments that would appeal to consumers. "Style has done much to help the war effort," observed the WPB's Frank Walton. There was an idealistic component to this perspective as well: Fashion, as an expression of individuality and freedom, marked the American way of life and symbolized one of the reasons "why we fight."[28]

Manufacturers of menswear generally seem to have complied with the government's conservation order, at least initially. "Relatively few appeals have been received from the clothing industry," reported a WPB staffer in August 1942. "Those that have been filed mostly relate to extra trousers, simulated cuffs and patch pockets, pleats and extra or abnormal sizes." The latter concerned work clothes for large men rather than jitterbug-crazed youth purchasing one size up. Investigators surveyed manufacturers in five major garment centers—New York City, Philadelphia, Chicago, Baltimore, and Rochester—to assess compliance, and found few serious violations. More than three-quarters of the 303 manufacturers they inspected reported that they obeyed all regulations; the majority of violations involved less than ten yards of cloth—extra fabric for cuffs, pleats, or a vest. Charges of infringement did not mention the zoot suit. Just as important, 60 percent of the firms reported the order posed no hardship. The WPB circulated these results, hoping for increased compliance as narrower styles, cuffless trousers, and suits without vests became the accepted fashion. Although government figures vary, production of men's wool suits dropped steeply from 1941 to 1944. According to one survey, only 36 percent of men over sixteen purchased one or more suits in 1943; many of those who did not, of course, had entered military service.[29]

Although the WPB's initial order did not specify the zoot suit by name, to some it portended the end of drape styles. One African American newspaper, the *Philadelphia Tribune*, sent its "inquiring photographer" to gauge the reactions of "Mr. and Mrs. Public." Several of those interviewed were sorry to "see the drape suits go out of style," but said they would support any measure to win the war. No one liked the new "defense style," with its narrow silhouette, however. One man who had contemplated new clothes now concluded, "I think I will make out with what I have." Another observed, "the man is the thing that counts, whether he has jitterbug suits or defense suits," and for most, induction into the army would mean a military uniform anyway.[30]

Despite the call for home-front sacrifice and the equanimity of these Philadelphia residents, the conservation order did little to stop the zoot suit craze. Joe Shephard, a reporter for the *Baltimore Afro-American*, found that one could still buy "yards and yards of the hepcat's delight." When he interviewed a zoot-suit purveyor about the government's clothing restrictions, the clothier turned the table. "Where'd you get those corny duds you're wearing?" he asked, and offered to make him a suit "as wide as you want 'em and as narrow . . . I'll make a real citizen out of you."[31] Manufacturers worked around the restrictions and continued to produce long, full jackets and trousers with high-rise waists and baggy knees. Some nodded to the order by making a more conservative "Victory zoot," featuring a single-breasted jacket, slash pocket, and fly front. One Washington tailor explained how he came within the letter of the WPB order: "We've still got the exaggerated shoulders. They can't touch those. You can't do much about the three-quarter length. That we got to put up with. . . . But you can get around that with this new one-button-roll double-breasted business. . . . Overlapping pleats we can't have, so we got stitched pleats in the pants. And the tight cuffs are still right there." With the limits on wool, customers ordered the zoot suit in rayon and cotton, fabrics that were not yet restricted and, as an added bonus, were manufactured in gaudier colors, rendering the style even more visible and outré.[32]

Over the summer of 1942, the growing popularity of zoot suits began to concern War Production Board officials. The final straw was a zoot-suit dance at a prominent hotel in Washington, D.C. Frank Walton worried that fashion-conscious youth were ignoring the wartime principle of "wear it out, use it up." If he did not squelch the zoot suit now, Walton warned, another youthful fad would arise and more resources would be squandered. "In a war we cannot afford the luxury of wasteful garments," Walton declared. The cloth was needed not only for the American military but also for Allied forces and refugees.[33]

Walton decided to lay down the law and put an end to the style. He ordered a crackdown on manufacturers and distributors of zoot suits. "We are going to put a stop to this waste of cloth," he said. "Every boy or girl who buys such a garment and every person who sells it is really doing an unpatriotic deed." In October 1942 the WPB further tightened the restrictions on wool and now included cotton, rayon, and linen in its new Limitation Order L-224 on menswear. This order specifically focused on the attributes of the zoot suit. It banned "high-rise trousers"—those with high waistbands—and limited their width at the knee; trousers with a 32-inch waist could not exceed 22 inches at the knee and 18½ inches at the bottom. It also fixed the maximum length for suit jackets; those in wool in a size 37 regular could be no longer than 29¾ inches. As one official put it, "the Order takes the droop and the drape out of 'zoot' suits."[34]

Thus the zoot suit became the exception to the government's policy of shoring up fashion and style. WPB regulations were designed specifically to eliminate it, and public officials depicted it as unpatriotic. Still, popular memory and scholarly histories alike have tended to overstate the zoot suit's illegality as they render it a "renegade" style. *Wearing* the style was never against the law. Only in Los Angeles was a ban on wearing the zoot suit debated. During the riot in June 1943, the city council considered such an ordinance, but did not pass it—a distinction most accounts of the riot do not make. The councilman who proposed the bill thought the style could be banned as a public nuisance, and compared it to local laws stipulating the length of bathing suits. The debate must have been memorable—the local black newspaper offered the headline, "City Council Goes Nuts"—but enough members knew that the proposed law would be unconstitutional that it was referred to the city attorney's office, where it quietly died. Ultimately, there was no recourse against the consumer. As a WPB official explained, "If these jitterbugs are buying their fantastic toggery in a black market, they have only their consciences to deal with."[35]

Government regulations were effective overall in conserving textiles for military use, but they did not stop the zoot suit. The WPB threatened retailers that they would be prosecuted and punished with a fine of $10,000 and a year in prison. To that warning, "local zoot suit dealers only smiled," reported the *Washington Post*. Indeed, the *Post*'s headline, with its syntax out of Damon Runyon—"Yon Clink Nods to Bootleggers of Zoot Suits"—suggested the threat had few teeth, and in fact enforcement was feeble. In the coverage of five major newspapers, there was only one reported instance of the government issuing an injunction against a zoot suit dealer—and this was in Los Angeles at the end of the riot.[36]

Instead, the WPB relied largely on the self-policing of manufacturers and retailers. Major department stores and reputable shops made a point of their adherence to the law, stating explicitly they would sell only styles "suited for victory." Even as they reassured customers that the "WPB is conserving without detracting from your clothes," an ad for Richman's clothing store in Chicago featured Civilian Defense guards declaring "I Play Safe! I buy my Clothes at Richman Brothers."[37] But despite the WPB's initial optimism, many firms flouted Order L-224. By 1944, M. S. Verner, director of the compliance division, complained that "circumvention, evasion, and outright violations of the restrictions of the Order are widespread," and he did not have the personnel to enforce it. Among the difficulties, Verner observed, was that the order "appears to have occasioned unusual resentment on the part of the public," which complained about everything from the quality of fabric to the rule against supplying two pairs of pants with each suit.[38] Wanting a "drape shape" was not the only desire that defied wartime conservation efforts. And it was easy enough to fulfill that desire: Young men could purchase ready-to-wear standard suits in a larger size, and tailors would cinch the trouser legs and let out the jackets for the draped effect.

How many tailors defied the law is impossible to document. The *New York Times* article profiling Clyde Duncan is one of the few that discusses a black market in zoot suits. It quotes menswear journal editor J. V. D. Carlyle, who stated that legal clothiers willingly stopped selling the garment after the limitation order went into effect, but "bootleg retailers still ma[d]e them." The notion of the bootleg tailor gestured to the Prohibition era. The *Men's Apparel Reporter* captured this aptly with a cartoon of a boy knocking at an alley hideaway: "Harry sent me! He said I could get a zoot suit here!"[39]

Scholars have fixed on the bootleg tailor, which heightens the cachet of illegality and transgression associated with the zoot style. Certainly there were tailors who set up shop in an apartment or home, similar to hairdressers who worked out of their households. But the zoot suit trade continued out in the open: If there were bootleggers, they were hiding in plain sight. A 1942 photograph advertising Van's Men's Shop in Washington, D.C., shows three zoot-suited white men jauntily strutting down a street, and other publicity shots of zoot-suited men appeared the following year. "Drapes" and zoot suits were continually advertised in black newspapers, including the *Chicago Defender*, *Pittsburgh Courier*, and *Baltimore Afro-American*, as well as such Spanish-language newspapers as *La Prensa* in Los Angeles. Burton's clothing store in Los Angeles hung a prominent sign with an image of a zoot suiter to promote its wares for months after the WPB orders, removing it finally in June 1943 after the riot made the style a target.[40]

Government restrictions even became a selling point for retailers. Clothing stores could sell their stocks of garments purchased before the limitation order, and some seemed to have an endless supply of zoot suits, judging from the numerous ads in African American newspapers.

"Certain materials needed by the Government will not be used in the future," warned National Clothing Stores, Inc. "Get yours before our present large supply is exhausted!" In Baltimore, tailor Elmer Liepman suggested buying drape suits "expertly tailored to last 'for the duration' . . . destined to become prized possessions." Some firms seemed to take delight in sharing their bad faith with their customers. "The government order is: Stop Drapes! And we back the idea wholeheartedly," insisted the Northwestern Loan Office, which carried new and out-of-pawn suits in April 1942, but "we looked ahead and contracted for a store full of the smartest drape suits in town." Similarly Kermisch's intoned that "without sacrifice on the part of all of us . . . VICTORY is impossible," but "here's some victory values that don't call for sacrifices." More than a year after the WPB had clamped down on the zoot suit, King Clothing Company in Chicago was still offering its "rhythm styled clothes"—men's zoot suits and pegged trousers—by mail order.[41]

"Cut off in a fantastic ascendancy, the zoot suit has given its all for the war"[42]—or so the government hoped. For the first and only time in its history, the state had become an arbiter of fashion. However, even as the zoot suit became the one style to be banned from manufacture, it was ever more an object of fascination, for wearers and observers alike. The production system in menswear allowed manufacturers and consumers to wiggle around the clothing limitation orders. At the same time, the government's official pronouncements had the unintended consequence of drawing attention to the zoot suit, giving it a level of exposure the style would not have had otherwise. Men who would never be seen in a zoot suit began to adjust their eyes and tastes to a fuller and looser style. In spring 1943, reputable Washington clothiers were selling clothes that were "less zooty but more drapey," suits that fit the WPB's regulations but preserved a roomy, swinging fit. A year later, a *New York Times* editorial writer, wandering around Times Square, marveled at the size and shape of men's attire. Topcoats were longer than they used to be, and "they seem to flap loosely more than half way down from the

Figure 6. National Clothing Stores advertisement, *Chicago Defender*, December 12, 1942. Courtesy of the *Chicago Defender*.

knee to the instep." He could not reconcile the "startling zoot-suit effect" with the rumor that menswear might be rationed; there seemed to
be a "clash between rumored shortage and actual superfluity."[43] Despite
the rumors, the unexpectedly high levels of textile production meant
that conservation measures began to be reduced in 1943. By October
1944, most restrictions on men's suits were rescinded, and the WPB
announced that the zoot suit could return. In fact, the style had never
left.

2

Going to Extremes

What drew young men, and even some women, to the zoot suit? Most historical studies depict the zoot suit as a "street style," devised by those whose experience of racial discrimination and prejudice led them to create distinctive sartorial responses to their situation. In these accounts, the zoot suit took flight in the streets and dance halls of Harlem and made a transcontinental leap to the *barrios* of Los Angeles. There, the social isolation of poor black youth and *pachucos* from the mainstream of American life not only created a subcultural space where a new aesthetic could flourish but also gave stylishness a political charge, making it a symbol of opposition and resistance. Although this interpretation has become axiomatic in discussions of youth of the 1940s, it rests on problematic assumptions about minority communities, the closed nature of subcultures, the direct relationship between style and politics, and most important, the consciousness and motives of those who wore extreme fashion.

The zoot suiters themselves left few explanations of why they wore zoot suits and what the style could have meant to them. No clothing surveys document their purchasing habits; no pollster interviewed them for their political views. Only rarely did zoot suiters put their style into words. For these youths, the clothing itself was the statement and means of expression. Contemporary observers and latter-day scholars alike have often relied on visual representations and textual descriptions of the zoot suit, "reading" the long coat, wide-brimmed hat, and dangling keychain as eloquent signs. These interpretations are important, indeed inevitable, but need to be treated with care, as they run the risk of imposing an alien meaning on objects that do not speak for themselves. With the rise of ethnic studies and growing interest in the war years, oral histories of Mexican Americans have delved into the attitudes of former *pachucos* and others to the role of dress in everyday life. These oral histories too pose challenges of interpretation, but their observations are invaluable. Unfortunately, we do not have comparable evidence for other young people who wore these styles.

Although the evidence is limited and elusive, an exploration of zoot suiters' own understanding of their attire and appearance is necessary if we are to gain a purchase on the meaning of a suit of clothes. To do so, we must not only focus on urban African Americans and Mexican Americans as the quintessential zoot suiters but also consider the range of youths—of different ethnic, class, and regional backgrounds—who embraced extreme style. A potent symbol of status and longing that fired the imagination, the zoot suit was not contained within specific subcultures of poor black and Hispanic youth. It spread like quicksilver, in dance scenes and music venues, along railway lines and on city streets, in the moment it took a youngster to weigh the look of pegged pants or a newly hired worker to splurge on a flashy jacket. The zoot suit meant many things in its early years, but the political valence of the style was not foremost in the minds of those who wore it.

*   *   *

Originating among African Americans, the zoot suit was initially adopted by specific groups of young men. In Harlem, early zoot suiters were not so much the "respectable" elements of the community but rather youths of the lower class, often marginally employed, who took pleasure in night life and spent their time in social clubs or gangs. The Depression-era world of streetwise youth has long been the subject of sociologists and historians, who have documented the social conditions of joblessness, racial discrimination, and class hierarchies within urban black communities. Against privation and despair came a range of inventive cultural responses. Only some lower-class black men wore zoot suits, however, which not only were expensive but also required a particular fashioning of self and appearance to carry off the style.

Those who did were known as "sharpies," who took extraordinary pains with their looks and wanted "to be dressed down to the bricks." Meticulous in the crafting of appearance, they were aware of the nuances of drape, silhouette, and ornament. In the war years, when the shortage of skilled labor and materials minimized tailoring flourishes, sharpies demanded that tailors make shoulders, jacket pockets, trouser bottoms, and pleats to their exact specifications. "The average zoot suit addict is most difficult to please," said Bill Cola, a Seventh Street clothing dealer in Washington, D.C. "They want the things just right." As the *New Yorker* put it, these young men "devoted most of their time and income to a life as sartorially intense as Lucius Beebe's," referring to a writer and legendary dandy. Decades later, one African American man in Norfolk lovingly recalled his zoot suit with stripes in two shades of blue "which caused a shadow effect on the suit." Indeed, the word "sharpie" became an early term for the zoot suit, a case of the man making the clothes.[1]

Some took their fashion cues from black celebrities, seen in person or the press. These were not "marginal men," isolated from the influence of mass media and consumer culture. Musician Duke Ellington and boxer Henry Armstrong were said to shape young men's taste for the zoot suit around 1939. The style rapidly spread among musicians, dancers, and other entertainers, then imitated by spectators. Others reworked displays they saw among screen stars and fashionable celebrities. Edward, Duke of Windsor, made a particular impression. "Many of the more

Figure 7. African American sharpies at a soda fountain in New York City, 1943. ©Bettmann/CORBIS.

daring of our Americans studied his garments before seeing their tailors," stated the *New York Amsterdam News*, which wondered if he was, in fact, the first zoot suiter.[2]

Zoot-suited busboy Clyde Duncan said his inspiration was Clark Gable in the 1939 film *Gone with the Wind*. As the dashing Rhett Butler, Gable wore a long frock coat, fitted at the shoulders and waist, with loosely draped trousers, a style that gave an impression of Civil War authenticity but that, in fact, merged the look of the 1860s with that of the 1930s. Was there a sense of irony in following the fashions of the plantation era? Gable's Rhett Butler—with his sardonic perspective, swashbuckling heroism, and degree of consideration for the film's black characters—might have seemed the image of hip masculinity. In any case, a punning Cab Calloway observed that the sharpies "were so impressed with Gable's long coat that they just 'followed suit.'"[3]

Mainstream magazines were also an important source of fashion news for Harlemites, available on newsstands and in barbershops and passed from one man to another. In 1939, *Life* magazine featured Lucius Beebe on the cover and reported that some affluent style-setters had revived wearing long gold watch chains, a story that may have influenced zoot suiters to adopt this accessory. One year later, an *Amsterdam News* reporter knew about the trend toward longer jackets for Easter because his "fashion scouts" had gone through issues of *Esquire* before they hit the newsstands.[4]

The phenomenon of sharp dressing occurred among lower-class men from other racial-ethnic minorities as well. Some were believed to have worn the zoot suit even earlier than African Americans. "Filipinos by the thousand have worn zoot suits around this town for years without hurting their own reputation or that of their haberdasher," wrote a *Los Angeles Times* columnist during the 1943 riot, advising readers not to assume the worst about the wearers of style. Although relatively few in number and confined to menial jobs as houseboys, chauffeurs, and bellhops, young Filipino men stood out for their sharp dressing and flawless grooming. In the 1930s they favored "McIntosh suits," double-breasted jackets with wide lapels and full shoulders worn with high-rise trousers and bright shirts. An abrupt departure from the traditional attire of Filipino men—the long, embroidered shirt known as *barong tagalog*—the McIntosh suit mimicked elements of the Hollywood gangster style and prefigured the zoot suit. They were so valuable that they could be pawned like jewelry in hard times.[5]

Mexican Americans were also thought of as early devotees of the zoot suit. "It's nothing new," actor Adolphe Menjou observed. "The Mexicans in California have been wearing them for generations." Like Filipinos, they had worn clothes with larger proportions and unusual tailoring. By 1940, many had adopted drape pants, with their high waists, full legs, and tight cuffs. Extreme zoot suiters went further, wearing large hats with a feather, long keychains, "ankle chokers," and fingertip jackets. In wartime Los Angeles, they frequented one particular shoe store where they would "double sole their shoes," recalled Mexican American Arthur Arenas. "They'd walk out with those shoes and right away they would dye them black, and shine them and keep shining them, and then the grain would disappear, and all you'd see is a plain, beautiful shine." Those who wore the full zoot suit ensemble embraced an identity as *pachucos,* combing their long hair in a "duck bill" style, speaking a hybrid slang called *caló*, and organizing their everyday lives around social clubs and peer groups. Some were so fixated on their appearance, explained Arenas, that they even refused to move on the dance floor. This was the "stationary *pachuco*": "He was *órale*, see? You know, it's my day, you know. He don't want to mess up his pants. . . . He didn't want to wrinkle the coat or nothing."[6]

Pachuco culture was a product of combined Mexican and Anglo American practices in the Southwest. Some historians argue that *pachucos* emerged in the 1930s or earlier in the underground and marginal economy operating across the Mexican and U.S. border. They formed gangs engaged in drug running and petty criminal pursuits, and used bilingual slang and such markers as dress and hairstyle to identify each other and carry out their activities. If the spreading use of *caló* is an

Figure 8. *Pachuco* Frank Lopez dressed in a zoot suit, San Fernando, California, 1944. Shades of L.A. Archives/Los Angeles Public Library.

indicator, *pachucos* moved back and forth from Mexico and throughout the Southwest along the Southern Pacific Railroad from El Paso to Tucson and Los Angeles. The drape style—sometimes referred to in slang as *tachuche*—is more difficult to trace in the 1930s or earlier. Unlike *caló*, developing as a subcultural language among migrants along the border, drapes seem to have emerged in the commercial and mixed social environment of Los Angeles and other Southwestern cities. Eduardo Pagán suggests that men known as *tirilones* may have picked up the zoot suit style in New York City when they traveled to supply jazz musicians with marijuana, and brought it back with them to the Southwest, where Mexican American agricultural laborers and city dwellers may have seen and emulated the style.[7]

The Mexican American middle class did not wear drapes, César Chávez observed: "People that wore them *eran los mas pobres* [were the poorest], the guys like us who were migrant farm workers." The musicians Eduardo "Lalo" Guerrero came in contact with were also poor youths, mainly busboys and waiters. During the war, Guerrero worked at an aircraft factory and played at the Mexicali Club in San Diego. He did not wear a zoot suit, and was unsure how it moved from New York to Southern California. Still, he observed that *pachucos* began to have a growing impact on musical taste and local culture. Nightclubs began to have "*pachuco* nights," and Guerrero wrote *pachuco* songs and boogie-woogie tunes with *caló* lyrics. "The boys were very neat, very clean, and they loved to dress up," Guerrero recalled. "They'd save for months for a tailor-made zoot suit that would cost two hundred dollars or more."[8]

The zoot suit touched the body differently from conventional men's attire, which was cut more narrowly and fitted more closely. Young African American men in Washington, D.C., prized the sack jacket which, "as one of the boys says, 'touches nuffin' but the shoulders,'" and swung loosely as its wearer strolled down the street or stepped out onto a dance floor. The zoot suit enabled the theatrical gesture. When Malcolm X bought his first zoot suit, he immediately modeled it for a drugstore

photograph, posing like a hipster "cool[ing] it," drawing his knees together, spreading his feet, and pointing his forefingers to the floor. "The
long coat and swinging chain and the Punjab pants were much more
dramatic if you stood that way," he observed. Tailor Harold Fox similarly remembered his young clientele who, after putting on their new
zoot suits, would strike a pose or swing the long chain for effect.[9]

The drape and fullness of the zoot suit mattered particularly on the
dance floor, and its emergence coincided with the craze for swing and
jitterbug. As one enthusiast put it, zoot suiters were "guys who could
really dance." Innovative dance steps at Harlem's Savoy in the 1930s
jump-started the trend, as dancers pegged their pants to keep from getting tangled with their partners and to accentuate their moves through
their trousers' ballooning effect. The speed and gymnastic moves of wartime dancing, Carey McWilliams observed, would have "meant disaster
to the average suit." The classic description of this scene, and the zoot
suit's place in it, appears in *The Autobiography of Malcolm X*. Working
at the Roseland Ballroom in Boston, Malcolm Little marveled at the
brilliantly dressed pairs, the whirling bodies, and the passionate dancing.
"Some couples were so abandoned—flinging high and wide, improvising
steps and movements—that you couldn't believe it," he wrote. "I could
feel the beat in my bones." On and off the dance floor, the zoot suit
made heads turn. Some African Americans even dubbed the extreme
suits "killer-dillers," using jive, the coded slang of jazz musicians and
swing devotees: "killer-diller" meant "a great thing," but it also referred
to fast dance numbers, and those who could perform the steps.[10]

In New York, Los Angeles, Chicago, and elsewhere, a dense commercial culture sprang up in African American neighborhoods and city centers that offered lower-class leisure pursuits, possibilities for social
mixing across racial and ethnic lines, and opportunities for small-time
hustling, vice, and marginal business activities. These entertainment districts were incubators of new fads in music, dance, and fashion, with the
line of influence radiating typically from African American trendsetters

Figure 9. Young men in zoot suits watching an act at the Savoy Ballroom in Harlem, late 1930s. ©Bettmann/CORBIS.

to other racial and ethnic minorities. By the end of the 1930s, as migrants journeyed to cities for war work, the jostling of pleasure seekers in these districts meant that new styles would be relayed quickly, even as racial and ethnic mixing increasingly became a source of anxiety and concern.[11]

During the 1920s and 1930s, for example, Filipinos in Los Angeles had spent their leisure hours in their own "Little Manila," enjoying gambling, boxing, and taxi-dance halls, where a dime paid for a dance with a white hostess. Fears of interracial social and sexual encounters led to a ban on Asian men in taxi-dance halls, and they began to frequent mixed-race "black and tan" cabarets. Contact with African American panache led many Filipino men to shed the McIntosh suit for the zoot suit. Although older Mexican residents did not venture far from their own neighborhoods in Los Angeles, Carey McWilliams observed, "the second generation was lured . . . into the downtown shopping districts, to the beaches, and above all, to the 'glamor' of Hollywood." In these places they saw the evolution of extreme dress, taking the measure especially of African American men's style.[12]

Some Japanese American men picked up the zoot suit style in Los Angeles's "Little Toyko" before the war and joined gangs that stayed together in the internment camps and after they regained their freedom. Investigating the resettlement of Japanese American internees in 1943, sociologist Charles Kikuchi interviewed several *Nisei* (second-generation) zoot suiters, known as *yagore*—literally "dirty." They had received work permits, left the internment camps, and moved to Chicago, living in mixed-race neighborhoods. There they socialized with Mexican American, Chinese, Filipino, and *Nisei* friends and lovers, taking pleasure in casual sex, drinking, and nightlife; some ran with gangs and made a living through gambling or pimping. These men imitated streetwise sharpies: Kikuchi described one who wore his hair *pachuco* style, owned several zoot suits, and, according to the sociologist, looked like a Filipino. Journalist Ayako Noguchi found resettled *Nisei* zoot suiters in Denver and Salt Lake City, who, in her view, drew an unwanted kind of attention to Japanese Americans. Wearing zoot pants and "pachook hairdresses," they looked "rowdy, cheap and shiftless" as they strolled down the street. She was shocked by their extreme looks and demeanor, which she described as far less conventional than even those of African American and Mexican American youth.[13]

For a number of young lower-class men—African American, *pachuco*, Filipino, and *Nisei*—incorporation of the extreme style into their lives was rich, substantial, and intense. Dress, music, dance, language, and gesture combined to convey a sense of identity and allegiance. It is in this sense that zoot suits may be seen as integral to specific youth subcultures, as an aesthetic that expressed and encompassed a way of being and living.[14] Clothing style was not necessarily the defining attribute of such a subculture—it is a misnomer to label this a "zoot culture"—but dress was one of a congeries of elements that made such youth recognizable, to themselves and each other.

At the same time, it would be wrong to consider the zoot suit a marker only of enclosed or isolated out-groups, a style belonging solely to an "underclass" of impoverished and disadvantaged minority men. As is often true with fashion, the style seeped into the everyday dress of many. Young men typically distinguished between extreme and moderate zoot suits using the tailors' taxonomy: "drapes," after the drape-cut suit, "semi-drape," for those who wanted a muted look, and "extreme drape," which went all the way. Arthur Arenas explained the difference in terms of trousers cinched at the ankles. "A semi-drape is not completely an ankle choker. It was maybe a 16 bottom, instead of a 14 bottom," he noted. He looked at the zoot suiters, with their "big hat and a feather and a chain dragging down there, ankle chokers," and decided, "I don't want to go extreme. I'll just go semi. You know, make it look different, a little different." He observed, "A lot of guys wore semi-drape." Educator and diplomat Julian Nava, who was fifteen when the Los Angeles riot broke out, recalled that about 30 percent of his peers wore drapes, but "there were great extremes in zoot suits—the peg of the trousers, the length of the coat, how much shoulder padding, how wide the hat brim." It was not only lower-class "sharpies" who wore versions of the zoot suit but African American collegians and professionals. John Kinloch, a journalist for the *California Eagle*, wore a "gorgeous" green zoot suit as his "pride and joy." Even *Nisei* men who shunned the *yagore* put on modified drapes for dances and parties in the Tule Lake relocation center and other internment camps. Newspaper photographers eager to render such camps harmless shot pictures of "jitter-bugging to evacuee bands," and instructed viewers to "note the 'zoot suit' pants."[15]

Taking root among urban Mexican American and African American youth, the zoot suit nevertheless spread quickly around the country. Even before Hollywood or the press noticed the style, it appeared in surprising places. After the *Men's Apparel Reporter* ran the picture of Clyde Duncan in early 1941, tailor James Brown submitted photographs of two *white* men who had requested similar outfits. Brown ran a clothing store in Anderson, Indiana, a small town between Indianapolis and Muncie and a production center for the automobile industry. Nothing he had seen in the trade journals compared with the long coats he was selling, "not to just a couple of boys who try to outdress anyone else, but to a large group of fellows." These jackets had fly-fronts, button center vents, "drape sleeves as they are not made anywhere in the state, and extremely loose full-draped bodies." The young men asked for brilliant color combinations, such as yellow coats and maroon trousers. "We have sold a number of iridescent red and green, red and blue, made the wrong side out so that the red is really the predominating color," Brown marveled.[16]

There is no way to know precisely what caused the fashion for zoot suits in as unlikely a place as Anderson. Brown's store may have advertised "clothes of renown," but it promoted ordinary menswear in the local newspaper. To be sure, the city had a small African American community, although Brown's letter made no reference to it. One clue to the puzzle may be that Anderson had become a boomtown in the early 1940s, as industrial plants converted from automobile manufacturing to war production. In similar places around the country, flashy attire appealed to war workers with spending money and the desire for a good time. These were defense workers in armaments factories, aircraft plants, and shipyards—riveters, punch-press operators, jigmakers, sorters, and checkers. They worked hard all day, then flocked to bars, nightclubs, bowling alleys, dine-and-dance places, and rollerdromes. Many of them took to the exuberant look of drape coats and pegged pants.

In Southern California, employees at Lockheed, Douglas, Boeing, and other factories gathered after hours at Zucca's on Hermosa Beach or the Trianon in South Gate, "a vast armory of a place, with acres of hardwood floor and miles of beer concessions." Many factories had put on an evening shift from 4 p.m. to midnight—the "swing shift"—and these workers danced and caroused when most people had long been in bed. With men earning $100 or more a week, and many of the women employed as well, they spent lavishly on entertainment and clothes. One master of ceremonies described his nightclub as a "regular democratic smelter pot." The working women often appeared in fancy dress— "more than half these fine mamas never wore an evening gown before"—with husbands and boyfriends still in their overalls or "the sports clothes they wore to and from work." Others wore drapes. The "oddest phenomenon of the new brand of California night life," observed journalist Walter Davenport, "is the zoot suit favored by the more ardent devotees of swing." In Chicago, "zoot suit audiences" made hits of such unlikely offerings as "Good Night Ladies" and "Maid in the Ozarks." The men and boys "in sweaters and zoot-suits and leather jackets" who packed the shows each night befuddled one theater critic accustomed to elite theatergoers. He commented, "The real reason for the triumph of these rowdy, caricaturish farces is their appeal to huge populations who never before laid eyes upon live actors, and yet who, now, in war-work prosperity, have plenty of cash and little to spend it on."[17]

The war had spawned new wants and predilections, including a desire for bigger wardrobes and luxury items like furs and jewelry. The clothing industry called it a "new aristocracy," with unpredictable taste. As one fashion columnist wrote, "It's the workers in industry who are responsible" for rejecting the "ancient austerity of their attire" in favor of unusual colors and such oddities as porkpie hats and cowboy belts. Retailers, style expert Henry Jackson warned, would not be able to "ritz them with gentlemanly fashion," but have to offer "something special, with flash." The two years before the United States entered the war were crucial to this emergent consumer sensibility. With the government's infusion of money and creation of jobs in the mobilization for defense, relief rolls declined and household income rose for the first time in a decade. "A lot of guys who've been just barely able to make ends meet for the past ten years, are suddenly finding themselves in the chips—but in a big way," Jackson observed. Many had paid off debts and bought practical items for their households. But others—young, footloose, and facing an uncertain future—took to living in the moment. After Pearl Harbor, the economic equation changed, with wages remaining high but consumption tightened. Unable to make purchases of major household goods or automobiles for the duration, consumers splurged on clothing. Newly flush, these men were "buying up," willing to pay $35 or $45 for a suit. Although racial discrimination continued to limit opportunities in high-paying defense jobs, many people of color nevertheless were seeing larger paychecks for the first time and treated themselves to clothes. Observed black journalist Frank M. Davis, the zoot suit was a form of "relief from Depression," when young men "had been forced to don cheap garb or hand-me-downs."[18]

The zoot suit had spread to white working-class youths and even to middle-class teens by the early 1940s. Young men of Italian and Eastern European descent eagerly took up the style. Harold Fox recalled that many Jewish boys frequented his shop on Chicago's West Side, drawn by the jazz musicians and the clothes. One psychiatrist found that four of ten middle-class boys in a Brooklyn high school wore zoot suits. Jive talk and drape shapes "went wild in Washington's high schools" and attracted teens in Midwestern towns and cities too; in Decatur, Illinois, high school students protested after the principal banned ankle-length watch chains. When Harry James's big band played at the Paramount in Times Square during Easter of 1943, teenagers in zoot suits came out in droves—"maidens in grown-up Easter bonnets tottering nervously on nascent high heels" and "goslings in finger-tip topcoats with manhood sprouting through in upper lips." Blocking traffic in front of the theater,

Figure 10. Teenage zoot suiters walking down a New York City street, 1943.
©Bettmann/CORBIS.

the concertgoers displayed "a riot of color with their zoot suits, shrunken ankle pants, green pork pie hats and sharply etched sport coats done in mauve and off-doe hues." Indeed, the zoot-suit phenomenon had caught on so widely that an educational journal even suggested how teachers could make their lessons more relevant by discussing it in class, especially if their school was in a "zoot suit locale."[19]

The fad took off at a unique moment, when economic and social transformation seemed to be articulated through vivid new forms of cultural expression. As the hardships of the Great Depression gave way to the supercharged economy of World War II, swing and jitterbug swept the country. Dance steps created by northern African Americans, most visibly at Harlem's Savoy Ballroom, were seen and imitated by white youths. Mass jitterbug dances, in particular, brought youths together in unprecedented ways: The Savoy was well known as a "melting pot," where "every night in the week, every race and nationality under the sun, the high and the low, meet," while a 1939 jitterbug contest in Los Angeles announced that "teams will include Mexicans, Jewish, Philipino, and all nationalities." In a regeneration of popular culture and music, historian Lewis Erenberg writes, swing "affirm[ed] personal experimentation, affluence, and ethnic and racial pluralism." While women usually adopted a casual look for these dances—circle skirts, bobby socks, and saddle shoes—young men often dressed up in long sports coats and drape pants. Swing's rhythm released a charge from hotel ballrooms to school auditoriums. After listening to editors bemoan modern youth's infatuation with jitterbug and swing, Orlando Suero, a seventeen-year-old office boy at the *New York Times*, wrote an essay in "swinguage" to explain the phenomenon: "You feel something come over you that cannot be controlled, your heart feels alive and gay, you jump with jive."[20] For many white youngsters, jumping with jive could only be done in a zoot suit.

Urban dance halls featuring black bands circulated clothing styles and dance steps that had originated among people of color. Cab Calloway was the most notorious of the snappy dressers among musicians, popularizing zoot suits and jive talk not only in the black community but also among white patrons. In Washington, D.C., zoot suiters strutted in the city's prominent hotels. They took the floor in the Victory Room at the Roosevelt Hotel and crowded Uline Arena to hear the best swing bands. The Washington Hotel held jitterbug contests and zoot suit balls "where no one could enter without a zoot suit for the boys and a 'juke coat' for the girls." Louis Redmond's "heppest zoot suit ever" won him five dollars and an appearance on the radio in August 1942. Even the Elks Club Dance, "the cleanest dance in town," attracted men in

Figure 11. A dancing zoot suiter twirls his partner at a Washington, D.C., dance, as photographed by Ollie Atkins in 1943. ©Bettmann/CORBIS.

drapes.[21] These were segregated venues: Only whites attended Uline Arena, the Washington Hotel balls, and the Elks Club, and there were many zoot suiters among them.

The style moved rapidly around the country in the early 1940s, as if it spontaneously erupted everywhere. It is virtually impossible to trace the movement of the zoot suit chronologically or geographically, from coast to coast, or from the metropolis to small towns. Traveling bands brought swing styles to Southern and Midwestern locales; in Anderson, Indiana, they played at the Paramount Theater and the Green Lantern, a popular roadhouse. Wherever there was swing and jitterbug, zoot pants and long jackets appeared: government photographers found the styles at a farm workers' community party in Yuma, Arizona; an affair thrown by watch-factory employees in Lancaster, Pennsylvania; and a WPA-sponsored scrap salvage rally and dance. As jobs in defense industries multiplied, the migration of men for employment also spread the style; this was true of black men in the small city of Opelousas, Louisiana, who traveled to Houston, Texas, for work and came back dressed in zoot suits. Sometimes, they would simply mail a photograph home, as Malcolm X did to his family, displaying a new big-city style.[22] Spectators watching musicians and dancers, ordinary men on the street glancing at a trouser leg, a conversation with an astute tailor—in the relay of looks, men gauged the effect of a long, loose jacket, wide-brimmed hat, and swinging watch chain. As their eyes adjusted to the silhouette and shape of drapes, what had once been outré became a desired fashion.

The zoot suit did not become a fad through a concerted marketing campaign or explicit promotion by advertisers and the press. However, newspaper and magazine coverage did circulate the style, first when the War Production Board assailed it in 1942, and then in the wake of the zoot suit riot, and this reporting contributed to its rapid rise. An elderly man recalled in 2005 how he had come to wear a zoot suit sixty years earlier in Oblong, a small town in downstate Illinois. Seventeen or eighteen years old, this self-described white Anglo-Saxon Protestant had seen photographs of the zoot suit in *Life* magazine and read about the attacks on *pachucos*. He tried to emulate the style by buying an oversized coat, pegged pants, and a brass chain used in light fixtures to serve as his long keychain. All in all, he said, "I thought I was pretty spiffy." He wore the zoot suit "as a rebellion . . . against the preceding generation" and also "in sympathy with the Mexican Americans" because he was studying Spanish in school.[23] His motives, remembered over the decades, combined a generational awareness, a sense of wanting to appear unusual, and an imaginative connection to disadvantaged youths whose lives were markedly different and far away.

Before the zoot suit became an overt public issue in Los Angeles in 1942 and 1943, however, the political overtones of the style are difficult to perceive. To be sure, the style scorned standards of respectability, violated wartime conservation measures, and offended elders. But should it be understood as a gesture of refusal to white supremacy and "hegemonic" culture? The evidence points in a different direction. Rather than wearing the zoot suit as an inchoate symbol of resistance to discriminatory treatment and racial prejudice, it was more often the case that men found in the style a compelling aesthetic that embodied a new sense of themselves at a moment of possibility and transformation.

For many, especially those who had migrated to cities in search of jobs, wearing the zoot suit signified a new urban identity, being modern, prosperous, and in the know. Malcolm X describes his transit from a small Midwestern town to Boston, where he saw his own provincialism through the eyes of street-smart youths and felt ashamed. "I looked like Li'l Abner," he said, evoking the popular cartoon character that epitomized the hick. "Mason, Michigan was written all over me." He quickly transformed his appearance, buying a zoot suit and conking his hair. As Malcolm X described it, wearing the zoot brought on many powerful feelings and desires—of shedding the past and reveling in a newfound sense of manhood and selfhood, of enjoying male comradeship and being sexually attractive to women. He was not alone in embracing fashion as a sign of urbanity and belonging. At age sixteen Lee Gilliam moved from a farm in Arkansas to take a high-paying job in a cannery in Oakland. "The first thing I did was went and bought clothes and started going to a [hair] process shop," he recalled, which "showed I had money and prestige."[24]

Young men described the zoot suit as a style that bedazzled, holding the eye and making a powerful impression. As one boy put it, "the idea of looking 'drape' is to look like a diamond." Some *pachucos* saw the zoot suit as magical, even superhuman. Among young Mexican Americans were skilled caricaturists and cartoonists, and a few of their drawings of zoot suiters survive. During the Sleepy Lagoon murder trial,

Figure 12. A caricature of a zoot suiter drawn by defendant Manuel Delgado during the Sleepy Lagoon murder trial, on the letterhead of the Sleepy Lagoon Defense Committee, whose ranks were filled with Hollywood stars and left-wing leaders, c. 1943–44.

Manuel Delgado, Sleepy Lagoon Defense Committee Records, Department of Special Collections, Charles E. Young Research Library, UCLA.

which brought notoriety to the zoot suit as the style of alleged Mexican American gangs, defendant Manuel Delgado drew an image of the zoot suiter on the letterhead of the committee defending him. The picture shows a tough, nattily dressed man; heavy outlining and cross-hatching emphasize his sharp-looking clothing. The man's facial expression is youthful and calm, yet determined and unwelcoming. Delgado linked his own name to Michelangelo and Rembrandt, with a palette as his trademark. The words surrounding the text underline the magnificence of the zoot-suited man—"Terrific as the Pacific!!" "frantic as [the] Atlantic!!"—and mark him as a member of the 38th Street gang.[25]

Other pictures used cartoon superheroes and comic book characters to stress manliness, swagger, sexual magnetism, brotherhood, and the strength of neighborhood. Four drawings appeared in *One Nation,* a series of essays highlighting different racial and ethnic groups in the United States. Compiled by Wallace Stegner and the editors of *Look* magazine, the volume was intended to foster tolerance in the wake of wartime racial conflicts. The images are undated, but drawn during the war years, and their creators are unknown; still, they offer a rare opportunity to see how some Mexican American youths at that time imagined themselves. In one, a muscular *pachuco* knocks out his opponent in midair. Another shows a "Mex" ready to punch an "Okie," who quakes with fear and pleads, "Now, let's be reasonable." The draped pants and vest emphasize the fighter's strength and build, while the Okie's narrow silhouette, rolled-up pants, and beads of sweat depict his weakness and provinciality. A third drawing elaborates on the Happy Valley "hep cat." Here the cigar-smoking zoot suiter seems beholden to Warner Brothers' edgy Daffy Duck. He pushes away a small and frightened birdlike creature as an admiring woman watches. "One side Long hair: let a Hep cat on the platter!" he says, using jive to say that straight types (long hair being equated with classical music) must step aside and let hepcats take center stage (on the platter, that is, a phonograph record). The picture depicts a strutting masculinity that mingles control, style, hero worship, and sex appeal. A final drawing portrays an archetypal zoot suiter, surrounded by the names of members of "La Loma," a Mexican American gang or social club. The names had the same intention as graffiti, marking a sense of belonging and place; like Happy Valley, La Loma was a particular locality in greater Los Angeles, with a poor Mexican American population. Although the cartoon portrayed gang affiliation, it may have also reflected a broader wartime fad among teens for writing their names on each other's clothing as a mark of friendship.[26]

There are other hints of fantasy and longing that fixed upon the zoot suit. José "Chepe" Ruiz, convicted for the Sleepy Lagoon murder, wrote activist and supporter Alice Greenfield about a conversation with his mother, who visited him in prison. His mother had tried to "psychoanalyze the reason for the actions that brought in the present trouble." She attributed individual action to the influence of culture, including fashion, and observed that people made moral judgments based on their reactions to style and appearance. She used the image of Don Juan in the movies as an example. "He leaves an impression of a sort . . . you arrived at a conclusion by the clothes Don Juan wore," she said. "So, for God's sake, son, give me permission to take the zoot suit of yours and have it made over into a dress." "After being revived," Chepe Ruiz replied, "Never, mother, never. I shall keep that suit for a keepsake. Who knows, perhaps in the 25th century someone may look at that suit, and say, WHAT DON JUAN WORE THAT?" Where his mother saw a dangerous sexuality that could be tamed only by turning menswear into a woman's guise, Ruiz imagined his historical legacy as a Latin lover, but with an underlying sense of suffering for a cause. Although he told Greenfield that this was a "true transcript," its theatricality and humor, with references to psychoanalysis, "savage" Africa, seventeenth-century France, and Don Juan, suggest the truth may have been embellished. Ruiz concludes, "Seriously, I am serving a long, long, time for wearing a suit like that."[27]

Conquering superheroes, admired hepcats, tough gangsters, the world's greatest lover and its most legendary artists: these images swirled around the zoot suit of the imagination. What is striking, then, is the

Figures 13 and 14. Two zoot suit cartoons drawn by Mexican American youths in Southern California during the war years.

Wallace Stegner, *One Nation* (Boston: Houghton Mifflin, 1945).

frequent disparity between this sensibility and the actual article of clothing. *The Autobiography of Malcolm X* does not include the drugstore snapshot of Malcolm "cooling it" in his Punjab pants, but it does reproduce two photographs of Malcolm wearing a long drape coat, peg-top pants, and narrowed cuffs. This zoot suit is much more staid than the

Figure 15. Mexican American youths in jail, detained for questioning, reveal an array of looks, c. 1942.

Los Angeles Daily News Negatives, Department of Special Collections, Charles E. Young Research Library, UCLA.

one of his reminiscence or, for that matter, the glorious costumes in Spike Lee's 1992 film version of the *Autobiography*. Photographs of Mexican American youth arrested after a brawl in 1942 also suggest a difference between what was imagined and what was worn. Jail officials ordered the lineup to put those wearing zoot suits in the front row, underscoring the link between style and criminality. A look at the boys' faces—some sullen, many open and approachable, all very young— belies the view of law enforcement that these were hardened criminals. They wear the long coat and pegged pants of the zoot suit, but the natural shoulders of the jacket, dark colors, and above all the quiescent pose, upend the images of masculine swagger drawn by Delgado and the *pachuco* cartoonists.[28]

Among men, the style marked numerous distinctions that spoke not only to differing images of masculinity but also to class, education, ethnicity, generation, and norms of propriety. Observers noted stylistic differences between zoot suits East and West, with Los Angeles drapes supposedly being more conservative in color and less exaggerated in shape than those seen in New York City. It is, in fact, difficult to substantiate these differences, as men around the country wore various versions of the drape style and the evidence is fragmentary. Men's ability to modify the zoot suit allowed them to draw a line, as they saw it, between looking sharp and looking ridiculous. But men were also making sociological distinctions in the drape of jackets and fullness of pants when they tied the embrace of the extreme to racial definitions, outsider status, and danger. Rudy Leyvas, the brother of Henry Leyvas, one of the Sleepy Lagoon defendants, wore drapes but observed, "Frankly we didn't consider ourselves zoot suiters because we didn't wear the extreme zoot suit that the blacks wore." In an interview, Johnny Rollonza, a Filipino who did not wear zoot suits, made a similar distinction when remembering life in Little Manila in the 1940s: "Sure, there were some Filipino zoot suiters in the city during the war, but only the 'panggulo' [copycats, troublemakers] wore them, because it was mostly the Mexicans and blacks who wore the suits."[29]

Zoot suits could be controversial within these communities of color even before they became items that provoked fear and anxiety among white Americans. The style threatened African American and Mexican American community leaders, who insisted that respectable appearance and appropriate behavior would help secure the safety and status of these groups. "Surely there is much clowning going on," warned Reverend J. L. Caston in 1941, fearful that black youth in Los Angeles were bringing trouble on themselves through tomfoolery instead of working hard and living a respectable life. Pointedly condemning "those extreme fashions called drapes," he worried about the "symptoms of tragedy which may lurk in a clown's suit." Some school principals banned zoot suits. "You couldn't go to school with them," recalled Arthur Arenas. "You'd wear them maybe on the weekend." Others stressed that the zoot suit was for dressing up. Mexican American youth wore a variety of clothes around the neighborhood and to school, especially pegged pants and large untucked shirts, observed one migrant daughter, but the complete zoot suit "was worn on special occasions" only, especially to public dances.[30]

The zoot suit figured in conflicts between generations, especially among immigrant parents and their American-born children. "Parents didn't like it," observed Carlos Espinoza, who lived in Los Angeles in the 1940s. "So some of the guys would go down to their neighbor's house and put the zoot suit on, and then go to the dance. And they would come back and take it off, and put their Levi's on and go home when they had trouble with it." Mexican Americans concerned about respectability within their own community and acceptance in the larger society understood the way that clothing conveyed social status. One middle-class women remembered that in the early 1940s, "we actually started seeing the drape pants around that time, but we didn't approve of it and we didn't dress that way." Zoot suiters, she said, "were really, really different; more dropouts, shall we say, with time on their hands. We kept away from them and they never tried to go to our dances or to our parties." The Japanese community, concerned to present a positive public image, reacted even more strongly to the *yagore*, who defied the expectation that *Nisei* be quiet, hard-working, and harmless. The *yagore*, writes historian Paul Spickard, "so embarrassed other Nisei that they appear nowhere in published accounts."[31]

If wearing the zoot suit required defying parents, ministers, and community opinion, not wearing it might cause young men to be labeled "squares" and "Pepsi-Cola kids." One young man embraced a *pachuco* identity from age fourteen to seventeen, beginning in junior high school in Los Angeles's Watts neighborhood, despite the disapproval of his parents and brothers. Peer pressure to wear drapes was intense. "You're a square if you don't," he observed. After two years overseas in the army, he returned, married, settled down, and gave up the style. César Chávez loved the "sharp and neat" look of the *pachuco*'s drapes. "It was the style, and I wasn't going to be square," he recalled. "I would have felt pretty stupid walking around dressed differently." He remembered being harassed by the police and scorned by some older people in the Mexican community. "We needed a lot of guts to wear those pants, and we had to be rebellious to do it," said Chávez, but "I was prepared for any sacrifice to be able to dress the way I wanted to dress." Julian Nava, also looking back on his adolescence, observed that the style was "associated with rebellious youth," those with what he termed "social adjustment problems." However, the appeal of the zoot suit "wasn't all negative," but for many reflected "a searching for something new and more meaningful." The deep attachment to the style is suggested in one journalist's account: When a judge punished two young Mexican Americans for rowdiness by ordering them to stop wearing their zoot suits, they broke down and cried in court.[32]

Chávez identified *pachuco* attire with working-class life, the importance of looking sharp, and an assertion of independence, but he drew the line at the suggestion that the style was a statement of political resistance. "Our rebellion wasn't the kind of rebellion they have today— students and young people rebelling against society," he explained in 1975. "Today these kids have an idea. We didn't know exactly what was happening. . . . You have to understand that I wore them as a style." The young middle-class woman who refused to date zoot suiters had the same perspective. "We figured it's an exaggerated style of dress that's going to come and go away, never expecting them to take over as much as they did eventually," she observed. "You saw them all over, but they weren't belligerent; they weren't that way yet."[33] Prior to the Sleepy Lagoon murder case and the zoot suit riot, the zoot suit served to uphold an alternative masculine style and to make distinctions among young men with respect to class and status. It was a focal point of generational tensions, and figured in the everyday policing of appropriate and respectable behavior. But it did not yet carry a political charge, not with a degree of consciousness to be associated with the term "political."

Although mainly men wore zoot suits, some women adopted elements of the style. During the war years, they were encouraged to wear slacks on their defense jobs, and women's clothing retailers offered an array of ready-made trousers. It became increasingly routine to see women going to work, shopping, and enjoying leisure dressed in pants, and some adopted the pegged style. Women wearing "juke jackets" also appeared at nightspots and hotel ballrooms. At the Trianon, where he watched war workers dance the night away, syndicated columnist Henry McLemore observed that "the girls wear 'zoot' suits too," calling them "defense drapes" and "defense capes."[34]

Mexican American women were among those who played with masculine extreme style. Known as *pachucas,* they developed a complementary fashion to that of their boyfriends and brothers, wearing pegged pants or long drape jackets with short skirts, along with elaborate pompadours. They also spoke *caló*, associated with male gangs, and formed their own groups or social clubs with such names as the Black Widows and Slick Chicks. Their most popular style of dressing, however, involved short skirts, fishnet stockings or bobby sox, and tight sweaters—a distinctive, even sexually provocative, look, but not so different from the "sweater girls," jitterbug-dancers, and pinups prized by servicemen. Historians Catherine Ramírez and Elizabeth Escobedo have shown how these styles went together with young Mexican American women's greater public presence in the workplace, at leisure venues, and on city streets. A new sense of Mexican American female identity emerged, which sparked concern both within the Mexican community and in white Los Angeles.[35]

Other women who adopted men's zoot suits were lesbians, whose clothing style directly challenged gender norms and sexual identities but who are generally ignored in discussions of style politics of the 1940s. As Elizabeth Kennedy and Madeline Davis explain in their study of Buffalo, New York's lesbian community, the growing acceptance of women wearing pants provided a cover for lesbians to express their sense of identity and erotic interest in women through their clothing. In a lesbian culture organized into butch/femme relationships, butches put on stiffly starched

Figure 16. The *pachuca* fashion for pegged pants and drape jackets, worn by Mexican American junior high school students in 1939.

shirts, tailored pants, and jackets, and some adopted the zoot suit style. One interviewee recalled a black woman whose tough look both frightened and fascinated her. She "was leaning up against the juke box, and she was swinging a key chain; and she had on men's spade shoes, black leather dress shoes, and maybe like a suit, or a vest, and a pair of trousers and a trench coat." Another, who typically wore feminine dresses and high heels, remembered that "once in a while, I'd get real . . . brave" and dressed in a zoot suit "with the long jackets and the chains and the pants that had the real tight legs and you had to take your shoes off to put them on." Wearing "full men's attire"—whether a zoot suit or not—frequently subjected lesbians to verbal harassment, beatings, and arrest for violating laws against cross-dressing. In Memphis, three black women were arrested for wearing men's clothing in a café; when one protested that "they were wearing slack suits and riding outfits, just like white women wear," the judge rebuffed her assertion and fined them $50 each for "wearing clothes of the opposite sex and loitering."[36]

Wearing a zoot suit conveyed many meanings in the early 1940s. The full ensemble offered a dramatic means of self-fashioning to men, especially but not only to African American and Mexican American youths, and appealed even to a small number of women. For sharpies and *pachucos*, it was an aesthetic integral to the rhythms of everyday life, bound up with their sense of personal and group identity, and a bond with like-minded peers. For some, then, this was an *intensive* cultural form. Appearing in public in such outfits sometimes required an act of courage, a choice to take a risk in order to assert one's self and desire, perhaps particularly so in Southern California, but elsewhere too. In Harlem and East Los Angeles, the zoot suit pointed to a variety of social differences, marking friendships, generational bonds, neighborhood affiliation, and a challenge to norms of respectability and conventionality. It sometimes designated the gang member or hustler, but it was more often worn by a subset of youths who, in circumstances of poverty and disadvantage, found pleasure in dressing up and gaining attention and admiration. But the frame of reference for understanding the zoot suit must be widened, for it was an *extensive* cultural form as well. Elements of extreme style spoke to many young men of different socioeconomic and cultural backgrounds, from newly flush industrial workers keen on flashy clothes to middle-class teenagers obsessed with swing bands. The street style was soon relayed through mass media and popular culture, a spectacular yet enigmatic image for a nation lifted out of the Great Depression by mobilization for war.

3

Into the Public Eye

Although the penchant for extreme drapes began to appear toward the end of the 1930s, neither the mainstream press nor the entertainment industry paid much notice at first. *Men's Apparel Reporter,* usually alert to trends in menswear, did not publish Clyde Duncan's 1940 zoot-suit photograph until a year after it was taken. In early 1941, the *New Yorker* gave one of the first accounts in a general-interest magazine when it presented a mock fashion report on Easter styles in Harlem, "the world's least inhibited fashion centre."[1] At that time, the style was attracting attention in the black press, occasioning humor, concern, and debate unseen by white Americans. By 1942, however, the zoot suit had come into the public eye across the United States. The push to conserve textiles brought the glare of publicity on a fad now deemed unpatriotic, and a host of news stories, songs, films, cartoons, and photographs suddenly spotlighted the zoot suit. In most of the country—outside of Los Angeles—these portrayals rarely tied the style to delinquency, violence, or the estrangement of young men of color prior to the riot in June 1943. As defense mobilization boosted the economy and swing music buoyed the culture, the zoot suit initially seemed an exotic expression of youth and an indecipherable style of African Americans—but not, in the first instance, a sign of menace and danger. Reworked by animators, songwriters, and journalists—most of whom witnessed the style rather than wore it—the zoot suit was an aesthetic that embodied the flux, dislocation, immediacy, and even ecstasy of American life in a time of war.

*   *   *

The zoot suit spread initially among African Americans through the everyday interactions of tailors and customers, jazz musicians and jitterbug dancers, street-corner style-setters and their friends. It was only around 1940 that the style became a frequent item of notice and comment among the wider African American public. *New York Amsterdam News* writer Bill Chase anticipated the *New Yorker*'s coverage when he described how stylish African Americans had taken the English drape coat and dropped it to the knees, created trousers the likes of which no one had seen, and wore wide-brimmed hats that could double as umbrellas. He could not make sense of the look. "Just what the Seventh avenue glamour boys' reasons are for togging the way they do is slightly beyond comprehension," he admitted. "Maybe, they feel they should look different just as a matter of a trade mark. They might possibly be under the impression that they're the last word, the dernier cri, or killer-dillers. Anyway, that's their business, but the ofays [whites] who ride Seventh avenue buses have had many a laugh at these strange get-ups." In early 1941, a rumor circulated in Memphis's black community that the police had banned "extreme English drape suits," high-waisted pants, and the wide-brim hats popular among the "coterie of snappy dressers." When Beale Street merchants called on the mayor to stifle these reports, which hurt their business, the police chief took pains to deny the "ridiculous and absurd" story. "No crepe on drapes," the black press reported, but noted that many had deemed the rumor credible, because local authorities had threatened blacks who were actively picketing white-owned stores.[2]

The zoot suit caught the fancy of a new generation of young African

Figure 17. Gordon Parks focuses on the pegged pants of African American students at Bethune-Cookman College, 1943.
Library of Congress, Prints and Photographs Division, FSA-OWI Collection, LC-USW3-014839-E.

American artists, who were attracted to scenes of daily life and leisure. Employed as a photographer by the Farm Security Administration, Gordon Parks took close-ups of the pegged pants of African American college students at Bethune-Cookman College in Daytona Beach, Florida. In the Philadelphia Print Workshop, a New Deal arts project, artists Raymond Steth and Claude Clark captured the style of juke joints and dance

Figure 18. Claude Clark's *Jumpin' Jive* depicts a jitterbugging couple at a Philadelphia nightspot. Color carborundum etching, c. 1941.

Print and Picture Collection, Free Library of Philadelphia. Courtesy of the Fine Arts Program, Public Buildings Service, U.S. General Services Administration. Commissioned through the New Deal art projects.

halls. Clark's *Jumpin' Jive* (c. 1941) portrayed the ecstasy of a jitterbugging couple, the man in drapes, with rolled cuffs and long jacket. Steth's ambitious *Evolution of Swing*, created around 1940, traced African American music and dance from its roots in Africa to the modern world of jazz; his athletic dancers pull against each other, the woman leaning back, her skirt creeping up, while the man jackknifes in the air, his drape pants ballooning and long jacket flying.[3]

African American cartoonists had a field day with a style ready-made for caricature. The *Chicago Defender*'s Jay Jackson loved the exaggerated silhouette, the broad brim hat, and swinging watch chain. His zoot suits, which began to appear in 1941, puffed out the pants and made the jacket into an overskirt. Jackson, along with E. Simms Campbell, Ted Shearer, and Wilbert Holloway, drew "togged out" sharpies and street-corner hustlers to comment on life in urban black communities. Such lower-class men were familiar types—the stuff of blues songs and everyday banter—but attired in zoot suits, they seemed, if anything, a more visible target for humor and ridicule as wartime mobilization began to take hold. Ted Shearer's *Around Harlem* cartoons for the *New York Amsterdam News* captured the moment when men exchanged their zoot suits for uniforms and the tension when some were drafted and others deferred. In one, a man walks out of a pawnshop wearing a barrel and says to his girlfriend, "But, Baby—where I'm goin' they don't use those kind of drapes"; another depicts street-corner men agreeing on the importance of deferments because "someone has got to look fo' fine women."[4]

Many cartoons in black newspapers zeroed in on the ways that the war unsettled the thorny relationships between men and women. Jay Jackson specialized in such commentary. In one cartoon, a woman talks on a pay phone to her girlfriend, explaining that since her husband went into the army she had moved to a smaller apartment; as she gives her new telephone number, the zoot-suited "wolves" lined up for the phone listen in and take it down. Typically these images mocked the pretensions and vanity of the zoot suiter, who firmly believed his style would attract the ladies. "Dig them cats; bet they think they're on," whispered one woman to another about two zoot suiters. The old figure of the seducer became a wolf in zoot-suit clothing: A father with a shotgun chases off his daughter's drape-shaped beau as she exclaims, "I said MY wolf was at the door, not A WOLF, Daddy." Other cartoons mocked men for expecting to live on wives' and girlfriends' wages. Jackson drew a zoot-suited man standing over his wife, a laundress who had fainted, and explaining to the doctor: "All I did was hand her my pay envelope and say, 'I got a job now and

SO WHAT? - - - - - - - - By Jay Jackson

But the government said to get rid of all non-essentials.

Figure 19. Cartoonist Jay Jackson's version of zoot-suited manhood. *Chicago Defender*, February 7, 1942. Courtesy of the *Chicago Defender*.

you don't need to work no more.'" In another, a woman in a divorce court points to her zoot-suited spouse and exclaims to the judge, "But the government said to get rid of all non-essentials."[5]

African American cartoonists seem to have tapped into a current of unease and tension that was signified by the zoot suit but hardly limited to it. One young woman told advice writer Abbé Wallace that her boy-friend had privately professed his love but ignored her when he dressed up in his zoot suit. Wallace condemned the behavior of "night-time wolves": "If he can't share the glamour of that zoot suit with you, why share your moonlight and roses with him?" Mrs. Chloe Bottoms berated *Amsterdam News* columnist Dan Burley for blaming the problems of childrearing on "barfly mothers" and reminded him that "no child has a proper chance whose father is a dressed up skunk." Young married men too often were "still thinking with a zoot suit mind and want[ed] to mix up rug-cutting, hanging on the corner with the boys, and staying out late at night," destroying domestic life and undermining their children's futures.[6]

Some journalists and columnists became enchanted with the zoot suit as a form of black cultural expression, part of the entertainment and sporting world they reported on and enjoyed. In his column *Back Door Stuff*, Burley told tales of "Zoot Suit Shorty," painted a "portrait of a hepcat getting 'sharp,'" and elaborated his lexicon of jive, which he published in 1944. Others, however, found the extreme clothes unsettling, viewing the riotous colors and exaggerated silhouettes with disdain. "The wearers in general look like men from Mars," observed Herman Hill in the *Pittsburgh Courier*. In a critique of the consumer market published in the *Defender*, a housewife blamed clothing merchants for assuming that African Americans liked loud colors, "those queer green shades and blaring reds that are unfortunately chosen by some of us." Hoping to counter aesthetic illiteracy, a fashion columnist patiently explained the colors African American men should choose for their suits depending on their skin tones.[7]

The criticism went beyond a matter of poor taste, however, and targeted indolent, hedonistic youth. The "Hi-De-Ho bunch," the *Atlanta Daily World* termed the phenomenon, using Cab Calloway's signature phrase. These "get byers" had embraced a "'zoot suit' philosophy of life." "They spend much to touch up the outside, but appropriate little or nothing for the development of the inside," railed an Atlanta minister. In a similar vein, A. L. Holsey, an official at Tuskegee Institute and the National Negro Business League, condemned "the 'Zoot Suit' policies of the race" during a war-bond banquet. Six thousand youths had gathered for a dance on the Tuskegee campus, but fewer than one hundred had attended an important economic conference the next day. He observed, "Too many Negroes are flocking en masse to pleasure-seeking spots, and too few giving consideration to the economic welfare of the group." One speaker at a Houston high school graduation stated flatly, "There is no place for the zoot suit, small legs, nineteen-inch chain in this war-torn world."[8]

The war had spawned new opportunities for African Americans, even as government policies and propaganda, which asserted freedom as a war objective, raised expectations of change. As historian Adam Green writes, there was an emerging sense of "national black feeling," at once racially distinct and consciously American. Hopes of economic mobility, improved race relations, and expanded civil rights were tempered by fears of growing hostility and violence as African Americans took defense jobs, entered military service, and competed for scarce housing. Even as black political leaders pressed for the government to safeguard African Americans, they advised workers to conform to employers' requirements. Wearing a zoot suit when applying for defense jobs was not advisable, warned George Robinson, the Negro Personnel Representative for Wright Aeronautical Corporation. When the War Production Board moved to ban the style, some black newspapers celebrated. Not only was it wasteful, unpatriotic, and "offensive to public taste," explained the Atlanta Daily World, but when worn by African Americans, it "set them apart as slicks, hep cats, and jazz boys," and caused employers to deny them jobs. One reader addressed a different problem, however, when he observed that young men on defense jobs now had spending money to embrace a pleasure-seeking, immoral life. "I wonder how any Negro mother feels when her son puts on his big pants, 10-gallon hat, zoot coat, puts his switch blade in his pocket, and steps out," asked George Neely, who called on the community to monitor the young. An item in the *Amsterdam News* seemed to confirm these worries when it reported on three Brooklyn brothers "whose $83.50-a-week defense jobs in upstate New York led them into a life of crime." After five weeks of fat paychecks, they had bought zoot suits and returned to Brooklyn to "do the town." When their money ran out, they began robbing local homes, committing more than thirty thefts before being caught.[9]

The *Pittsburgh Courier*, whose Double V campaign linked the war against fascism to the fight against racial discrimination, ran many stories that included zoot suiters among the "malefactors of our race," as columnist Joseph D. Bibb put it: "bad actors and devotees of the arts of crap shooting, gin drinking, loud talk, rug cutting, and zoot suiting." Bibb believed whites were gathering data about African American behavior—"peering into the innermost archives of our lives"—in order to deny black equality and civil rights. Criticizing the conduct of lower-class youth and rural migrants in particular, he condemned them for "forging their own fetters by their zoot-suited, aboriginal monkey shines in public places." Such references to a newfangled slavery appeared most dramatically in an editorial cartoon by Wilbert Holloway depicting "Uncle Toms: Young and Old." Slave master White Supremacy held in chains the slave of 1843, bent-over and wearing rags, and the zoot suiter of 1943, wearing a long coat, drape pants, smoking a cigarette, and affecting a cool pose. Holloway wrapped the black mens' heads in bandannas or do-rags, a headpiece normally not worn by zoot suiters but which would have connoted to respectable black readers the mark of slavery, as well as the lower-class fashion for conking hair. Accompanying the illustration was an editorial excoriating the "young Uncle Tom who has flourished since World War I." Such men hindered African American progress by flouting standards of public decorum, playing racist stereotypes in theater and films, endorsing segregation in print, and currying favor with whites for personal gain. Here the

Figure 20. Wilbert L. Holloway's powerful "Uncle Toms: Young and Old" condemns the zoot suiter. *Pittsburgh Courier,* February 27, 1943.
Courtesy of the Pittsburgh Courier Archives.

zoot suiter took on great symbolic weight, as the *Courier* linked street-corner sharpies to various social types perceived to be detrimental to the race, at a moment when African Americans were pushing for greater opportunities and equal treatment.[10]

*   *   *

Such expressions of unease and hostility to the zoot suiter, articulated in the context of black mainstream political aspirations, were largely invisible to most white Americans. The style entered their consciousness through the youthful craze for swing music, jive talk, and jitterbug. White audiences would have seen swing band musicians wearing such clothes on stage. Cab Calloway was famous for adopting the style, switching from the tuxedoes he wore in the 1930s to the zoot suit in the early 1940s. But other jazz musicians also took up the fad for drapes. "You're not hep these days unless you're wearing a zoot suit, is the report among swing musicians today," observed *Down Beat*. Calling himself "pretty dandified," Dizzy Gillespie wore "drape suits like everyone else." In 1943, Midwesterner Johnny Otis "couldn't wait to get to Los Angeles to get me a zoot suit"—"brown chalk stripe, thirty inches in the knees, with fourteen-inch bottoms and a coat down between my knees"—but when he showed up at the Club Alabam, his fellow musicians laughed at the sight. "I guess I looked like something out of a corny, hepcat movie," he recalled, and changed back into his band uniform.[11]

The first theatrical performance to call explicit attention to the style was Duke Ellington's 1941 *Jump for Joy*. Ellington had created this musical review with an overtly political purpose, "to correct the race situation in the U.S.A. through a form of theatrical propaganda." Showcasing African American entertainers, it challenged performance stereotypes, addressed racial conditions, and celebrated black life. *Jump for Joy* was a show ahead of its time, and Ellington would later call the review his "hippest" entertainment. In it, he brought the zoot suit to center stage as a symbol of expressiveness, fluidity, and freedom. A sketch called "Made to Order" was set in a tailoring shop and featured comedians Pot, Pan, and Skillet, who bantered in jive about their outrageous zoot suits "with a reet pleat and a stuff cuff and a drape shape, shoulders extended, eighteen as intended; padding—Gibraltar; shiny as a halter; streamlined alignment; pipeline the pocket; drape it, dig it, sock it, and lock it—fifty three at the knee and seven at the cuff." As to the suit's color, "Daddy, let the rainbow be your guide." After this sketch came a number called "Sharp Easter," with a parade of stylish fashions. According to white screenwriter Sid Kuller, who worked with Ellington on the show and wrote "Made to Order," teenagers began coming to the theater wearing loud zoot suits, hoping to outdo the comics onstage. When *Jump for Joy* opened at Los Angeles's Mayan Theater in July 1941, it drew enthusiastic audiences but also hostility and threats of violence. The show closed after only 101 performances, but Pot, Pan and Skillet toured with the Duke Ellington Orchestra and continued to perform "Made to Order" through 1942.[12]

Soon after the Ellington show, white songwriters Ray Gilbert and Bob O'Brien released "A Zoot Suit (for My Sunday Gal)." They probably picked up the idea—and the opening lyrics—from "Made to Order," although the tune had nothing to do with Ellington's broader affirmation of African American dignity and freedom in *Jump for Joy*. Planning a big date on their day off, Sam rushes to his tailor and Sal to her seamstress, looking for clothing that will impress and attract the other. Singing in the rhyming slang of the day, Sam wants a "zoot suit with a reet pleat" to appeal to his dream girl, while Sal croons for a "brown gown with a zop top" to entice her man. In this hepcat's gloss on a traditional date, the twist is that both sexes are fashion conscious: it is Sam who wants to be a "walkin' rainbow." Written in 1941, the song quickly became a hit, sung in nightclubs, on the airwaves, and in recordings. "Watch out for the sky-rocketing of the latest whacky tune based on swing lingo," advised the *Washington Post*'s entertainment column in March 1942.[13]

By then, a few reporters had begun to notice the style. Among the first was Henry McLemore, a syndicated columnist based in Los Angeles. In February 1942, he dressed up in a zoot suit and went out to the Trianon, a vast ballroom and nightspot, to see the phenomenon for himself. The previous week McLemore's column had harshly called for the immediate internment of Japanese Americans and had urged his countrymen to "quit worrying about hurting the enemy's feelings." Now he was moved by an energetic mass of oddly dressed war workers who worked and played hard: "A new life for them. New hours. New entertainment. A new crop of Americans. . . . 'Zoot' suits. Swing bands at those hours near dawn. No natural life. Girls, boys, all thrown out of line by a nation at war. But girls and boys accepting that fact and making the most of it."[14] McLemore celebrated extreme clothing as a sign of youthful exuberance that would help the Allies win the war.

Five months later, journalist Walter Davenport found that the managers of dine-and-dance palaces and smaller speakeasies in Southern California had grown wary of zoot suiters, who tended to get into fights and harass women patrons. Some dance halls began to enforce a dress code, with coats no longer than the fingertips and trousers at least seventeen inches at the ankle. Eyeing the suit, bouncers took the measure of the man. As one put it, "If a bug's coat is any longer than the ends of his fingers with his arms hanging down at his sides, he's apt to be a character and make trouble." "If the zoot suit is extreme, so is the character inside it," echoed *Newsweek*, reporting on the "superzoots" seen on the West Coast.[15] The term "character"—straight out of Damon Runyon and evoking his world of colorful theater people, gangsters, and hustlers—made the zoot suiter a recognizable Broadway type.

Attention to the zoot suit escalated sharply when the government moved to ban the style in September 1942. Indeed, the term first appeared in the *New York Times* in its report on the War Production Board's press conference announcing that tighter restrictions were in the offing. WPB officials strangely introduced a jive-talking employee to "puzzled reporters . . . who never had seen any of these strange garments affected by the jitterbugs." The deadpan young man explained that the zoot suit was "a creation also known as a 'solid set of threads.'" Some jitterbugs, he observed, wore a coat hanger inside their jacket so that after they had spent the evening listening to music and smoking marijuana, they could easily hang up their jackets. A more straight-laced WPB spokesman, asked if the zoot suiters would find a way around the restrictions, observed that "anybody who could conceive such a paragon of bad taste as the zoot suit . . . is capable of anything."[16]

Serious journalists gave their reporting a Runyonesque treatment, using an arch, convoluted idiom that joined the zooters' jive vernacular to a parody of courtliness. They marveled at the "needle nuts," "solid senders," and "zoot suit gentry" who wore such outlandish clothes. Commenting on the fact that the WPB had not put the lighter-weight rayon fabric in its limitation order, the *Washington Post* remarked, "Ingenious lads that they are, the characters were even talking of donning long handled underwear, come the wintry winds, to compensate for the lack of warmth in their woolless garments." After hearing the government's "ukase," Washington journalists went to the commercial district on Seventh Street to interview local zoot suiters and their tailors, and typically reported their stories in the slang of the day. The *Afro-American*'s Joe Shephard explained to a couple of sharpies that "the Old Guy with the Whiskers is hangin' crepe on the drape shape and putting the chill on frills." "Man, man, that ain't right," one replied, "think of civilian morale." Even the *Wall Street Journal* offered its white-shoe readers a lesson in jive, albeit with a dose of sarcasm. Describing the zooters' trousers with their tight cuffs, its reporter noted that "this sometimes causes a slight stoppage of circulation above the ankle, but no bug minds making this light sacrifice for his art." Despite the WPB ban, the *Philadelphia Inquirer* ran a set of fashion photographs, "How You Look in a Zoot Suit," showing three poses by a tailor's assistant playing the jitterbug. Similarly, *Life* magazine published a photo spread of wholesome white teens in their zoot suits, criticizing their appearance as "solid arguments for lowering the Army draft age to include 18 year olds," yet publicizing the look.[17] It was much harder to be unaware of the style after the WPB banned it.

In issuing their restrictions on the zoot suit, the WPB had made it the one fashion deemed unpatriotic during wartime, and some pressed this theme in the months that followed. "I don't know how this zoot suit thing got started," a columnist in Hartford, Connecticut, wrote, "but it certainly shouldn't be tamely accepted as being one of the four freedoms." Lichty's *Grin and Bear It* cartoon, syndicated in a number of newspapers, showed the Japanese high command pleased to hear the latest intelligence report from their secret agent: "Hon. spy investigating new development in U.S. . . . Maybe like brown shirt movement in

Germany . . . Report great number of youths clamor for 'Zoot suits with drape shape.' " In the months that followed, editorial cartoons occasionally featured a zoot suit to symbolize puffed-up Nazi claims or swollen wages and prices, its very style conveying a sense of exaggeration and ill-fit.[18]

Some producers of popular culture disseminated the message that citizens were duty-bound to reject the zoot suit. A 1942 song by Carmen Lombardo and Pat Innisfree, "Since He Traded His Zoot Suit for a Uniform," contrasted the comical appearance and vanity of the drape-shaped civilian with the manly good looks and sex appeal of the soldier in uniform. Jazz vocalist Mildred Bailey sang it on *Treasury Star Parade*, a radio program sponsored by the Treasury Department to promote war bonds, but the song did not catch on. A more prominent effort for the Treasury Department that accentuated the official view of the zoot suiter was the Walt Disney cartoon *Spirit of '43*. Disney had created a similar film promoting Americans' wartime duty to pay taxes and buy war bonds in the weeks following Pearl Harbor. When a Gallup Poll declared it a success, he produced a second film a year later, this time fastening upon the zoot suiter to make this point. In *Spirit of '43*, Donald Duck is tempted to spend his high war wages, but his thrifty Scottish uncle—a precursor to Scrooge McDuck—warns him to save his money and pay his taxes if the Allies are to triumph. Pulling Donald in the opposite direction is a zoot suiter, who entices him into a saloon. Donald begins to succumb, when he sees the barroom door become a swastika and the zoot suiter transformed into Hitler. Thoughtless male pleasure-seeking and conspicuous consumption, the cartoon shows, made the zoot suiter a turncoat. At once Donald comes to his senses and punches temptation in the jaw; renewing his civilian duty to Uncle Sam, Donald watches his tax dollars produce the arsenal of democracy. A vast audience saw Disney's view of the zoot suiter: movie exhibitors across the United States had agreed to show the cartoon.[19]

Letters to newspaper editors reveal that not everyone agreed with the WPB's decision. Some questioned the motives of officials who would ban the jitterbug's outfit yet permitted other excesses. Louis Redmond,

Figure 21. Walt Disney portrays the zoot suiter as America's enemy in *Spirit of '43*. Walt Disney Productions, 1943.

winner of the zoot suit contest that had finally pushed WPB official Frank Walton into action, complained: "You stop tailors from making long coats and putting on cuffs, yet women are wasting material in all kinds of uniforms for dress. Why don't you get wise and stop wasting the taxpayers' money?" Using jive vernacular, one man asked, "Why the official puss fuss about glad rags and not an eyebrow to the swallow-tail monkey outfits?"—that is, the tuxedoes worn by government dignitaries to official events. When the *Washington Post* polled the members of the Senate, most sensed they were treading on treacherous political ground. They were "about evenly divided on whether zoot-suiting was a crime or a peccadillo," with Southern senators most opposed to the style. Only one would speak on the record, Democratic senator Guy M. Gillette of Iowa, who supported the teenage jitterbugs and thought the WPB had gone too far. "As long as these zoot suits aren't hurting the war effort, I say let them go ahead and wear them," he opined. "Individualistic clothes are one of the prerogatives of young people."[20]

Focused on conserving textiles needed for the war, the WPB's action against the zoot suit in the fall of 1942 had the unintended consequence of mobilizing fascination with the style. Tin Pan Alley and Hollywood quickly exploited the craze. Songwriters tried to reproduce the success of "Zoot Suit (for My Sunday Gal)" with several zoot-themed tunes. Animators found the style's extremes perfectly suited for the wild antics of cartoon characters. Motion pictures had long featured actors in English drape suits and even extreme styles in gangster movies. However, the zoot suit appeared on film as an identifiable fashion largely after the WPB had singled it out. Indeed, Hollywood required exemption from the clothing limitation orders to permit the drape shape in gangster films and comedies. When comic duo Stan Laurel and Oliver Hardy filmed *Jitterbugs* in 1943, the portly Hardy received a special dispensation from the government to use the fabric required for his zoot suit.[21] As a whole, the entertainment industry found in the zoot suit's outlandish appearance a way to consider and symbolize an unsettled time, in which old cultural types clashed with new images and conditions.

The zoot suit was often presented as an aspect of black identity and culture, but its depiction ranged widely at a time when African Americans confronted racial stereotypes more vigorously and wartime politics promoted in some measure an ideology of cultural pluralism. Movie cartoonists, for whom caricature could easily devolve into racist imagery, were fascinated by swing culture even before the war. The frogs in MGM's 1937 *Swing Wedding* impersonate actual jazz artists, including Cab Calloway, Louis Armstrong, and Ethel Waters, but their speech and appearance reflect racial stereotypes; their tuxedoes may have seemed zoot-like to viewers. Warner Brothers' 1943 *Coal Black and de Sebben Dwarfs*, an all-black parody of the Snow White fairy tale, turned the Prince into a zoot suiter. Filled with the kind of minstrelsy and stereotypic images that now render it too offensive to be broadcast, *Coal Black* is a remarkable cartoon for other reasons, notably its jazz rhythm, rhyming dialogue, risqué elements, and exuberant animation. Director Bob Clampett not only wanted to create a parody of Walt Disney's 1937 *Snow White* but had been inspired by Duke Ellington's *Jump for Joy*, whose cast encouraged him to create this swinging version of the fairy tale.[22]

Feature films too created demeaning stereotypes of African American zoot suiters. In *Star Spangled Rhythm* (1942), which starred such headliners as Bob Hope and Bing Crosby, comic actor Eddie "Rochester" Anderson wore an overblown suit with large checks in the musical number "Sharp as a Tack." Rochester proudly struts before admirers in Harlem and pairs up with dancer Katherine Dunham, but she is attracted instead to a serviceman in uniform. Anderson's zoot suit was not at all like those worn on the streets, in which the jacket formed an inverted triangle that emphasized the shoulders and implied masculine strength. Instead, Anderson's enormous outfit puffed out and minimized his body, rendering him clownish. It is no wonder that at the end of the sketch he changes his zoot suit for an army uniform and dances off with Dunham. However novel the zoot suit, to African American and white liberal commentators, it seemed merely a new twist on old stereotypes. John T. McManus, film critic for the progressive newspaper *PM*, excoriated Hollywood for *Star Spangled Rhythm*, whose "zoot-suit sequence proves that Negroes can be made their worst caricaturists." The film *Cabin in the Sky* (1943), starring Anderson with Ethel Waters and Lena Horne, similarly received criticism for promoting racial stereotypes, including those of the zoot-suited hustler and low-life.[23]

There were other performances in which a purported zoot suit bore little resemblance to the real thing. A 1942 "Soundie" of "Zoot Suit (for My Sunday Gal)," featuring Dorothy Dandridge and Paul White, offers one example. Soundies were short, 16-millimeter film reels that were shown on coin-operated projection machines in bars, bowling alleys, and nightspots from 1940 to 1946; they often featured black entertainers at a time when their opportunities to appear in feature films were limited. White and Dandridge sing "Zoot Suit" as they try on their sharp clothes at the tailoring shop and dressmaker, then meet on the street decked out in their new outfits. White's attire—jacket with narrow shoulders and little drape, a checked vest, and small cap—was hardly what the fashionable zoot suiter was wearing. While the performance is light-hearted, White's mugging for the camera, along with his clothing, carried more than a hint of minstrelsy.[24]

Other Soundies presented the zoot suit style as the hepcat's delight. In *Jack, You're Playing the Game* (1941), the Delta Rhythm Boys offered a primer on looking sharp, attracting women, and enjoying good times. Getting a shoeshine, two zoot-suited Rhythm Boys chide the shoeshiners as squares who work for a living and lead drab lives. Their advice is to "go out late and stay till dawn / Your life is gay, you're never forlorn." First they visit a tailor for the latest in Harlem design, "coat way long and pegged so fine." Their girlfriends willingly pawn their watches to pay for the men's attire and a night out dancing. The shoeshiners are convinced, and head off to Harlem Credit Clothing for the same treatment. With their "front solid," new dates, and a night at the Café Pom-Pom, they're "playing the game." The idea of the togged-out man avoiding work and seeking pleasure was familiar to anyone who read black newspapers; one intriguing detail of this 1941 Soundie is a picture frame with the word "peace" hanging near the shoeshine stand. Released before the U.S. entrance into the war, it may have reflected a common sentiment of isolationism among many African Americans, or linked antiwar sentiment to the zoot suiter's irresponsibility.[25]

At other times, the zoot suit seemed not only the epitome of African American panache and modernity but also, remarkably, a symbol of patriotism. Released in early 1943, *Stormy Weather* made the style integral to the history of black performance and part of a confident African American culture on the home front. The film featured an array of dazzling black performers, including Bill "Bojangles" Robinson, Lena Horne, Fats Waller, Katherine Dunham, and the Nicholas Brothers. Bandleader Cab Calloway appears in a white zoot suit, complete with long watch chain, as he talks jive with Robinson, sings his well-known song

Figure 22. *Stormy Weather* featured zoot-suited dancers entertaining servicemen in uniform. Twentieth Century Fox, 1943.

"Minnie the Moocher," and presides over the swing orchestra. The final sequence of the film, set in a USO cabaret where black soldiers and their dates watch the show, brought out a troupe of dancers, the men wearing zoot suits and women in juke jackets, swinging and gliding to the song "Ain't That Something." A zoot-suited family, the small children in matching drapes, skip across the stage, and when the announcer calls out "everybody dance," zoot suiters and servicemen fill the frame, symbolically unifying home front and battleground.[26]

Sometimes the racial connotations of the zoot suit were disguised. The song "Zoot Suit (for My Sunday Gal)" began with a line about stepping out in Harlem, and its rhyming slang derived from African American jive. These associations were confirmed by the sheet music, whose cover featured racial stereotypes drawn in a modernistic style.

Nevertheless, as performed on radio and in recordings by a host of white performers, including the Andrews Sisters, Bing Crosby, and Art Lund—usually omitting the opening line—the zoot suiter and his Sunday gal could have been any modern young couple. The jive talk that surprised adults had spread, by the early 1940s, into the world of white middle-class youth. At play in many depictions of the zoot suit was a common-place dynamic of American popular culture, described by Eric Lott and other scholars as a white appropriation of black style that simultaneously renders racial specificity invisible or diminished.[27]

These appropriations are often difficult to identify, and in some cases, at least, the racial component of the zoot suit seems obscure or absent. Comedians wore the outfit in films to comic effect—not only Laurel and Hardy in *Jitterbugs*, but also Ole Olsen and Chic Johnson in the zany 1944 film *Ghost Catchers*, in which nightclub owners Olsen and Johnson help their neighbors exorcise their haunted house with a swing parody of Edgar Allan Poe's "The Raven." Frequently men's extreme clothing figured in commentary on masculine identity and sexuality that was not overt in its racial identification. In *Red Hot Riding Hood* (1943) and *Swing Shift Cinderella* (1945), Tex Avery's cartoon revisions of classic fairy tales, the lecherous Wolf, dressed in an angular, zoot-like tuxedo, pursues the alluring women who populate a sexualized home front. Re-versing the ideal of female innocence and virtue, Avery drew self-assured female war workers, sultry songstresses, and even a randy grandmother, all of whom get the better of the Wolf. *Red Hot Riding Hood* caused concern within the NAACP, discomfited by the "crossover" of black style into mainstream popular culture, but such perceptions barely registered with whites. Although without Avery's taste for sexual aggression and menace, animators William Hanna and Joseph Barbera produced a Tom and Jerry cartoon, *Zoot Cat* (1944), that tied the zoot suit to masculine sexuality and competition. Tom tries to woo a female cat steeped in jitterbug culture, but the finger-snapping feline rejects him as a square. Hearing an ad on the radio for zoot suits, Tom transforms an orange-and-green hammock into stylish drapes. His hepcat looks, jive talk, and rug-cutting succeed in winning his sweetheart, until Jerry foils his rival by throwing a bucket of water on the zoot suit to shrink it down to mouse-size. Devolving into a typical cat-and-mouse chase, the cartoon, released after the Los Angeles riot, presented a joking and innocuous view of the zoot suit.[28]

For many, the zoot suit phenomenon was not much more than that. Colorful fads and slang, along with hyperkinetic dance and nonsense music, distracted Americans and gave them a laugh as the burdens of mobilization and sacrifice set in. Into the spring of 1943, the antics of zoot suiters seemed part and parcel of this cultural fizz, even as journalists reported continuing demand for the frivolous fashion. In Washington, D.C., hotel dances drew " 'Zoot Suits' bouncing to 'jump' tunes," zoot-suited comics appeared on skates in the Ice Follies, and an egg painted to look like a zoot suiter won the Easter egg decorating contest at a boy's club. Photographer Ollie Atkins won the grand prize at the first White House Photographers Association exhibition with a shot of a dancing zoot suiter (see Fig. 11), much to the dismay of Vice President Henry Wallace, who could not understand why one of the "important pictures pertaining to the war effort" hadn't been selected. Journalists describing zoot-suited youngsters who lined up for tickets to a Harry James concert emphasized their appealing innocence. They were "mild and good natured as they skittered about like grasshoppers, clicking their leather heels and smiling up at the mounted police." This benign throng seemed more a miracle of nature than a fraught social phenomenon: "Every bus and subway train brought more of them as by some call of instinct, which police say can be likened only to visitations of locusts and Japanese beetles, the swarming of bees, or the wonderful migrations of birds." Explanations for the spectacle ranged from mob hysteria to an "anti-minuet revolt," but sensible experts deemed it harmless.[29]

Witnessing the wacky pleasures of youth, columnist Malvina Lindsay would call the zoot suit fad part of the "American tradition," one of the "little things that absent men must now remember," along with corner drugstores and sweater girls. Thus the zoot suit could even be incorporated into a national understanding of wartime purpose, the fashion's very eccentricity a sign of American freedom and individuality. This was, strikingly, a pervasive theme in the coverage of the zoot suit, reflecting not only propaganda against the lockstep of fascism but a broad discomfort with the growing regimentation of American life. Americans, it seemed, would swing off to war: "Fighters with a boogie beat," and "the dancingest Army and Navy ever," exclaimed an article in the *New York Times*. The Andrews Sisters' hit 1941 song "Boogie Woogie Bugle Boy"—"he makes the company jump when he plays reveille"—highlighted a free spirit as quintessentially American, even if it must be put to collective national purpose.[30] A similar theme, albeit one with a more serious social and moral dimension, appears in Robert Abrahams's poem "The Zoot-Suit Kid," published in the *Saturday Evening Post*. At home, the Kid was poor and "gutter-bred"; he danced and played, amusing the hepcats but confirming the elders' sense that he would ultimately die in jail. Instead he went to war, where his smart-aleck ways turned into courage under fire:

> No the Zoot-Suit Kid they couldn't teach,
> Until that day they took the beach,
> When the Zoot-Suit Kid he found his reach—
> There on the sand dune, humming a swing tune, all the long
>   forenoon,
> Fighting well.

He died on the battlefield, buried alone, "lying long," yet surviving in song, as if the Americans were fighting to a syncopated beat: "The tide brings a rhythm to that far-off shore, / And the Kid swings with it, though he doesn't know the score."[31]

Like Abrahams, many saw the zoot suiter as a youth in transition, not opposition. One teacher wrote the *New York Times* to say that his students' passion for dancing and drapes did not mean they were unaware of their wartime responsibilities; in addition to taking classes, they worked in different jobs and organized bond drives. Maureen Daly, author of the bestseller *Seventeenth Summer* and a *Chicago Tribune* columnist, recognized the temptations of a turbulent time and advised young men to do their schoolwork, have fun, and avoid false maturity and sophistication: "Be careful not to become too zoot-suit-minded—just hitch up your watch chain and act the same way you would if you had on your old work trousers and a sweat shirt." During the zoot suit riot, Louisiana representative Edward Hebert even read into the *Congressional Record* a newspaper editorial about an archetypal "lad named Joe," who was not much as a civilian, but "strip him of his bizarre zoot suit, take him out from behind the ribbon counter, the lathe, or the adding machine," put him in the armed forces, and he would become the backbone and future of America.[32]

African American poet and essayist Sterling Brown offered one of the most sensitive observations of the world of zoot suits and jitterbug by attending to the emotional temper of black youth. He had begun to speak on the zoot suit not long after the War Production Board's ban, attributing the style to young people's disillusionment with the world their elders had made, and to black rejection of white popular culture. Later, during an Earle Hines concert and dance in Atlanta, Brown was startled when Billy Eckstine began singing the haunting ballad "Skylark" and the crowd went wild, singing along to "their greatest juke-box favorite":

> At first I wondered what these kids in their zoot-suit drapes, their jitterbugging costumes almost as uniform as athletic suits, had to do with valleys green with spring, or meadows in the mist, or with Keats and Shelley, even disguised in Tin-Pan Alley garb. What did these kids, lost in the cramped tenements of Atlanta's Darktown, have to do with Skylarks? . . . But as Eckstein [*sic*] repeated his chorus on demand, I caught what I felt to be the simple, deeper meaning. The will-of-the-wisp and "the gypsy serenading the moon" business might be foreign, but the "lonely flight," "the wonderful music in the night," those phrases were their language, and something deep in these young ones answered.

Then the dancing began in earnest. Absorbed in the steps, their faces impassive, the couples moved as one: "She was always there, he was always there, each anticipating the other, each knowing the other's improvising." Reflecting upon the stereotype of the "happy, carefree" black dancer, Brown thought the jitterbugs' joy "wasn't free of care, the way I saw it; it was defiant of care instead." Children of the Great Depression, they had lived their lives in poverty, and now the army beckoned. "Tomorrow was coming for these kids with a sick thud," he wrote, and "they had to grab their joy where they found it and hold on frenziedly, today."[33]

Before the Los Angeles riot, the extreme style even found its way into the military. Soldiers "zooting" their uniforms appeared especially in the black press but also in *Time* and other mass-circulation magazines. Cartoons featured recruits standing ready for inspection, wearing long keychains and trousers cuffed tightly around the ankles. "I don't care if you *did* have it made up special," the officer exclaims in one. "You'll have to forget about zoot suits from now on." Cartoonists may have been inspired by several newspaper reports about African American soldiers who customized their uniforms. At Fort Huachuca in Arizona, a large training camp whose segregated facilities kindled racial tensions, such alterations were reported to be a frequent breach of army regulations. Recently arrived from civilian life, "some have had their uniforms tailor-made in 'Drapes' and long coats resembling the 'Zoot Suit,'" stated the *New York Amsterdam News*. In Washington, military police arrested a black sergeant wearing "a coat of expensive officer's gabardine material . . . full flared at the skirt, with puffed sleeves and a finger-tip length," along with "chest-high and ankle-fitted trousers." Others, like former musician Floyd Jones, simply posed zoot-style in his regulation uniform—feet spread apart, forefingers pointing down—to show his friends back home "he's doing all right and looking the same."[34]

Zoot argot found its way into military life. One aircrew called their Flying Fortress "the Zoot Suiters." Both the marines' camouflage in the Pacific and the makeshift uniforms of the Women Airforce Service Pilots, made out of army-surplus mechanic's overalls, became known as "zoot suits." A WASP song was called "Zoot-Suits and Parachutes," which humorously told the tale of a former working girl, now a member of the Army Air Forces Flying Training Detachment, seduced by a pilot in the cockpit of their plane. And according to the *New York Times*, the style even helped a patrol in Rome capture two German spies with the question, "Are you a zoot-suiter with a reet pleat?"[35]

How servicemen felt toward civilians in zoot suits before the Los Angeles riot is hard to know. Some griped about them as slackers and wastrels. One Yank "somewhere in the Pacific" explained what was on the minds of servicemen abroad—doing their jobs, looking forward to mail, thinking about home, and "ridiculing zoot-suit wearers and high-living war workers." A similar kind of ridicule appeared on the home front. In Washington, D.C., army and naval officers went to Uline Arena, a sports and entertainment venue, "for the apparent dual purpose of dancing to Jack Coffey's music and watching the riffing of the 'zoot suiters.'" Photographer John Ferrell captured the servicemen's quizzical stares at a hepcat's threads during a Woody Herman concert there in June 1942. Their reaction seemed more bemused than hostile; as one captain cracked, "Those kids will scare the Japs to death, anyway."[36]

Throughout the spring of 1943, it is difficult to discern the building tension over a suit of clothes in the press or popular culture, except in Los Angeles itself. The wartime simmering of racial conflict—on army bases and in civilian life—did not, at this point, seem explicitly connected to a style of clothing. Government efforts to label the zoot suit an unpatriotic style were inconsistent and undermined by the array of images that appeared in popular entertainment and the press. Many Americans would have seen the zoot suit portrayed in a harmless light, in such films as *Jitterbugs* and *Stormy Weather*. Even more might have followed the comic strip *Li'l Abner* through April and May, when cartoonist Al Capp drew the leading character as "Zoot-Suit Yokum."

In Capp's convoluted story, zoot-suit clothing manufacturers plot to sell the new fashion to male consumers by creating "a great national hero who performs incredible deeds of valor—always dressed in a Zoot-Suit." American men and boys will want to emulate such a hero by

Figure 23. Soldiers encounter zoot suiters at a Woody Herman concert in 1942.
Library of Congress, Prints and Photographs Division, FSA-OWI Collection, LC-USF34-011543-DLC.

adopting his style, and the zoot-suit manufacturers will make millions. They search for someone dumb enough to put himself constantly in harm's way, and they find Li'l Abner; not only does he have the lowest IQ among American men, but he genuinely, and innocently, wants to do good. Throwing himself down a mineshaft to rescue a miner and his watch, he emerges a hero. Zoot-suit mania sweeps the country, and Zoot-Suit Yokum is nominated for the presidency. The plot is so successful that the conservative clothing manufacturers decide to fight back by finding a crook to commit crimes while impersonating Zoot-Suit Yokum. Opposition is stirred, the fad comes to an end, and the last remaining zoot suit is given to the Smithsonian Institution.[37]

Did these depictions portend the social tensions that erupted over a suit of clothes? Historian Mauricio Mazón, reading backward from the

Los Angeles riot that June, interprets Capp's cartoon as a symbolic fore-
shadowing and unconscious influence on the riot: "It may not be a
breach of historical reality to suggest that more than any other individual
or institution Capp was responsible for introducing the American public
to the perils of zoot-suiterism." In his view, the comic strip adumbrated
the symbolic and psychological structure underlying the riot: "The split-
ting of images into antipodal frames—life/death, patriotism/disloyalty,
annihilation/ regeneration, innocence/corruption, and hero/villain—
anticipated the themes that servicemen and civilians reenacted through
the Zoot-Suit Riots."[38] Yet Mazón admits that it is quite difficult to establish the influence of "Zoot-Suit Yokum"; his reading of symbolic opposition is so universal that it seems impossible to apply to the actual
historical moment. Capp did not anticipate the riot but rather was a
caustic observer of American manners and mores, attacking the absur-
dity of fads, the professional engineers of public opinion, the exploitation of heroes and celebrities, and the herd instinct of the populace.
These were all easy targets of the war years. The meaning of the zoot
suit, Capp shows in Li'l Abner, could be readily manipulated, a symbol
of the heroism Americans yearned for one week, a sign of criminality
and disillusionment the next.

During the war, the press expressed growing alarm about juvenile
delinquency, including street gangs and criminal behavior of minority
youths. With the significant exception of Los Angeles, however, big-city
newspapers before the riot carried relatively few reports pinpointing zoot
suiters committing serious crimes, although there were some cases of
murder, assault, and attempted rape that involved perpetrators or victims wearing the distinctive style. For example, the New York Amsterdam
News reported that a teenage youth, "dressed in drape fashion," was
arrested after attacking a fourteen-year-old girl at knifepoint at a school
dance; the Philadelphia Tribune characterized a victim killed by "one of
North Philly's most notorious gamblers" as a "boy in an extreme 'zoot
suit.'"[39] Most accounts described petty crimes by zoot-suited thieves,

such as one "wearing a big apple hat, a blue-green zoot suit coat, and tan trousers" who robbed a delicatessen of five dollars. There were also a number of humorous squibs. In one, a Chicago zoot suiter tried to sleep on an elevated platform but could only lie down by removing his tightly cuffed pants; scandalized passengers called the police, who arrested him for disorderly conduct. In another, "a panic-stricken man telephoned the police station that he could not dance any more, somebody had stolen his jitterbug coat and his tan gabardine trousers." The allure and prestige of the style led some men to steal zoot suits from clothing stores for themselves or to sell to others. In one case, five thieves stole the suits from a railway loading platform and were caught peddling them for ten dollars each. One of the worst crimes of this nature was the robbery and murder of a Chinese laundry worker by four youths, including a sailor AWOL from his ship, who wanted money to buy zoot suits and go on a hunting trip. Most of the men in these crime reports were African American. These stories received no sustained coverage and often appeared as filler in the back pages of the newspaper. Strikingly, the Sleepy Lagoon murder and trial, which made Los Angeles obsessed with zoot suiters, received little coverage beyond that city.[40]

The most publicized criminals in drape shape outside Los Angeles were two Italian American teenagers in Brooklyn, Neil Simonelli and Joseph Annunziata, factory workers who were "addicted to the peg-topped, long-coated clothing of jitterbugs." On October 2, 1942, they visited the junior high school they had once attended with the intention of making trouble. They went to the men's room to smoke and told a student to inform math teacher Irwin Goodman. Goodman arrived, and after a quarrel he brought them to the assistant principal, who ejected them from the school. Simonelli and Annunziata returned with a gun and shot Goodman to death. The press quickly deemed them "jitterbug killers" and "zoot suit murderers." In jail, they regaled the other prisoners with "the intricacies of the zoot suits they were wearing when arrested and still wore," comparing their pegged pants with exactitude. Annunziata's trousers, measuring fourteen inches at the ankles and twenty-eight inches at the knees, were the most extreme. With his stylish clothes, dancing ability, and "hair cut in 'sharpie' fashion," Annunziata boasted that the "girls had been 'crazy' about him," and he told reporters to call him by the moniker "Handsome." The press pointed out that the twosome lost their swagger when they appeared in court, becoming a "pair of frightened, rumpled, and subdued boys." The judge deemed one youth particularly incorrigible, calling him "defiant of authority" and "anti-social," terms that would be applied more generally to those wearing zoot suits in the wake of the Los Angeles riot. Although the prosecution asked for the death penalty, the pair were convicted of second-degree murder and given prison sentences of fifty years to life. The judge pointedly blamed the killers for their own moral failing, not the social environment in which they were raised.[41]

Such reports were notable for being rare in most of the country. On the eve of the Los Angeles riot, opposition to the zoot suit in the national media and popular culture had not congealed. Even though the War Production Board had tried to ban the style and render it unpatriotic, American youths embraced the trend and many adults tolerated it, if only half-heartedly. Like other fads of the war years, it was an object of humor and a quizzical sign of the times, a momentary distraction from the national campaign for victory. Commentators and cartoonists had a field day with the extreme styles and the "characters" who wore them. Associated with lower-class urban culture, especially but not limited to African Americans, the style was still more bewildering than outright sinister. Only in Los Angeles did the presence of zoot suiters generate not the rhythms of jive but a drumbeat of concern and opposition. There, the coverage of an extreme style would be called both a symptom and cause of the zoot suit riot.

4

From Rags to Riot

On the night of June 3, 1943, a band of fifty sailors armed themselves with makeshift weapons, left their naval base, and coursed into downtown Los Angeles in search of young Mexican Americans in zoot suits. For many weeks, name-calling and small-scale skirmishes between the uniformed men and the zoot suiters had escalated until the situation seemed intolerable. Now the servicemen were determined to strike. The posse prowled the streets, searched nightclubs, and invaded movie theaters, forcing the managers to turn on the lights so they could identify youths by their attire. When they found a zoot suiter, they beat him, stripped him of his pants, and tore his jacket. The next day, servicemen hired a convoy of taxicabs to go to East Los Angeles, where they accosted *pachucos* on the street and even pushed their way into private homes. Over the next few days, crowds of white civilians joined in the rampage, targeting mainly Mexican American youths but also some African Americans and Filipinos. Spurred by police bulletins, newspaper reporting, and radio broadcasts, 5,000 people jammed the downtown area on the night of June 7 as the melee continued. While many Mexican Americans retreated into their communities, some fought back, borrowing cars and traveling into the commercial district to confront the servicemen and their civilian allies. The city's district attorney called it "a state of near anarchy." As the violence escalated and spread, the Los Angeles police finally raised a riot alarm and began arresting scores of Mexican American youths, seeing them as instigators and believing law enforcement could quell the conflict by taking them off the streets. On June 8, military authorities declared Los Angeles out of bounds for servicemen, and the city finally quieted down. Although no one had died in the conflict, at least ninety-four civilians and eighteen servicemen were treated for serious injuries. Of all the servicemen who had taken part in the violence, the police arrested only two. The earliest press reports described these events as the "zoot suit riot," and the label stuck. Although not all the victims in the Los Angeles riot wore zoot suits—in fact, many did not—it was this style that focused the rage of the attackers and framed public debate over the riot.[1]

Many historians have examined the Los Angeles riot and together offer a full assessment of those days and the events leading up to the crisis. The riot climaxed years of growing apprehension in white Los Angeles over racial and ethnic minorities. Never known for racial tolerance and harmony, the City of Angels reached the breaking point during the war years. Southern California had become a hub of wartime production and a destination for thousands of workers, including large numbers of African Americans and whites from the South and Midwest. African Americans increasingly gained employment in armament factories and shipbuilding, and white hostility to their presence caused frequent conflicts in the workplace. Migration from Mexico also grew substantially when the government reversed its policy of repatriation, begun during the hard times of the Great Depression, to meet growing needs for agricultural and other manual workers. At the same time, Japanese and Japanese American residents, nearly 37,000 in Los Angeles County alone, were forcibly relocated from their homes to internment camps in 1942. The destabilizing effects of these migrations in and out of the city, reconfiguring the mix of racial and ethnic groups, cannot be overstated. Long-time and newly arrived Angelenos jostled for space, breaching traditional borders dividing racial-ethnic communities. After the Japanese internment, the growing African American population expanded into Little Tokyo. The Mexican community began to spread out from their long-time residency in the Plaza district and made inroads into the downtown commercial zone, where movie theaters, variety stores, and small shops all "began to 'go Mexican,'" as the activist and writer Carey McWilliams put it. Adding to the flux were armed forces personnel on military bases in Long Beach and elsewhere. Training and preparing for embarkation to the Pacific, soldiers and sailors crowded into the city's entertainment venues when on leave. "Los Angeles was just a beehive, twenty-four hours a day," remembered one resident. "Any time would be Saturday night."[2]

As historians George J. Sánchez and Eduardo Pagán have explained, the shifting status and identity of the Mexican population, and the response to those changes by white Angelenos, provided the backdrop against which the zoot suit riot occurred. By World War II, American-born children of Mexican immigrants constituted a majority of the Mexican community in Los Angeles. Mindful of their rights as citizens—an awareness heightened by the numbers of Mexican Americans who had enlisted or worked in defense plants—they chafed at the daily experiences of racial bigotry and discrimination, from restricted job opportunities and police harassment to decaying schools and segregated swimming pools. How these assertions became manifest varied, with some educated young Mexican Americans joining organizations that fostered respectability, assimilation, citizenship, and upward mobility. Others, especially working-class youths, grew estranged from those goals, and many opted instead to seek out everyday pleasures as best they could. Enjoying American popular music and dance, aware of African American culture, yet holding on to identifiably ethnic practices of their own, they embraced the zoot suit or took up aspects of the style. A small but visible number formed themselves into neighborhood gangs. Marking and defending their turf, these close-knit peer groups were usually a harmless source of sociability, security, and social identity, but at times they engaged in petty crimes, drug use, and other illicit activities.[3]

The response of the local police and the press to these developments, contemporary commentators and historians agree, aggravated the racial and ethnic tensions that led up to the riot. Beginning in the 1920s, Edward J. Escobar has shown, the Los Angeles Police Department increasingly targeted Mexican American youths, linking together what they perceived to be racial characteristics with propensities to criminality. By the onset of the war, patrolmen arrested *pachucos* in growing numbers for drunkenness, petty thefts, and disorderly conduct. In the summer of 1942, the murder of twenty-two-year-old Jose Diaz at a house party incited a media frenzy and police crackdown on Mexican American youths. At the Sleepy Lagoon reservoir, an area of rural Los Angeles County inhabited mainly by agricultural workers, an evening of dancing and music at the home of the Delgadillo family turned deadly. As in many cities, neighborhood gangs skirmished over turf, women, and reputation. In this case, 38th Street gang member Henry Leyvas and his girlfriend had been assaulted on the street by some of the Downey Boys, a rival gang; Leyvas collected his own gang to retaliate, and they drove in search of his attackers. They finally decided to crash the Delgadillo party, but were attacked by guests there. Diaz was found dead, but who had killed him was unclear. Typically the authorities ignored violence within the Mexican community, but this time the police rounded up hundreds, charging twenty-two young men with murder. The trial dragged on for three months, as the press and prosecutors fanned local fears of crime, gangs, and violence by demonizing Mexican Americans as delinquents and criminals. Twelve were convicted of murder, and five of lesser counts, verdicts later overturned on appeal.[4]

A cycle of street skirmishes, harsh policing, and incendiary reporting heightened social tensions. Initially this was low-level antagonism, the sparring of different social groups newly arrived for war work and military training in a city unprepared for the rapid influx of such diverse peoples. Managing shore leave became a difficult task for the military, which repeatedly placed bars and dance resorts off limits; these orders came if the building was deemed a firetrap or otherwise unsafe, if there were "unattached women" and "undesirable conditions," or to prevent potential conflicts from the mixing of black and white patrons. In early 1943, Mexican American youths increasingly harassed sailors who went into their neighborhoods and commercial districts. A training school for the all-white navy had been located in Chavez Ravine, which had a large Mexican population, and its presence there exacerbated tensions. Men in zoot suits and sailors' uniforms traded insults and bridled when "their" women were harassed by the other. Verbal taunts escalated into fistfights: From winter to spring of 1943, Pagán found, clashes increased from once a week to daily. When these conflicts finally escalated into a riot in early June, one petty officer volunteered to the *Los Angeles Examiner*, "We're going to do what the police haven't been able to . . . we're going to make the streets of Los Angeles safe for sailors, for sailors' girls, and for the general public." According to the *Chicago Tribune*, the rallying cry was different: "We'll destroy every zoot suit in Los Angeles before this is over."[5]

All this might have occurred without the fixation on the zoot suit as a symbol and source of Mexican American delinquency and disorder. Los Angeles was the first in a string of cities where racial conflict erupted in the violent summer of 1943. In Beaumont, Texas, black and white shipyard workers fought when a white woman accused a black man of raping her; the riot that broke out in the city left several dead and the black community devastated. Racial tensions exploded into a riot in Detroit, sparked by conflicts at an amusement park called Belle Isle; in the course of three days, thirty-four people were killed. Not long after, tensions came to a breaking point in Harlem when rumors that the police had killed a black soldier led to rioting, extensive looting of local stores, six deaths, and hundreds of arrests. The violence in these cities was more severe than that in Los Angeles. In these places, too, the civil disorder was frankly defined as race riots or, in the case of Harlem, intraracial violence that had been sparked by racial discrimination.

The situation in Los Angeles was far more confused. The zoot suit had become the focus of social conflict and interpersonal antagonism, even cathexis, seemingly to the point of causing civil unrest. Why would an article of clothing be deemed such a provocation in *this* city? A style that elsewhere communicated a range of meanings became in this place indistinguishable from Mexican American youth and tied to criminality. Marking a distinct social type, the zoot suit generated a host of reactions from those who wore the style and from those who did not. From a style associated with dance halls and nightspots, the zoot suit now appeared on police blotters and in courtrooms, in the mayor's office and admiral's headquarters. It took on an enormous symbolic weight as it moved into these political domains. Understanding how this occurred is crucial to any assessment of the zoot suit as an expression of political commentary or resistance.

*   *   *

Several developments coalesced in the zoot suit riot to make the clothing seem not only a symbol but also an instigator of disorder. Face-to-face interactions in the workplace, at leisure, and in the streets came to be interpreted through the prism of style and gesture. Certainly the multi-cultural populace of Los Angeles figured prominently; this was not a biracial city, in which behavior could be read in black and white, but one with an extraordinary number of ethnic and racial groups. Added to that was the concentration of media know-how and self-consciousness about image-making peculiar to Los Angeles, the home of the motion picture industry. A highly competitive press played a striking role in defining the riot. Local politicians, activists, and ordinary citizens under-stood this and showed a remarkable sophistication in manipulating rep-resentations to their own advantage. As wartime politics—local, national, and international—played out in Los Angeles in 1943, the zoot suit, with its air of mystery, came to serve a range of public views and positions.

Signs that the zoot suit spelled trouble began to appear in Los Angeles in the early 1940s. Some managers of movie theaters, ballrooms, and other entertainment venues, connecting the style to disorderly conduct and inappropriate behavior toward women, had banned the "zoot suit element" outright, while others refused "extreme" or "superzoots." Although the zoot suit was known as a style of racial minorities, "swing shift" nightspots attracted white war workers decked out in draped coats and pants who were deemed troublesome. The social dynamics of the wartime home front—tensions over fraternizing, dating, and sexual language as women and men crowded the city's public spaces—were exacerbated by the unprecedented mix of racial and ethnic groups working and living side by side. The erotic charge, racial tensions, and fraught psychology of Los Angeles may be glimpsed in Chester Himes's 1945 novel, *If He Hollers Let Him Go*. The novel follows the rise and fall of a black foreman, Bob Jones, newly promoted to supervise his work gang in a Southern California defense plant. Proud of his skills, dreaming of success, and filled with sexual longings, he dresses and feels sharp, but is brought down by daily encounters with racial bigotry and, ultimately, a trumped-up accusation of rape by a Southern white woman worker.[6]

Zoot-suited men turned up at dances and nightclubs, flirted with women on the streets, and gathered together in groups, making themselves a conspicuous part of the Los Angeles scene. *Pachucos* in particular were newly visible to white Angelenos, who had long celebrated the tourist's version of the region's Spanish heritage while staring past the working-class Mexicans in their midst. Guy Nunn, regional director of the War Manpower Commission's Minorities Branch, recalled the growing resentment of the white population as members of the Mexican community took defense jobs and ventured outside the *barrio*: "Mexican youth, mobile, subject to the draft, cultivatedly 'different' in hair style and dress, often rebellious against parental meekness vis-à-vis Anglo authority, given to gang-type social organization, were the easiest and most visible objects of Anglo anxiety."[7] Tales of servicemen dating Latinas and zoot suiters accosting Anglo women grew more and more exaggerated.

The earliest clashes involving zoot suiters took place in 1941. Testifying in one of the post-riot investigations, Police Chief C. B. Horrall and his administrative assistant Captain Joe Reed recalled a series of small disturbances, largely confined to the Mexican community in Los Angeles. Young men demanded service in bars or tried to invade another group's dance, leading to skirmishes. "Whenever there was a party or a dance or home gatherings, these groups would travel around in caravans of cars and pull up in front of the house and demand everything they had to eat in the house or drink," Reed explained. Repeatedly, zoot-suited youths and servicemen squared off. One gang attacked a group of sailors in San Pedro. Another broke up a USO dance in Venice. Scuffles occurred in the streets when *pachucos* took offense at seamen making advances to Mexican women. None of these incidents foreshadowed a riot. "Quite a few of the boys had their clothes torn off, but the crowds weren't particularly hard to handle," Horrall observed. "The feeling in general among them was one of fun and sport rather than malice." Although these actions hardly seem innocent, *zoot suiter* was not yet a stigmatizing label or social identity.[8]

In Los Angeles, the association of zoot suits with Mexican Americans, criminality, and deviance took hold during the Sleepy Lagoon murder investigation and trial, over the second half of 1942. The young defendants were clad in assorted clothes when they were arrested, with most in draped pants and many in zoot suits. When the prosecutor in the case insisted that they not be permitted to change their clothes or cut their hair when they stood trial months later, defense counsel accused him of "purposely trying to have these boys look like mobsters, like disreputable persons, and . . . trying to exploit the fact that they are foreign in appearance." Nevertheless, the presiding judge agreed with the prosecutor's argument that "haircuts are distinguishing gang characteristics." To the judge, Eduardo Pagán observes, "their very appearance was a significant fact in the case."[9]

In the midst of a circulation war among the city's daily newspapers, the Hearst-owned *Examiner* and *Herald-Express* spearheaded a campaign depicting Mexican youths as "baby gangsters" and "zoot suit hoodlums." Other newspapers joined in, reporting a surge of gang disturbances and street violence. The police fed stories to reporters and editors printed them without further corroboration or questioning other sources. Conceding this point years later, Nick Williams, the night editor of the *Los Angeles Times* in the midst of the tumult, said ruefully, "At the time, we thought we were objectively covering the news." An official in the sheriff's office, Clem Peoples, even offered his version of the Sleepy Lagoon murder and Mexican juvenile crime wave to the tabloid *Sensation,* which reportedly sold more than 10,000 copies in December 1942. That fall, an investigator from the Office of War Information and the Coordinator of Inter-American Affairs, along with a representative from the Mexican government, went to Los Angeles to express their concern about this situation. The OWI asked newspapers to stop describing gangs and crime by nationality, because the government did not want to undermine its Good Neighbor Policy with Latin America. In response, editors substituted "zoot suiter" or "zoot gangster" for "Mexican" in their coverage.[10]

Thus the police and the press, often working in tandem, bore a particular responsibility for shifting the meaning of the zoot suit from a harmless, if extreme, phenomenon to a symbol of deviance and danger. Likewise, they narrowed perceptions of those who embraced the style. Around Los Angeles, African Americans and Mexican Americans were most likely to put on zoot suits, but it was also a costume of war workers, Hollywood actors, and jitterbugging high school students, including whites, Filipinos, and Asian Americans. Among the newspaper-reading public, the Sleepy Lagoon coverage and everyday crime beat made *zoot suit* and *zoot suiter* almost exclusively the symbols of young Mexican American delinquents and offenders.[11]

Police harassment and public fear-mongering sharpened resentments among Mexican American youths. Along with young African American men, they defiantly embraced the style that marked them, finding in it a heightened sense of group belonging. Several sources point to the increasing numbers of Mexican American men who wore drapes in the wake of the Sleepy Lagoon case. Some of these were members of gangs, identified by neighborhood, who wore the style as a way of upholding affiliation and identity as *pachucos.* Others gravitated to draped pants and long coats because they proclaimed their presence and legitimacy in public: Official Los Angeles had made it a point of honor to wear a zoot suit. Still others found the aesthetic appealing, as an item of fashion. Although it may have seemed that everyone was wearing a zoot suit, estimates range widely, from as many as one-third or even two-thirds of Mexican American youth, to a much smaller figure of about 3 to 5 percent. As Pagán observes, few men arrested in the Los Angeles riot were wearing zoot suits.[12]

For some minority youths, extreme styling had gained a political meaning. Condemning discrimination and prejudice in the wake of police roundups and arrests, the Youth Committee for the Defense of Mexican American Youth specifically criticized the press for "mak[ing] fun of zoot suits." One young man, Alfred Barela, had been arrested for disturbing the peace in an incident in May 1943; before the case was dismissed for lack of evidence, Judge Arthur Guerin scolded him for being a disgrace to his people. In a letter to Guerin, Barela shot back: "We're tired of being told we can't go to this show or this dance hall because we're Mexican or that we better not be seen on the beach front, or that we can't wear draped pants or have our hair cut the way we want to." He pointedly asked the judge why he did not criticize the police for false arrest. Freedom was their birthright as Americans, and that meant not only speech in the public square but the right to dress as they pleased. At the time of the riot, this sentiment could be heard repeatedly. "This is supposed to be a free country," observed Rudy Sánchez, a Mexican American sailor. "We don't go around beating up people just because we don't like the clothes they wear." A young man at a meeting held by left-wing newspaperman Al Waxman agreed: "Isn't this a free country? Can't we wear the kind of clothes that we like? Must we be disrobed at the order of other men?"[13]

The political implications of the zoot suit were apparent to African American youth as well. Days before the zoot suit riot began, the principal of Dorsey High School in Los Angeles condemned the style and sought to ban it from the classroom: "I don't want any of that low zoot suit stuff from the Eastside on this campus!" he told a school assembly. Black students, their mothers, and the NAACP's Junior Council protested the action. The campaign against the style gave "a false impression of degeneracy to those who prefer long coats," when in fact, "every generation selects clothes different from preceding ones." The real purpose of this measure was to stigmatize and exclude minority students from the "palatial new school." The zoot suit, they argued, had become a political weapon of reactionary forces, including the police and the mainstream press, which sought to criminalize minority youth.[14]

These young Angelenos had politicized the zoot suit, deriving their claims from rights to schooling, recreation, and public spaces, and a right to self-expression through clothing and appearance. As a costume featured in street fights, arrests, and court appearances, the zoot suit also figured in a critique of the police, the judicial system, and the press. When young men spoke of the style in this way, they directed their grievances to the racial prejudice and discrimination they experienced day to day. In these ways, wearing the zoot suit involved a self-conscious degree of opposition.

Still, the political valence of the zoot suit to its wearers should not be overstated. There is little evidence that young men incorporated the zoot suit, explicitly or implicitly, into a stance of opposition to the state, the war, or capitalism. Many young men wore the style while waiting to be inducted into the army. As historian Kevin Leonard writes, they "described themselves as patriotic Americans, not as criminals." Rudy Sanchez strikingly observed, "Thousands of former 'zoot suiters' are fighting for Uncle Sam." Although they were well aware of the discrimination they faced, they insisted their clothing choices were aesthetic, not sociological. They would wear the style until their induction into the armed forces. "Nobody is going to make me take off this zoot suit" until then, said one. The rights these young men demanded were claimed in the name of American ideals, all the more so in the context of wartime. Liberal groups and civil rights activists repeatedly tried to draw larger political implications from the situation, a view that was not necessarily held by young people themselves. Thus, the report on the Dorsey High School protest in the *California Eagle* quoted its own writer John Kinloch, who was also an NAACP Youth Council member. He railed against police brutality and crime reporting that was "smearing minority groups because they wear 'zoot suits'—this is all part of a scheme to disrupt and divide the war workers of Los Angeles." This viewpoint was not explicitly promoted by the high school students themselves. In a similar vein, Alice Greenfield, a leader of the Sleepy Lagoon Defense Committee who regularly visited the convicted men in prison, praised one for having written an article that "showed a good understanding of the case in its broadest aspects." She hoped he would help the other, less politicized, men "to understand more clearly the tie-up between this case and the fight against discrimination generally."[15]

Even as the zoot suit took on a more politicized meaning for Mexican American men in the weeks leading up to the riot, it was being reinterpreted by white servicemen stationed in Southern California. It was not only a charged threat—the "zoot gangsters"—conjured in the newspapers, but an embodied style that affronted them. At first, perhaps, soldiers and sailors in Los Angeles may have been like their counterparts around the country, mildly offended or even amused by the peculiarity of the zoot suit. In spring 1942, they were razzing those who wore it by "stepping up to zoot suit wearers and politely asking: 'May I have this dance, Miss?'"[16] Soon, however, the style had acquired the cachet of menace and danger. Encounters with Mexican American zoot suiters became more troubled, marked by taunts, scuffles, and fistfights.

Moreover, baseless rumors circulated throughout the city about the depraved behavior of *pachucos*. In a secret investigation of racial conditions in 1943, FBI agents claimed they had received reports of "wives of Navy men being robbed and raped by 'zoot suiters.'" A police captain similarly testified after the riot that "in many cases they grab a young couple, tie the escort up, rape the girl and then urinate on them." These rumors reached the servicemen posted in the Los Angeles area. One had written his mother, Mrs. Fred Holley, in Vernon, Texas, just days before the rioting began, telling her that several sailors had been beaten and killed by "3 of these zoot-suits as they're called." Holley wrote her congressman, Ed Gossett, on June 4, 1943, outraged that the government would "take your sons away from a safe, respectful home and place you in a state like that," but "*can't* clear the *highways* and *places of recreation* the boys have to attend, of gangsters such as these." Gossett sent the letter to Secretary of the Navy Frank Knox, who forwarded it to Admiral David W. Bagley, Commandant of the 11th Naval District. By then Bagley had his hands full trying to quell the riot. He finally answered Gossett on July 2, informing him that Holley's information was "grossly exaggerated" but acknowledging "attacks by small groups of hoodlums on service men on liberty from the Naval Reserve Armory in Los Angeles which finally resulted in men from that station getting together and going out seeking retaliation against the zoot-suiters."[17]

Such rumors, a rehash of racial myths and white fears, received reinforcement in the press and on the street, in the encounters between sailors and assertive young Mexican American men. In Los Angeles, they concentrated fear and rage on a peculiar form of dress. In the heat of the moment, the zoot suit enabled first servicemen, then white civilians and police, to identify a target. When worn by dark-skinned males, the outfit had a kind of heuristic value, providing a visual indicator of crime, guilt, and punishment.

Ripping the jackets and pants off the bodies of Mexican American men was essential to the servicemen's modus operandi. If not necessarily premeditated, that act suggests a measure of motive and design to the chaos of the riot. Where did this practice originate? In many cultures, including those in early modern Europe, forced disrobing, exposing the vulnerable body to ridicule, was a form of ritual shaming and social coercion; rioters in early nineteenth-century Baltimore, for example, stripped the finery off the social and political elite. In the 1920s, "debagging" was a custom among upper-class English students who wanted to humiliate men wearing "Oxford bags," an extreme style of menswear sometimes seen as a precursor to the zoot suit. These bullying customs unclothed men to put them in their place, even as they confirmed the status and bonds of their attackers. Hazing rituals in fraternities and athletic teams that involved coerced stripping had a different purpose: that of initiating novices into membership. Still the practice would have been familiar to navy men, who endured various debasing rituals, as when they first crossed the equator or International Date Line. Although trying to tamp down the violence, navy officials nevertheless referred to the " 'collegiate' spirit of their young seamen."[18]

Nor was the practice of tearing clothes limited to the military. Carey McWilliams testified that months earlier, when the police had begun to associate the "pachuco suit" with criminality, some officers affixed razor blades to their nightsticks to rip the jackets. Young men arrested for loitering were ordered by a judge to cut their duck-tail hair styles and surrender their zoot suits. The embarrassment of public nakedness and exposure, as well as the destruction of a revered possession, must have been deeply humiliating to zoot suiters, who were particularly sensitive to the power of clothes to create impressions. Thirty-five years after the riot, Rudy Leyvas recalled how sailors pulled an acquaintance from a streetcar, beat him, and stripped off his clothes in his mother's presence: "That really got me steamed, that they would do something like that in front of his mother." Yet the ritual of removing and destroying clothing may have deflected sailors and civilians from worse violence. Although there were numerous serious injuries, no one died in Los Angeles, unlike the riots that followed in Beaumont, Detroit, and New York City.[19]

The servicemen's invasion of theaters, amusement piers, and other resorts contributed to the ritualistic aspects of the riot, transforming violence into spectacle. One eyewitness saw a mob enter a cinema, compel the manager to turn on the house lights, and force men in the audience to stand and show their trousers. In Long Beach, the newspaper *PM* reported, four hundred sailors chased a zoot suiter into a theater: "He scooted down an aisle, but couldn't shake off his pursuers. He leapt to the stage, swarms of sailors right behind him. There, to the cheers of the audience, they stripped off his baggy pants." Even on the streets, the

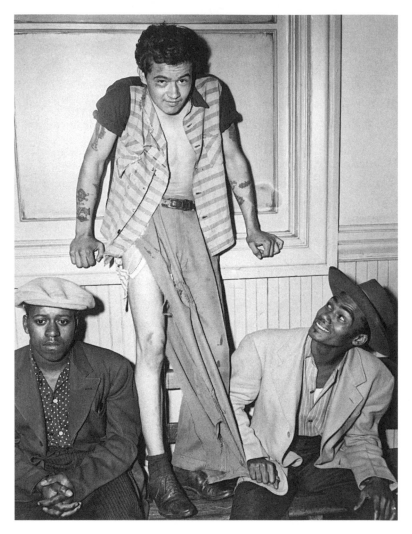

Figure 24. This image of a *pachuco* in torn clothing, with two black men in zoot suits, ran in a number of newspapers during the 1943 zoot suit riot; his facial expression is at odds with his appearance, the result of violent treatment at the hands of rioters. ©Bettmann/CORBIS.

theatricality of these attacks is striking. In one case, the police stopped a car full of young African American men, including an inductee, as they drove through downtown, only to stand by as soldiers stripped them of their pants. "It is believed the attack committed on the youths before the gaze of hundreds of downtown shoppers was prompted by the presence of a young white woman in the machine," related the *New York Amsterdam News*.[20]

Accounts of incidents on the streets and streetcars also suggest that the focus on the zoot suit caused many moments of cognitive dissonance, with sailors and civilians unsure about the objects of their attacks and searching for answers in clothing. A reporter for the *Chicago Defender* described white servicemen's attitude of hostility to any form of sharp dressing, especially by African Americans: "whether clothes are collegiate, English style drape (whence originated the zoot suit), or modernistic to any degree—especially California sports clothes—the wearers should be attacked." White women too derided "Negroes dressed in the modern style and accus[ed] them in overtones of being 'zoot suiters.'"[21] This fashion-conscious journalist perceived distinctions in menswear many could not.

As they roamed Los Angeles, sailors made split-second decisions about whom to beat up or pass by. *PM* published the following item: A young African American man, attending a pre-flight training program, was returning home on a streetcar when a group of sailors got on. The sailors spied a Mexican shipyard worker wearing a helmet and work clothes, dragged him off the trolley, and undressed and beat him. Then they went up to the African American: "One guy said 'you one of them zoot suiters too?' I said no, and pointed to my clothes, ordinary street clothes. I said I was in the Air Corps Reserve and they said they didn't care a damn what I was." They pulled him off the streetcar, but fled when a police patrol arrived. Some men wore overalls over their drape pants to avoid detection. Searching for signs of criminality at times took a comical form, as in a *Los Angeles Times* report that gangs were congregating at the beach: "How to tell a zoot suiter, when he isn't wearing his zoot suit, became a puzzling problem for Santa Monica lifeguards yesterday," a dilemma solved for the time by keeping alert for duck-tail haircuts. In one case, servicemen stopped and questioned a black lawyer who was not wearing a zoot suit, but released him when they decided "he was apparently a learned gentleman." A black college graduate, stopped by an MP who asked why he was wearing a zoot suit, answered that "he had bought and paid for it and that no one was going to tear it from him." The MP backed down.[22]

The police also battened on clothing as evidence of criminal guilt. Sociologist Edward McDonagh interviewed an African American college student who recalled his encounter with rioters a few months before he was to be inducted into the army. One Saturday afternoon, he was walking with three Mexican men down a thoroughfare in a town near Los Angeles when "a cab drove up to the curb and four Marines hopped out. One of the Marines said 'let's give these 4-F zoot-suiters some combat training.' There was nothing else to do but fight." When the police came, he was taken into custody. "My guilt as a zoot-suiter was determined by a careful measurement of my trousers!" he remarked. "My trousers proved me innocent. However, one of the officers phoned my mother and warned her that I should not be seen in public with Mexicans who apparently were zoot-suiters."[23]

A fixation with the width of trousers is one sign of the mindset of Los Angeles officialdom, which insisted repeatedly that the zoot suit itself had triggered the violence in the city. Police officials and sheriff's deputies took umbrage at news reports from outside Los Angeles that many of the men who had been attacked or arrested did not wear this style: "A desk sergeant, in a particularly lively section, where scores of arrests were made, said that 99 per cent of those seized 'wore zoot' suits." Seeking a misdemeanor charge for anyone caught wearing a zoot suit, members of the Los Angeles City Council believed that "by removing the identifying garb the attacks by sailors on the zoot-suited hoodlums would be halted." Despite unanimous support, the proposed ordinance was not passed.[24]

What percentage of men attacked or arrested wore zoot suits is subject to dispute, but in most cases, dark skin color—and being in the wrong place at the wrong time—was all a man needed to be beaten or thrown into a police van. One unlucky African American, taking the streetcar home from work, was wearing his defense-plant uniform and identification badge when attackers pulled him to the street and gouged his eye with a knife. The liberal press and left-wing commentators repeatedly observed that a majority of the Mexican American youths who had been attacked were not wearing zoot suits. "First, Mexicans, and then Negroes were attacked regardless of their garb," reported Thomas L. Griffith, Jr., the head of the local NAACP, on June 9, 1943. "I have no information of a single instance in which a White zoot suiter was attacked by either civilians or service men."[25]

The doggedness of Los Angeles officials, in the face of evidence to the contrary, was a determined effort to downplay the racial basis of the riot. "There is insistence on every side that the problem presented by their scraps with the Navy is not intrinsically one of race; that it is merely unfortunate, that the wearers of the zoot suits are chiefly Americans of Mexican descent, along with some Negroes," observed one journalist. The *Los Angeles Times* editorial page stated bluntly that it was "their weird dress and not their race which resulted in difficulties."[26] The label "zoot suiter" aligned with the cultural style of young men of color, but it permitted a deflection of race as incidental, sidestepping the extensive evidence of discrimination, prejudice, and social tension.

Los Angeles's daily newspapers, "snatched up eagerly on downtown street corners," played a crucial role in broadcasting this view to white residents. At their most sympathetic, they described the zoot suiters' psychological makeup, social origins, and family relations to place their style and behavior in context. Although filing stories riddled with racial stereotypes, *Los Angeles Times* reporter Timothy Turner was more sensitive than most. Writing in the months before the riot, he explained the "zoot-suit gangster" as a "social problem of first generation Americans," and told readers that "the zoot suit is no label of juvenile delinquency" but was also worn by hard-working, church-going youths. During the riot, many reporters painted a far more lurid picture that aimed to expose a harsh truth behind the seemingly harmless fad. The average person "doesn't know the real zoot suiters," explained the *Los Angeles Examiner*, "the ones who must subscribe to a startling code of ethics that demands that both boys and girls be tough and hard, that the male members must be bad sports willing to fight at any provocation, who are willing to steal and swear, smoke and lie, and flunk out of school." As Kevin Leonard documents, only rarely did journalists interview zoot suiters to understand their point of view.[27]

Newspaper reporting likened the home-front riot to a war zone, with such phrases as "zoot suit offensive," "mopping up action," and "punitive task force" sprinkled liberally in their coverage. The *Los Angeles Times* ran a front-page photograph of two zoot suiters who had been beaten and stripped, their heads bowed and faces covered, with the caption "unconditional surrender." The *Herald-Express* even printed directions on how to "de-zoot": "Grab a zooter. Take off his pants and frock coat and tear them up or burn them. Trim the 'Argentine ducktail' that goes with the screwy costume." At the same time, the imagery of the entertainment industry bled into the portrayals of violence, with chase scenes and drubbings played for laughs, Hollywood-style. The *Los Angeles Times* called Mexican American youths "gamin dandies," as though a diminutive rendered innocuous the beatings they received. "In Keystone Comedy fashion yesterday, two sailors pursued two zooters through downtown streets and through a crowded market, overturning stalls and spilling produce," reported the *Examiner*. Another story described how "impromptu tailoring and haircutting jobs were performed on the suspected pachucos, sending them into custody begging to be kept safely behind bars." Pictures of zoot-suited prisoner Alex "Largo" Rodriguez made the point visually: one photograph depicted a sheriff inspecting his haircut, and another featured Rodriguez and a deputy sheriff chatting and smiling behind an assortment of weapons.[28]

The bemused and jocular coverage of the riot in turn contributed to the servicemen's sense of administering rough justice. In a conversation with Admiral Bagley, Captain S. F. Heim observed that the perpetrators were not the "old timers" but the young reservists "egged on by civilians telling them what a fine job they are doing and by the press." He described how "a draft of men came through the station and read about this in the papers and 8 men got out and left; they were supposed to wait at the station for their train, but they started a band and looked for zoot-suiters and started some trouble. The Patrol round them up and locked them up but it just shows how excited they get about it from just reading the papers."[29]

Notably, the zoot suit riot sparked public debate over the news media's representation of the disorders, creating an unusual self-consciousness about the relationship between image and action. This was arguably the first case of civil unrest in which much of the conflict played out in the press. The police believed the zoot suiters were publicity hounds. "We had no difficulty until the zoot suit gangs were given recognition by the press," one officer said. "If one got his picture in the paper, he became a shining example to the others." In response, the African American and liberal press expressed outrage at the inflammatory language and misleading photographs that filled the mass-circulation dailies. Carey McWilliams condemned the Hearst papers' use of the "familiar Harlem crime-wave technique," intended to scare readers and boost circulation. Some editors reinterpreted the crime photos or presented alternative images. "These are what the downtown sheets call 'baby gangsters' and 'murderous hoodlums,'" observed the California Eagle, a local African American newspaper, commenting on a photograph of young Angelenos during the riot. "They are just kids, as you can see. Some of them are delinquent. Most of them, average American boys." Such awareness of the power of the image extended beyond activists and editors. When reporter Peter Furst went to Central Avenue, an African American man confronted him, "You gonna take pictures of us so you can put them in them damn Hearst papers and call us gangsters again?"[30]

An article that portrayed Mexican American women as diseased prostitutes especially provoked anger. When mainstream newspapers refused to publish a rebuttal from a group of young Latinas, the leftwing East

Side Journal ran their story with a photograph. These were high school graduates who worked in defense plants while their male relatives served in the military. Attractively coiffed and attired in dresses and suits, they were the picture of respectability, yet the press had questioned their moral character. "We have not been able to have our side of the story told," they objected. Another group of thirty—"half of us girls were zooters and the other half Squares," one recalled—protested by marching to Juvenile Hall. "These girls insisted that they should be examined, as a group, by an officially appointed board of physicians so that they could prove that they were virgins," Carey McWilliams wrote. "Long after the riots, I have seen Mexican-American boys pull creased and wrinkled newspaper clippings from their wallets and exhibit this slanderous story with the greatest indignation." The young women, meanwhile, had "made a *corrido* [ballad] about it—so we won't ever forget that paper."[31]

As the riot ended, reporter Marcia Winn portrayed a city on edge—scanning the night skies for an air attack, seething with anger toward the Japanese, compulsively spending war wages, and uneasily returning to the abnormal patterns of home-front life. Street encounters remained fraught with the possibility of violence. Winn described coming upon a group of zoot suiters and "slick chicks" near city hall, the men dressed in "amazing creations" and ducktail haircuts: "The eight came, four abreast, down the narrow sidewalk. They slowed their pace, glared ominously. . . . We moved uneasily from the sidewalk to the street. So did two young soldiers. . . . They hastily crossed to the other side of the street."[32]

Some defense workers in Southern California refused the night and swing shifts, or carried weapons with them to work. They not only feared zoot suiters but dreaded meeting servicemen, who sometimes shouted epithets, called them slackers and draft dodgers, and even beat them up. "Most civilians just 'grin and bear it,'" San Diego Councilman Charles Dail wrote Admiral Bagley, but "every civilian, no matter what type of clothes he is wearing, should be safe on the streets." An African American electrical engineer found the situation to be too much, abandoning a high-paying job at a submarine base to return to the all-black community he had left in Oklahoma. "There were just too many foreigners and poor white trash working with me out there and I stayed tense and was constantly afraid that a fight at the base might break out any time," he observed. "When the 'zoot'-suit riot started, then I said this is no place for me. I'd rather be in poverty and have peace . . . than to make plenty money and probably lose my life."[33]

Mexican Americans too endured an uneasy atmosphere. Threatening handbills appeared in high schools with large numbers of minority students: "Big Sale. Second Hand Zoot Suits. Slightly Damaged. Apply at Nearest U.S. Naval Station. While they last we have your Size." According to a city councilman, the police department had asked the local Selective Service board to draft "particularly obstreperous devotees" of the zoot suit. Songwriter and musician Lalo Guerrero likened the atmosphere to a natural disaster: "Even in San Diego we could feel the vibrations of the violence, like being on the edge of an earthquake."[34]

Recriminations within the Mexican community, building since the Sleepy Lagoon case, spilled over. The *Mexican Voice*, a publication of educated, upwardly mobile youth, criticized Mexican Americans for failing to assimilate, noting, "We Mexicans have found it difficult to dismiss our cultural heritage, our Spanish language, our food habits and the like." It worried that, "regardless of who is to blame, these teensters . . . are giving our group a bad name," and challenged Hispanic servicemen to redeem the community. Newspapers prominently featured Vera Trujillo, the mother of a teenager who had been wounded in the riot. Visiting him in the hospital, she condemned his association with older zoot suiters and tore his "natty peg-top black trousers . . . seam from seam," right before his eyes. "We tried to keep him home but he kept slipping away and what has happened to him is his own fault," she said. A contrasting view came from another mother, Amelia Venegas, who had been on her way to buy milk for her baby when she got into an altercation with police. They had been questioning a group of zoot suiters near her home, and when she cursed them for harassing the youths, they arrested

her. Venegas had a husband in the navy, but defended the zoot suiters'
right to be in public places.[35]

Many zoot suiters and *pachucos* chose to back off in a tense situation.
On June 12, 1943, six cars filled with zoot-suited men and several young
women, flying white flags and the American flag, drove through the
downtown and stopped at police headquarters. A number lined up in
their zoot suits to give blood at a Red Cross facility and have their photograph taken doing so, an event mentioned by the left-leaning press as
proof of their patriotism. Young men who had been arrested during the
riot appeared for their court dates in ordinary clothes and without their
ducktail haircuts. Among them was Luis Verdusco, who announced,
"I'm through zooting." As the *Hollywood Citizen News* reported,
"Throughout the city zooters were assimilating a like attitude." When
the Los Angeles County grand jury began a probe days after the riot,
seeking to establish the extent of the *pachuco* gang problem and the
possibility of subversive activity, they called several young men in flamboyant outfits as witnesses. Each declined to draw the connection between their dress and the riot: one liked zoot suits because "they are
easier to dance in," and another declared, "I'm not a rowdy; I just like
this style." Both men were about to go into military service.[36]

"We're good Americans," said one Mexican American youth to Captain Joe Reed, when the cavalcade of zoot suiters called its truce. The
press reported this unmistakable declaration of patriotism, but the
young man's next comment to the police captain was not so clear. "We
want you to know we're passing the word along to cut out the rough
stuff," the *Washington Post* quoted him. "We want you to pass the word
along to cut out the rough stuff," reported the liberal *Hollywood Citizen
News.*[37] In a single pronoun rested an entire interpretation of the riot.

Many places in the United States witnessed the kinds of social tensions that led to civil disorder in Los Angeles: the war boom destabilized
local economies, put pressure on traditional neighborhoods, and threatened the customary status of social groups. The obsession with the zoot

Figure 25. Mexican American teenagers wave white flags and "surrender" at the end of the 1943 zoot suit riot; their cheerful faces and "V for victory" gestures emphasize their innocence and patriotism. ©Bettmann/CORBIS.

suit as a danger was in the first instance a local phenomenon. The city had a remarkably diverse and volatile population that was difficult to understand and control. The zoot suit became a material, tangible emblem, distilling the everyday encounters and cultural clashes of ordinary men into legible signs. Similarly, the institutions that oversaw Los Angeles, from the mayor to the police and the press, found the zoot suit a ready-made symbol. The city's preoccupation with style and image—typically directed at tourists and investors—made the zoot suiter even more visible as a potential threat to civic welfare and local interests.

It had become a clothing style with political implications, which were recognized especially by the elites of Los Angeles but also, in no small measure, by the young men who were attacked for wearing it.

The assaults on zoot suiters in Los Angeles reverberated in the streets of other cities that June. On a Philadelphia subway platform on June 10, several drunken sailors, inspired by their comrades on the West Coast, beat up two members of Gene Krupa's dance band when they mistook the band uniforms for zoot suits. These musicians were white. Two days later in the City of Brotherly Love, twenty-five white teens described as "corner loungers" attacked four black youths wearing brightly colored shirts, ties, drape trousers, and pancake hats. Three of the African American men were planning to show a visiting New Yorker the town when the attack began. One reported that "during the melee the other boys tried to rip off their trousers." The black men—not the white attackers— were taken into custody "for their own protection." On the same day, high school students in Detroit fought sixty-five teens wearing zoot suits and white armbands. In Baltimore there was a report of a zoot suit gang that went around smashing milk bottles, while in Richmond, Virginia, three sailors attacked a shipyard worker in a café after he had protested their "slighting remarks" about his zoot suit.[38] National headlines, radio broadcasts, and swirling rumors undoubtedly spurred copycat crimes, policing of zoot-suited youth, and reporting focused on what many now perceived as a sinister style. These incidents were quickly overshadowed by the more destructive rioting in Detroit and Harlem. As zoot-suit warfare finally quieted down, government officials, community leaders, activists, investigators, and academicians were left to ponder how a suit of clothes could spark a riot.

5

Reading the Riddle

ven as the Los Angeles riot was quelled, a war of recrimination
erupted. Local and state officials began a series of investigations,
while newspapers, opinion journals, and radio networks avidly covered the story in its aftermath, trying to account for the unrest on the
home front. Governor Earl Warren immediately appointed a citizens'
committee to study the violence, the Los Angeles County grand jury
issued a set of findings and recommendations, and the state government's Joint Fact-Finding Committee on Un-American Activities in California held hearings. A host of local organizations also put out reports.
A number of these studies probed the nature and extent of discrimination against Mexicans in Los Angeles, from employment and housing to
education and recreation; they focused especially on the problems of
second-generation youths who had grown up in the United States and
increasingly objected to the prejudice they faced. Other investigations
fastened on the political overtones of the riot. One school of thought
identified the handiwork of Mexican *sinarquistas*, members of a right-
wing Catholic movement that the U.S. government believed to be collab-
orating with the Axis. Adolfo de la Huerta, inspector-general of Mexican
consulates in the United States and a former president of Mexico, called

the riot "the work of Nazi-Fascist agents attempting to destroy continental solidarity." Others believed the zoot suit had been designed by Red tailors. After taking extensive testimony, the Joint Fact-Finding Committee on Un-American Activities in California found little evidence of police brutality, racism, or *sinarquismo*, but concluded that the fad presented "a golden opportunity for Communist racial agitation."[1]

Whether questioning political factors or probing the racial angle, everyone felt obliged to comment on the bewildering clothing for which the riot was named and to consider what the style might signify. Seeing a Communist conspiracy, the district attorney of Ventura, California, declared that "zoot suits are an open indication of subversive character." In contrast, Pastor Francisco Quintanilla, known as the "little mayor of Watts," believed that fascist Fifth Columnists, hoping to arouse servicemen's ire and public discontent, had enticed Mexican American men into adopting a style that discouraged them from enlisting or being inducted. Mississippi segregationist John Rankin took another tack, perceiving the conflict between Anglo sailors and Mexican American youths through the lens of Southern race relations. Rising in the House of Representatives to condemn "zoot suit rapists" and "savage brutes," he praised the servicemen "for the manhood and the courage they have displayed in stripping the masks, as well as the zoot suits, from these loathsome criminals and protecting innocent American girls from their beastly attacks." Here Rankin tapped into powerful and familiar white racist imagery—pure white womanhood, the black rapist, retribution through lynching, the minstrel mask—and warned of an outwardly innocuous fad that camouflaged evil intent; for him, this style disguised biologically rooted racial inferiority and danger.[2] In these cases, the zoot suit fit into established templates of interpretation.

For many others, however, the zoot suit's import in the wake of the riot was not readily grasped. Early in 1943, Ralph Ellison had wondered aloud about the "riddle" of the style and what political meanings it might conceal. After the riot, this question was on the minds of many.

The *Washington Post* did not perceive any immediate political overtones, but the unrest "might easily and quickly acquire them." An editorial warned, "The whole situation is full of explosive possibilities." Commentators repeatedly called the style baffling, a mystery they were at a loss to understand. Could the zoot suit still be viewed as an ephemeral fad, a mere object of mirth? The riot had turned the style into something more. Across the country, legions of experts, politicians, commentators, and ordinary citizens reached for ways to explain the zoot suit. In the process, an article of clothing became mainly understood as a representation of some larger reality, one often at a distance from the lived experiences and awareness of street-corner sharpies and *pachucos*. "Most people seem to be more eager to 'label' the phenomenon, than to find out what it is like," social psychologist Fritz Redl observed. As semanticist S. I. Hayakawa declared, "The 'zoot suit' is a symbol"—but a symbol of what?[3] This battle over the zoot suit would be fought on another front, of words and image. In the churning discussion that followed the events in Los Angeles, the zoot suit transmuted into a riot of symbolism, simultaneously resonant and unfixed.

For all the disagreements over the meaning of the zoot suit, the social and behavioral sciences provided much of the language for the debate. "With us such a phenomenon as a zoot suit becomes a symptom of a deep-rooted sociological malady and a theme for sober politico-economic articles and editorials," the *Washington Post* remarked. A *Chicago Tribune* columnist called for the experts: "If all the sociologists were not planning Utopias and all the psychologists were not testing military aptitudes, we might get a plausible explanation of the zoot suit business from rags to riot." The sociologists and psychologists managed to find the time, for the zoot suit was an irresistible magnet. Some, such as Emory S. Bogardus, a prominent sociologist at the University of Southern California, were already on the scene. Others traveled to Los Angeles to see for themselves. The University of California engaged Franz Alexander, founder of the Chicago Institute for Psychoanalysis, to study the zoot suiters, while a team from Fisk University's Race Relations Department, led by psychologist Herman H. Long, went to Los Angeles to survey racial attitudes. The personality traits of zoot suiters became a focus for well-known social psychologists such as Redl and Kenneth B. Clark. Specialists in education, criminology, social work, and psychiatry also investigated the zoot suit and explored its connection to youth, race, gender, sexuality, crime, and the war. "The wearing of extravagant and extreme styles seemed an innocent thing a few months ago," observed columnist Joseph Bibb, but now "all kinds of deep conclusions are reached about big breeches and balloon hats."[4]

That the experts rushed in to explain what had been viewed in most parts of the country as the folly of youth bespeaks the heightened authority of the social sciences in the 1940s. As Americans mobilized for war, researchers undertook opinion polling, testing of recruits and servicemen, studies of home-front morale, and psychological profiles of the enemy with a sense of urgency and mission. Consideration of the zoot suit took shape at a moment of fertile rethinking in many areas of the social sciences. Psychology, urban sociology, and anthropology were growing fields of inquiry that offered insights into the behavior and attitudes of racial minorities and adolescents. Particularly important were anthropological approaches to culture, and the increased attention to group rituals and meaning-making activities. At the same time, semanticists and philosophers had created a greater awareness of the way human beings continuously create symbols to make sense of their experiences. These intellectual disciplines encouraged scholars and laypeople alike to "read" a phenomenon like the zoot suit for its underlying meaning.[5] Public officials, journalists, and ordinary Americans drew heavily on these new ideas and concepts to explain the zoot suit in the wake of the riot.

Much of the immediate response to the zoot suit focused on the nexus of youth, criminality, and race. Since the Sleepy Lagoon murder case—and even before—Los Angeles officials and the press had linked the fashion to Mexican American gangs, crime, and social disorder. This had been the justification used by rampaging sailors and civilians meting out rough justice to zoot suiters during the riot, and it lay behind the decision of the police to arrest Mexican American youths almost exclusively. In the post-riot investigations, the police testified repeatedly that the zoot suit marked Mexican youths' criminal intent. Supporting this view, an assistant to the police chief stressed, was the fact that 134 suspects wearing zoot suits had been charged with crimes in the eighteen months prior to the riot. Reported on its own, that fact said nothing about the number of offenders wearing ordinary clothing, or about police profiling of zoot-suited men.[6]

Snaking through this insistence that the zoot suit reliably denoted crime were evolving views of Mexicans as a race and Mexican American youth as a distinct demographic group. During the Sleepy Lagoon case, Edward Duran Ayres, head of the Foreign Relations Bureau of the Los Angeles Sheriff's Office, infamously used turn-of-the-century ethnology and evolutionary science to explain the apparent rise in Mexican crime. While acknowledging the effects of employment discrimination and segregation, he insisted that the tendencies toward violence and lawlessness had a biological basis and should be seen as racial characteristics Mexicans shared with Indians and Orientals. Alluding to Rudyard Kipling, he concluded that "one cannot change the spots of a leopard," and predicted not only a crime wave but a race riot. When the riot came, however, city leaders, the press, and the police backed away from the subject of race, repeatedly denying that it had anything to do with the violence. "There is insistence on every side that the problem . . . is not intrinsically one of race," reported the New York Times.[7]

Instead, they fastened on the zoot suit not merely as a cultural marker of Mexican American youth but as the cause of the unrest. The police maintained that "the zoot suit, elsewhere merely a garment affected by jive-bitten adolescents, has become here in the last few months a uniform for roving gangs of Mexican-Americans and Negroes from 16 to 25 years old." In the midst of the riot, reporter Julian Hartt reinforced Mayor Fletcher Bowron's criticism of "zoot gangsters" by pointing to the symbols and rituals that expressed their sensibility: the use of slang "based principally on Spanish but unintelligible to the un-initiated," graffiti "chalked on buildings and billboards in their respective 'territories,' and the practice of the young hoodlums of claiming 'molls' who dress with equal group individuality—usually in short black skirts and long black socks or mesh stockings." By calling these attributes *group individuality*, Hartt drew on a concept in social psychology developed by Edward A. Ross, a pioneer of the discipline in the early twentieth century, to describe what today would be termed a subculture.[8]

Some of the investigating bodies in Los Angeles took a more benign view of the extreme style. The Los Angeles County grand jury found "no inherent connection between wearing zoot suits and juvenile delinquency." Rather, it was a "passing fad," "merely one manifestation of a disturbed time in our national life." The citizens' committee appointed by Governor Earl Warren agreed that many wore the style, and warned it was "a mistake in fact and an aggravating practice to link the phrase 'zoot suit' with the report of a crime." Attorney General Robert W. Kenny, head of the committee, waxed eloquent to the press: These were merely "kids running together, bent on devilment, something like the old Clancy Street gang going up against the guys over on Vesey Street. . . . There are lots of good kids among them." The native Californian had never actually lived on New York's Lower East Side, but he may have seen the film comedy *Clancy Street Boys*, which was playing in Los Angeles at the time of the riot. This kind of language had circulated already in sympathetic portraits of the Sleepy Lagoon defendants that called them "downy-cheeked youngsters" although half of them were twenty years old or older. Those who invoked "good kids" rather than "zoot hoodlums" stressed the underlying social and economic conditions in which Mexican American youths grew up in Los Angeles: the poor schools, segregated recreational facilities, limited employment opportunities, and racial prejudice. For them the zoot suit was not the uniform of troublemakers but simply a fashion. It was "something to hang the blame on," observed the *California Eagle*: "the zoot suits which these Mexican kids inhabit hold no mystic affinity with crime."[9]

Still, the preoccupation of Angelenos with the zoot suit made many outside the city impatient. Only a minority of local observers, like social activist Carey McWilliams, seemed to address the broader circumstances that led to the riot, let alone the actions of white servicemen and civilians. The press had "treated readers to long-winded speculations concerning the origins of the 'zoot suit,'" the liberal journal *Christian Century* wrote, but had failed to explain the gravity of the riot: Race "had everything to do with it. No white wearers of these bizarre clothes were disturbed. Hundreds of Mexicans and Negroes who were not wearing zoot suits were attacked." "Zoot riots are race riots," African American writer Chester Himes stated flatly in the *Crisis*. From a different political perspective, the *Chicago Tribune* heaped scorn on Los Angeles's "excursion into euphemism," an old habit of Californians who "once concealed an outbreak of bubonic plague, and chronically call a torrential downpour a mist." Far from being a "glorified roughhouse," this was a race riot, the latest in a "very bad record . . . in race relations" against not only Mexicans but also the Japanese, Filipinos, and African Americans. The most prominent critic, Eleanor Roosevelt, did not even mention the zoot suit but rather emphasized that the riots had resulted from "a mixture of race and youth problems" that all Americans would have to confront.[10]

The mixture of race and youth problems was, in fact, the object of intense research and analysis at this time. In the interwar years, social scientists had moved away from a biological framework for understanding race to one that centered on social processes and culture. Beginning in the early twentieth century, the Chicago School of sociology had created dynamic models to explain how ethnic, racial, and underprivileged groups achieved or were thwarted in their efforts to adapt and integrate into mainstream society. Its practitioners developed urban ethnography as a form of research to map the cultural and behavioral responses of different social groups in the city. Studying the urban black poor and working class, some academics focused on social and economic barriers, but others developed a new interest in culture and social psychology. They considered the heritage of slavery, retention of African customs, characteristics of marital relations, and a mentality shaped by caste status as factors in the incomplete assimilation of the black masses. Even when scholars delineated the structural determinants of African Americans' subordination, a concern with the damaged psyche, and its individuated and collective impact on social relations, appeared throughout the applied social science of the war years. Thus Gunnar Myrdal, in his momentous 1944 work, *An American Dilemma,* called black culture "a distorted development, or a pathological condition, of the general American Culture."[11]

The focus on psychology and culture also informed the expanding interest in the problems of youth, which brought together academics and practitioners in criminology, education, psychology, psychiatry, social work, and sociology. Investigations of juvenile delinquency, begun in the early twentieth century, continued, but there was a new interest in "normal" youths whose lives had been buffeted by economic insecurity and the mobilization for war. With an eye to postwar readjustment, researchers studied how adolescents were handling the upheaval in family life, greater economic independence, and the freer sexual climate of the home front. Concerns about young people and racial minorities intersected in the work of the American Youth Commission of the American Council on Education, which sponsored such studies as *Color and Human Nature* (1941) and *Color, Class, and Personality* (1942). Of particular interest was the personality development of adolescent African Americans who were socially isolated, blocked from economic opportunities, and victimized by racial prejudice. Notably, researchers found that they "have their own culture to which they respond," a culture that affirmed them psychologically yet was considered criminal and deviant by white society.[12] This scholarly interest in the psychology and culture of youth, especially those from racial minorities, became mobilized by the strange events of the zoot suit riot.

Among the most sophisticated analysts was Fritz Redl, who had been informally gathering data on the zoot suit phenomenon in Detroit as early as 1942. Redl, an Austrian émigré, specialized in adolescent development, group work, and delinquent children, and was closely tied to social welfare agencies in Detroit. When the Los Angeles riot broke out, Redl's views appeared in a widely cited article by Agnes E. Meyer in the *Washington Post*—an article Senator Rankin specifically denounced as sympathetic to "zoot suiter termites." Redl told Meyer that he found the phenomenon "baffling" and considered his findings "extremely tentative." This was a youth movement without any discernible organization or leadership. It had begun among a "haphazard lot of jitterbugging youngsters" who at times, and increasingly, solidified into unified and dangerous gangs. The zoot suit had become "definitely a symbolic expression of potential unity of attack." Redl and other social psychologists feared that, in the worst case, zoot gangs might be similar to what Dr. Ernest L. Talbert called the "rootless, restless adolescents" who had formed the Hitler Youth. Still, Redl cautioned adults to avoid "glamorizing the situation by calling every zoot-suit wearer a delinquent."[13]

Later, in a publication read largely by social welfare workers, Redl offered a detailed description of the zoot suit generation. In Detroit, they were African American and white youths, ranging in age from sixteen to twenty-five, some from the middle class but mainly the children of the Depression who were suddenly able to earn money in the wartime boom. Redl divided them into four groups. There were those who loved dancing and were devoted to the precision and excellence of their performances. Another group of zoot suiters took pleasure in strutting the streets and being seen, sporting the style as an "expression of independence." Some wore the zoot suit as a uniform of group identification, presenting themselves as tough young men in revolt against the adult world; these zoot suiters "came closer to the psychology of college boys," except that their socioeconomic circumstances led them to act out in other ways. Finally, there were those who put on the zoot suit as a "disguise for delinquent gang formation," which he saw as a distinct problem. Redl wondered about the "reasons for the peculiar amalgamation between music and dress [and] the symbolical meaning of parts of the zoot suit outfit," moving toward a notion of a cultural style grounded in social identities and relations.[14] Despite the many-shaded portrait he rendered, Redl worried that he had not really understood the bizarre youth fashion he described.

Other experts had fewer scruples. Joseph Catton, a psychiatrist and Stanford professor, contrasted the "perfectly normal" reactions of the serviceman who felt "a righteous pride in his military garb" with the "overwhelming inferiority complex" of the zoot suiter, which had led him subconsciously to design his own uniform to gain attention. Ralph S. Banay went further and interpreted the zoot suit as a symptom of deep psychological disturbance—"an index of emotional immaturity and sexual maladjustment rather than of a social revolution or of an organized youth movement." Banay, a psychiatrist at Sing Sing prison during World War II, wrote frequently on youth, crime, and mental hygiene, and at various times scrutinized style and appearance in psycho-analytic terms. Because the zoot suit was worn not only by criminals and the underprivileged but also by middle-class high school students, he argued that the fad was not an economic or sociological problem but rather "a psychological manifestation of chaotic sexuality." Adolescents' developmental problems—their immaturity, aggressiveness, and feelings of inadequacy—had only intensified in a time of war. Too young to enlist, they acutely felt their helplessness in the campaign for victory. Banay contrasted the sailor's tight-fitting uniform to the zoot suit's "masking of masculinity." The baggy pants and long coat hid the geni-tals, and the wide-brimmed hat, pointed shoes, colorful fabrics, and longish hair added to an aura of effeminacy, making the zoot suiter akin to the buffoon in Italian comedies or the eunuch in a Persian harem. The extreme style thus marked gender and sexual deviance, a point made vividly by a juvenile court judge in Washington, D.C. Describing the population of young gangsters, he lumped together zoot suiters with marijuana smokers, truants, 4-F draftees, and homosexuals—"a rouged and mascaraed 'cuddle bunny,' a juke-joint queen"—as responsible for the surge of adolescent crime. Others tied the outré fashion to dangerous heterosexuality, with the press reporting on the "growing wave of sex crimes by men wearing zoot suits," at a time when the sexual psychopath had become a target of the law and a monster in the popular imagination.[15]

It was more common to link psychological abnormalities to the changing social environment of the younger generation, who experienced a rending of established roles and customs during the Great Depression and World War II. The new prosperity among workers, women's growing presence in the labor force, and the odd combination of social freedom and greater regimentation on the home front all exacerbated family tensions. To sociologist Ernest R. Mowrer, the result was a cross between a nervous disorder and a communicable disease: "psychic epidemics" had broken out among youth, whose symptoms included the zoot suit and the "present wave of tarantism, in which the so-called 'jitterbugs' dance in the aisles of motion-picture theaters." Emory S. Bogardus thought the Mexican American zoot suiters were similar to the youth posses described by Frederick Thrasher in *The Gang*, a classic ethnographic study of the Chicago School published in 1927. Mexican Americans had picked up the zoot suit from a range of sources— jitterbugs, movie stars, Filipinos, and African Americans—and now wore it to convey a sense of group belonging and a desire for social freedom against the customs and wishes of their parents. This was a classic problem of immigrant parents and their Americanized children, he wrote, exacerbated by wartime conditions: "Warfare is in the air, and in consequence the gang grows more warlike."[16]

Although social psychologists grounded their analyses of the zoot suit more directly in the social and environmental context, they often stressed the strangeness and difference of the zoot suiter. Kenneth B. Clark and James Barker called it the "zoot effect in personality." They intended this concept not to be moral or evaluative but rather one that "indicates a complicated process of personality organization within a given set of field forces." During the Harlem riot, Clark and Barker had interviewed a young black man—"one of the brightest"—who had taken part. He dressed for the interview in a zoot suit and, with slang and swagger, told how he had been in the "Harlem Dump theater" when he saw a man running by and carrying "15 of Crawford's and Howard's suits, and pegged pants, a root suit with a reet pleat, and a stuffed cuff."[17] He went on to describe the riot, looting, and tense encounters between locals and the police.

From this interview, Clark and Barker discerned a personality in the process of disintegration. Discrimination, routine humiliations, and social isolation had created an "observable deviation in style of life" among those "living within but not a part of the larger cultural and societal context." The zoot effect produced a dehumanized and uncaring psychic makeup, even as it "involve[d] a pattern of conscious or unconscious protest against society-at-large."[18] The emphasis on psychological damage as a result of discrimination and prejudice had become a key finding in liberal social science on race. At the time of the riot, Kenneth Clark and Mamie Phipps Clark were already engaged in the doll experiments that would seemingly confirm such damage and become vital evidence in the 1954 landmark desegregation case, *Brown v. Board of Education*. At the same time, Clark and Barker characterized the style and behavior of such youths in a way that anticipated later interpretations that viewed the zoot suit as a subcultural phenomenon expressing an inchoate political meaning.

Strikingly, this damaged personality was hard to discern from the young man's own words. He had a regular job as a Civilian Defense messenger and was about to be inducted into the army. He regularly read the *New York Daily News* and *Batman* comics, and had an active social life, attending the movies, the YMCA, and a neighborhood "cellar club." This raconteur told the story of the riot with bravado and humor. The interview provided ample evidence of his criminal activity and hostility to white authorities, yet he pointedly distanced himself from the worst excesses of the rioters, even as he opportunistically participated.

Several rioters had appeared in newspaper photographs wearing top hats and tails they had stolen; he warned one that "he'd better take 'em off." At another moment, he observed some rowdies "messed up in sugar, walking in it, pissed in it, and one woman come up there with a bag and just pushed the messed up sugar aside with her hands and filled up her bag." She told him that sugar was scarce—indeed, it was rationed—and he replied sheepishly, "Yes ma-a-am."[19]

Other African American experts probed the meaning of extreme style along the lines of Clark and Barker, highlighting the psychology and culture of disadvantaged youth while also considering the political implications of the zoot suit. Horace R. Cayton, Jr., was a journalist and sociologist trained at the University of Chicago and was undertaking a major study of that city's "Bronzeville" with St. Clair Drake. In his regular *Pittsburgh Courier* column, he interpreted the zoot suit in light of studies of youth, urban pathology, and social psychology, seeing zoot suiters as a specific constellation of young lower-class men—a "depression crop of adolescents" of African, Mexican, and European immigrant descent—who mixed socially and had more in common with each other than with higher-class members of their own racial/ethnic group. He wanted to probe what outer appearance said about the inner self: "It's the mentality, not the fact that someone has a toilet chain for a key ring that reaches to his ankles." The zoot suit was a form of exhibitionism for those who had no other means of expression, akin to Bigger Thomas, the troubled, violent protagonist of Richard Wright's *Native Son.* Cayton worried that conventional leaders would have difficulty reaching them: "Their mentalities are so different and their drives for recognition and security are so foreign to one another that I doubt if they can communicate."[20]

Although recognizing the antisocial behavior of some "hep-cat delinquents," Lawrence Dunbar Reddick, an African American educator and historian, understood the situation differently. At the time of the riot, he observed that the zoot suit was an extreme version of the English drape, that is, it bore a relationship to adult styles. As such, it reflected youth's yearning for attention; for minorities and the poor in particular,

" 'sharp' sartorial get-up ha[d] become a badge of defiance . . . and a symbol of belonging." In the months that followed, Reddick's interpretation took on a political edge. Black youths in the North had totally rejected racial subordination—psychologically, if not yet sociologically—and were demanding equal rights and full participation. When the young people were frustrated in these aims, their resentment took the form of vulgarity, jive talk, zoot suits, and petty criminal behavior. "These phenomena are, also, social protests," Reddick declared: "protests which are not permitted to find expression within the legal framework of the social order."[21]

From another discipline, that of semantics, came the call of S. I. Hayakawa to understand the zoot suit as a cultural and psychological symbol. Hayakawa, born in Canada to Japanese immigrant parents, was a professor at the Illinois Institute of Technology, and he wrote a column for the *Chicago Defender* at the time of the race riots in the summer of 1943. He had been trained in English literature, but his interests gravitated to semantics, psychology, and anthropology, especially the theory of general semantics developed by Alfred Korzybski. Hayakawa published *Language in Action* in 1941, which was widely read and chosen as a Book-of-the-Month Club selection. Concerned about Hitler's demagogic ability to mobilize the German people, Hayakawa offered readers a critical approach to understanding propaganda and hate speech.[22]

In two *Defender* columns, he applied the principles of general semantics to the inflammatory symbol of the zoot suit. To Hayakawa, the Los Angeles riot resulted largely from a misreading of a symbol, caused by prejudice and fear. Loud clothes were not, in themselves, "signs of low moral character" or delinquency but rather "symptoms of youthful dissatisfaction." He urged readers to take the zoot suit seriously, reminding them that, as Korzybski put it, "men run themselves on symbols" and that clothing styles "symbolize the way we regard ourselves, whether as 'sports,' 'plain working men,' 'glamor girls,' 'ladies,' or 'gentlemen.' " In a similar manner, Hayakawa saw the zoot suit as a symbol to poor Italian, Mexican, and African American youths, rebelling "against the dreariness of slum life, . . . a symbol of the dash and glory which these young people would LIKE to have, but CANNOT GET. And because these kids don't belong anywhere in our society, it is their symbol of belonging at least to the society of their own creation." The zoot suit marked the distance between expansive American ideals and possibilities and the shrunken reality of prejudice and discrimination. "Give us kids something SIGNIFICANT to do. Give us jobs in something besides car-laundries and shoe-shine parlors. Give us GOALS that we can work for," he imagined the voice of zoot-suited youth. "Stop dangling before our eyes all the glamor of American life in your movies, your advertisements, and your radio programs, at the same time as you tell us that we can't have any of it because we are 'wops,' or 'dagoes,' or 'niggers.' "[23]

Newspaper columnists and opinion makers took up and circulated the experts' perspectives on the zoot suit. Agnes Meyer's piece in the *Washington Post* not only drew on Redl's investigations but also applied anthropological insights from the culture-and-personality school, notably Ruth Benedict's *Patterns of Culture.* She described the zoot suit phenomenon as Dionysian, with its ecstatic dance, cultlike behavior, and tendency to violence: "It is the expression of an unconscious desire to escape from our hard, purposeful, rational life into an atmosphere where the only competition is for artistic prestige." Social-science language even infused the writings of those who disagreed with an approach that tended to ascribe blame for the riot to the failings of society, not the individual. Columnist Westbrook Pegler, for example, condemned the liberal view that Mexican American youths were "misunderstood or the victims of social yearnings," but nevertheless he adopted Benedict's language, calling the zoot suiters a "cult." He saw nothing but trouble in the "degenerate exhibition of youthful mass hysteria which began on Broadway with hundreds of them writhing, twitching and howling gibberish to the horrible squeals and squawks of the jive bands." Responding to moralists like Pegler, jazz columnist Bill Gottlieb cautioned readers, "Don't blame swing music for [the] sins of modern youth," but treat it as a "symptom of the underlying pathological state of our younger generations." Young people had turned to a "medium developed by the Negro out of his long-standing frustration," and had embraced swing's "subtle lament" against a society "too inflexible to cope with unprecedented material change."[24]

Gottlieb and others drew upon the psychological concept of "compensatory response," a term used in theories of classical conditioning that had entered into the vernacular. Educator Lillian Gray explained that Mexican American youth, "denied the glamour of a uniform, . . . took compensatory flight in the zoot-suit costume." Walter White, a leader of the NAACP, took the same tack in an unpublished letter to the *New York Times*: "In a highly mechanized society like ours extremes of dress are worn by a good many people to lift them . . . out of the dead rut of nonentity," especially those who feel rejected by society. Such apparel was "psychologically significant," but did not account for criminal activity, which was better explained by poverty, segregation, and discrimination.[25]

Even some in the fashion industry focused on the "psychological implications of the zoot suit," as editor J. V. D. Carlyle titled his article in the *Men's Apparel Reporter*. Carlyle had followed the remarkable rise of the style closely, and was the one who had brought Clyde Duncan, the zoot-suited busboy in Gainesville, Georgia, to the attention of the press. Unlike many journalists, he saw the style not as a manifestation of social alienation or racial pathology but as a positive means of self-expression available to minority and poor youth: "In my opinion, the Zoot Suit was—and is—a rebellion of the young men of the less fortunate class against the every day environment. The boys who were quick to take up the Zoot Suit wanted, first of all, to express themselves. And they found the Zoot Suit a perfect medium for doing so. The Zoot Suit was different; it was colorful; it had definite character. The Zoot Suit and Zoot accessories marked the wearer as a young man of taste, distinction and dash. The Zoot Suit enabled each young man to definitely express his personality; to show that he was in the know." Carlyle thought the style had the potential to expand an entirely new market for men's fashion, but its future was unclear. He questioned whether the zoot suit deserved to be viewed as the "badge of hoodlums," but acknowledged, "from now on, people will associate the reet pleat and the drape shape with disreputable characters."[26]

Ordinary Americans also weighed in, writing letters to newspapers and radio stations in an attempt to understand the strange style and its role in the riot. Their views varied considerably. A number could not come to terms with the sheer expense and excess of the zoot suit, a recurrent theme in the press, which pointedly printed prices far above those in typical clothing ads of the time. For example, a photograph of *pachuco* Frank Tellez, arrested for vagrancy, ran with a caption that his drape coat and pegged pants came from two different suits costing $75 and $45. These prices had a decided effect on the public, exemplified by the response of one soldier stationed in Nebraska to a photograph featured in *Time* magazine. "To a soldier who has been taken from his home and put in the Army, the sight of young loafers of any race, color, creed, religion or color of hair loafing around in ridiculous clothes that cost $75 to $85 per suit is enough to make them see red," he wrote.[27] The price tag alone—not the style's association with a particular social group—was sufficient to render judgment on the morals and patriotism of those who wore the zoot suit.

However, others believed zoot suits and uniforms had a deeper meaning, and drew on social scientific insights to consider clothing as a manifestation of adolescent development, a portent of racial problems, and a symbol of psychological and social disturbance brought on by the war. Agnes Meyer's column in the *Washington Post* generated much soul-searching among readers. One sympathized with young people who had to find their own moral compass in wartime circumstances, "when such qualities as ruthlessness, belligerency and general 'toughness' are constantly being extolled in editorials, radio programs and, alas, in schools and pulpits." A woman who had come of age after

World War I looked back to the disillusionment following the "war to end all wars" to explain the current unrest. Her contemporaries rejected their elders' faith in high culture, etiquette, and correct grammar, "all of which smacked of the leisure and indifference to the things that really mattered and which led to the holocaust of which our generation is taking the brunt." William C. Lee thought the zoot suit might simply be a foolish style but also considered whether it was a way to express "the feelings of classes who do not, or who even think they do not, have a fair show." If this was the meaning of the zoot suit, then "the attempts to suppress such ideas by force [are] wholly wrong." Joseph Bougere, who had recently worked on the "Negro in Illinois" study of the Federal Writers' Project, held a stronger political view: "Numerous young Mexican, Negroes, and Filipinos affect these exaggerated suits," but that did not justify violence against them by whites. He condemned the "racial hypocrisy of such patriotic Americans, who did not pay attention to black soldiers dying in the war or being lynched in the south."[28]

Some focused not on the zoot suiters but on the men in uniform, whose drinking and rowdiness exacerbated local tensions. Two city-bred GIs now on the front lines sent a letter to *Newsweek* criticizing "the shore-duty jerks who can find no better way of occupying their time than mauling a bunch of high-school kids." They added, "Maybe we're a little more broad-minded and don't care what the other guy wears." Sergeant William D. Eastlake, an MP during the riot, wrote *Time* that servicemen had ganged up on the civilian youths: "I found the zooter on most occasions outnumbered 200 to one." Eastlake was an unusual observer—a hobo in the 1930s, then a participant in the left-wing culture of Los Angeles, and eventually an important writer on the West and World War II. Using the psychological idiom of the day, he focused on the servicemen's personalities and reversed the interpretation of clothing offered by psychiatrists like Banay: "Regimented, and in his drab same uniform, he resents the attention the zooter is paid when garbed in his nonmilitary, free-choice, albeit outlandish, getup." He concluded that these were soldiers with "an inferiority complex" and a "subconscious bitterness towards all civilians."[29]

The debate over the meaning of the zoot suit was especially lively in the African American press. Columnists focused on the racial dynamics of the conflict in Los Angeles—especially as other riots broke out across the country in the summer of 1943. They discussed conflicts over inter-racial sexuality in the leisure activities of young servicemen and civilians, analyzed the underlying conditions of discrimination, and articulated the fear that a subgroup of black youth would hold back African American progress at a critical juncture. Some, like popular historian J. A. Rogers, were simply content to excoriate the "shallow-brained revolt" of youth, but many summoned notions from the social sciences to make sense of the drape shape and its wearers. The *Chicago Defender* observed that the riot showed that "zoot suits are a community, rather than an individual affair," and underscored "the need for drastic action to curb the unbridled minority of our race." Civil rights lawyer Marjorie Mc-Kenzie gestured to work in educational sociology when she called zoot suiters a marker of "group cultural incompetence." Langston Hughes was especially reflective. He specifically acknowledged the expertise of psychiatrist Joseph Catton, who had stressed zoot suiters' inferiority complex, but he deflected a view that tended to pathologize youth. He reminded readers that "the zoot suiters were depression's kids," and when they were finally able to buy clothes, "it made them feel good to go to extremes."[30]

African Americans who wrote to the newspapers often moved away from a psychological explanation of zoot suiters to a more political one. Ed Peterson thought zoot suits were "extremely ugly," yet suggested that, especially for the disadvantaged, "these embody the new freedom thought." Private Clifton Searles rejected the idea that only the criminal element wore zoot suits and wrote the *Defender*: "I attended one of the finest Negro schools in the country to study for the ministry. At least 75 per cent of the students wore 'zoot suits,' but they were honest, hard-studying fellows." He pointed the finger at white supremacists' violent

opposition to racial progress, especially the presence of African Americans in the military. The attacks were "directly aimed at Negro Yanks," who were "fighting the world over so that men may wear any type of clothing they care to; speak that which is on their minds, and ride on or in anything they can pay to ride." Searles was outspoken in his condemnation of racism: Six months earlier, he had written Eleanor Roosevelt that he had been refused service at a drugstore soda fountain in Washington, D.C., then given a Coke in a paper cup while a white customer received a glass. Searles attached the cup to his letter and observed, "When I might see a white boy dying on a battlefield, I hope to God I won't remember People's Drug Store on January 11th." Another African American soldier agreed with Searles's view that the attacks on zoot suiters presaged other racial violence. Signing himself V.V., for the Double Victory campaign, he observed to NAACP leader Walter White that "the word Zoot Suiter isn't only used in discriminating civilian newspapers but also in the USA [U.S. Army] papers as well."[31]

The zoot suit's role in the riot sparked extensive discussion of race relations and troubled youth but inspired less examination of the motives and lives of the *pachucos* whose extreme styles had seemed to trigger the unrest. Although an important group of social scientists had written about Mexicans in the United States during the 1920s and 1930s, their situation was unknown to most white Americans. After the riot, some of these experts offered their perspective, drawing on current theories of ethnicity and race to explain what had occurred. No doubt thinking of Edward Duran Ayres's grand jury testimony, educator and activist George I. Sánchez railed against the use of old racial theories and "witch-hunting in anthropological antecedents" to explain the problems of juvenile delinquency. He directed attention instead to persistent patterns of segregation and economic exploitation. "The pachuco is a symbol not of the guilt of an oppressed 'Mexican' minority but of a cancerous growth within the majority group which is gnawing at the vitals of democracy and the American way of life," he argued. "The pachuco and his feminine counterpart, the 'cholita,' are spawn of a neglectful society—not the products of an humble minority people who are defenseless before their enforced humiliation." Emory Bogardus's study of Mexican American gangs highlighted Mexican intergenerational conflict but also emphasized the barriers to integration caused by white racism; in his view, humiliating zoot suiters would exacerbate a problem that required culturally sensitive policing, accurate press reporting, and the intervention of social workers.[32]

Versions of these views appeared regularly in liberal or reform publications, as in Thomas J. McCarthy's report from Los Angeles in *Commonweal*: "The problem is purely a second generation one intensified by maladjustments in the homes of foreign parents whose economic status is low." *Look* magazine editors made this point visually in *One Nation*, a 1945 book of photo-essays intended to foster racial tolerance. They depicted the hardship and discrimination Mexican Americans faced, then sympathetically called zoot suiters a "lost generation" caught between two worlds, whose "whole desire, unconscious though it may be, is to belong." As the disorders ebbed, newscaster Chet Huntley offered a striking editorial on the CBS radio show *The World Today*, calling the riot a moment of reckoning: "It doesn't make sense" that white Americans acted on their prejudices against Mexican Americans, but took pleasure in Hispanic music, art, and cuisine. They needed to provide education and opportunities for Mexican Americans to "amalgamate these people into our society" and for everyone to realize the promise of American ideals. The next day he reported a heartening reaction to the broadcast, with favorable comments from all but one listener.[33]

The zoot suit was ultimately a footnote in social scientific inquiries into race relations, as the riots during the summer of 1943 turned investigators away from style and more toward analyses of economic disparities, social interactions between racial-ethnic groups, and the effects of prejudice on psychology and behavior. Still there were some, mainly local activists and professional social workers, who kept the spotlight on *pachucos* and drapes. These individuals had direct contact with members of the Mexican American second generation, often through youth groups, schools, churches, casework, and political organizing. Carey Mc-Williams, Alice Greenfield, Ruth .Tuck, and Beatrice Griffith created a distinctive picture of *pachucos* and their world in liberal journals such as the *Nation*, *Survey*, and *Common Ground*, and in books published after the war. They used personal observation and ethnographic description to argue for greater tolerance and understanding.

McWilliams, an author and lawyer turned radical during the Great Depression, had already exposed the problems of migrant labor and racial minorities in California when he helped lead the effort to overturn the convictions of the Sleepy Lagoon defendants. In testimony before the Los Angeles County grand jury about the "problem of Mexican youth," he tackled Edward Duran Ayres's racial theories and, citing anthropologist Ruth Benedict, rejected the term "race" as "being almost meaningless." He observed, "Tendencies toward certain types of behavior are to be found, not in the blood stream of a people, but in their cultural heritage." His analysis of the zoot suit riot grew out of these experiences. Months before the unrest he wondered aloud whether *sinarquistas* were influencing Mexican American gangs, and he denounced the press for stirring up public opposition to minority groups. But he also had an eye for the telling details of daily life. In *North from Mexico*, published in 1949, he described the cross-border mix of goods and tastes in the American homes of Mexican migrants and charted the Mexican population's advance into the central commercial and leisure districts of Los Angeles. This formed a backdrop to his treatment of the *pachuco* generation, whose embrace of "drapes"—the preferred term—was part of this broader cultural encounter.[34] Alice Greenfield (later McGrath) also served on the Sleepy Lagoon Defense Committee as its executive secretary, and she developed personal friendships with the convicted youths. Greenfield's articles in the *Daily World*, a Communist newspaper, described in detail the styles of *pachucos* and *pachucas* and emphasized that "the wearing of the 'drape' is no sign of delinquency." She pointed instead to the heartbreak and disillusionment of Mexican migrants and their children cut off from the mainstream of society.[35]

Ruth Tuck and Beatrice Griffith came to their knowledge of Mexican American youth through social work. Tuck underscored the sharp break between these young people and their immigrant parents, and the cultural contradictions they experienced. Watching them playing war games and noting the high level of enlistments, she observed that "the impact of war on Mexican youth was terrific." Clothing styles did not indicate criminal intent. "The wearing of exaggerated clothing as a means of achieving distinction and recognition denied in other fields is a well recognized phenomenon," she wrote. "'High rise' trousers and bell bottoms were worn by the same groups a few years ago, but no mention was made of a high rise crime wave." Indeed, she reminded readers that the *Los Angeles Times* had run the *Li'l Abner* comic strip "which glorified the wearer of a zoot suit as a sort of Superman."[36]

Among these commentators, Beatrice Griffith stood out for her empathetic accounts of Mexican American adolescents and their dilemmas and dreams. Rejecting the distanced perspective of the sociological observer, she insisted she had written the true stories of the youths she had met to convey the immediacy of their lives. At the same time, her selection of ethnographic detail, creation of composite characters, and fictionalized narratives combined to create a benign picture that, for example, diminished *pachucos'* criminal activity and violence, and turned those in their late teens into children. "In the Flow of Time," published in the progressive journal *Common Ground,* describes the zoot suit riot through the eyes of two young men taking a last hunting trip in the hills beyond Los Angeles before being inducted into the army; they return to find their community invaded by rampaging sailors and civilians. In contrast to the newspaper reports that emphasized the public spectacle of the attacks on the streets and in theaters and bars, Griffith set the scene inside the home, as attackers broke down doors and interrupted family dinners. The first-person narrator, speaking slang with a Spanish cadence, gave an insider's view and made the story of the riot urgent and personal. Griffith's early essays and short stories on the *pachuco* generation would be published in 1948 as *American Me*, a title that rejected notions of Hispanic youth as isolated outsiders. In it, she emphasized the hybrid culture of a second generation caught between two ways of life.[37]

Familiar with social scientific perspectives, these analysts of Southern California underscored how much racial stereotyping and discrimination had limited the life chances of Mexican American youths even as they served in the American military and held to ideals of freedom and democracy; moreover, the processes of migration and generational change contributed to the difficulties they faced. Although they acknowledged that the cultural style and practices of *pachucos* grew out of a sense of the contradictions and alienation they faced, they were reluctant to define the zoot suit solely or even primarily as an emblem of psychological damage or pathology. In their descriptions of *pachuco* life, drapes, *caló*, dance, and promenading appear as creative cultural responses— "their own world of 'Pachuquismo,'" Griffith called it—an aesthetic that expressed a sense of individuality, possibility, and connection among young people in an uncomprehending and often hostile world.[38]

In the years after the war, social scientists would return on occasion to the zoot suit, treating the style as a symbol that revealed the psychological and social dynamics of those in and out of the American mainstream. One investigation showed how symbolic communication played a key role in mobilizing and legitimizing crowd behavior, using the Los Angeles riot as a case study. The press had stripped away "alternative connotations" in its references to Mexicans, concentrating on the symbol of the zoot suiter as criminal and deviant. "Hostile crowd behavior requires an unambiguously unfavorable symbol," sociologists Ralph H. Turner and Samuel J. Surace argued, and the figure of the zoot suiter effectively sanctioned violent behavior by sailors and civilians that was usually inhibited by social norms. A question about zoot suiters appeared in the surveys used in *The Authoritarian Personality*, one volume in the vast research project sponsored by the American Jewish Committee that examined the relationship between personality traits, racial and religious prejudice, and the potential for fascist or authoritarian regimes. Interviewees were asked whether they agreed with various statements about Jews, African Americans, Asians, "Okies," and, surprisingly, those who wore extravagant styles: "Zootsuiters demonstrate that inferior groups, when they are given too much freedom and money, just misuse their privileges and create disturbances." The psychologists who de-signed the "E-scale" measuring ethnocentrism understood how the zoot suit had become intertwined with ideas about lower-status minority populations deemed too irresponsible for equal treatment and citizen-ship rights. Another statement underscored the sense that clothing was a revelatory sign: "Filipinos are all right in their place, but they carry it too far when they dress lavishly, buy good cars, and go around with white girls." Meanwhile, folklorists in the Southwest delved into the sub-culture of *pachucos*, fascinated by its unique language, dress, drug use, and menace. The "aristocrats of the Borderland underworld," one called zoot-suit gangs, even as he emphasized their effeminacy and homoeroti-cism.[39]

After the riot, experts in the social and behavioral sciences proposed a method of understanding the zoot suit that saw style—wide shoulders, drooping pants, a long keychain—as symbols that marked a particular psychological makeup and cultural practice, stemming from racial op-pression, adolescent marginality, and the strains of the collective war effort. If they drew on concepts of social pathology, damaged personal-ity, and deficient individual development, they also elaborated a concept of subculture, aware of the uses of style to signal group identification outside the mainstream. This term would not come into common usage in American social science literature until after World War II, but the extreme fashion of the zoot suit, and its prominence in social unrest and public commentary, moved experts and opinion-makers toward that analytical frame. For some, particularly African American social scien-tists and commentators, the style took on a political charge, although one difficult to comprehend fully. The effort to explain a strange or unknown phenomenon and the perception of it as a symbolic one laden with meaning—and the recognition among many of the inadequacy of interpretation—distinguished the response to the zoot suit in the wake of the riot. Its riddle generated a nascent discourse—linking style, subculture, youth, marginality, and defiance—that would eventually become a conventional mode of interpretation in and outside the world of scholarship.

From his perch in Harlem, columnist Dan Burley watched a parade of academia's finest, only to offer a jaundiced view of the experts: "Little Mose and Big Mose and Big Mouth Mamie are getting a thorough going over by such anthropological aces as Ruth Benedict, Gene Weltfish, Ralph Linton, Margaret Meade [*sic*], Natalie Joffe and some of the 'better minds' inhabiting 'Camp Happy' in East Harlem," he observed. They had come to analyze African American clothing, foodways, hairstyles, and other aspects of culture, and to Burley, it seemed an easy gig that, nonetheless, failed to take the true measure of its subjects' daily lives. "Anthropology is a heluva subject," he concluded, "in that all you gotta do is to look out the window at the nearest zoot suit or drape shape and write what you think is on his mind as he dodges streetcars, police, his gal's old man, crumbling walls of rotten tenements, jumps out of windows in the middle of the night to keep from being burned up, and runs like hell all the time to get out of the dangerous shadow of his own color!"[40] For all Burley's humor, his observations—about the challenges scholars faced when they applied the research designs of the social sciences to everyday life, and the partial understandings that resulted—may have been on the mark.

6

Zooting Around the World

"**S** ome authorities feel** that the only thing to do is to let the whole mysterious business wear itself out and disappear through inner exhaustion of its possibilities," reported Agnes Meyer in the wake of the Los Angeles riot.[1] In fact, it was much harder than those authorities thought to shrug off the zoot suit. During the war and for decades thereafter, this style traveled across time and place, appealing to youths whose lives otherwise diverged. It turned up in wartime Great Britain and Australia, despite orders by their governments to conserve cloth for the duration. Bahamian farm hands, brought to Florida to pick crops, surprised their hosts by appearing in zoot suits. Canada had its own versions of zoot-suit unrest in the summer of 1944, and in occupied France, *zazous* sporting long coats and narrow trousers outraged officials. After the war, young people in other countries—from the *stiliagi* of the Soviet Union to the *tsotsis* of South Africa—picked up and adapted elements of an extreme style that had originated in American culture.

The zoot suit was never a leading cultural product or intentional export of the United States in an era when the nation's films, music, and consumer goods were reaching around the globe. Yet this seemingly ephemeral fashion traveled to many places during and after World War II. It is a telling example of a commodity that circulated

without marketing campaigns and advertising but rather along obscure routes and through informal networks of influence—a process
that has likely been more common than studies of consumer culture
have recognized. Captivating the imagination of young men across
continents, the zoot suit's strange features and hybrid identity—as a
generational marker, an emblem of racial-ethnic minorities, and a
quintessential American style—made it an unstable container of meanings. Although American journalists and commentators called *zazous*,
stiliagi, and other fashion-conscious youth "zoot suiters," this was not
the term used by the young men themselves. They made extreme styles
their own, although there was always something in them that referenced an imagined America and served as a touchstone even in indigenous cultural and political contexts. As in the United States, these
young people sparked public controversies and official concern over
antisocial behavior and the role of youth in securing the future. The
specifics of these debates differed significantly from nation to nation
as the war years gave way to peacetime reconstruction. Inevitably, the
American zoot suit—or a reasonable facsimile—became the focal point
of larger desires and fears.

                              *   *   *

The zoot suit quickly appeared among the closest neighbors of the
United States, part of the flow of goods, images, and people in the
Western hemisphere. The Mexican borderland was believed by many
to be the *pachucos'* point of origin. Although the zoot suit was most
apparent in Los Angeles, cross-border migration and communication
of style and behavior made drapes and pegged pants familiar to Mexican youths by the early 1940s. Still, the Los Angeles riot in 1943 led
Mexican officials and the public to scrutinize the style in a way they
had not before. The attacks on *pachucos* threatened to undermine co-
operation between Mexico and the United States, which had recently
resulted in trade and labor agreements, including the Bracero Program

that enabled Mexican migrants to work in American agriculture. The Mexican government responded cautiously to the events in Los Angeles, expressing concern but issuing no official protest to U.S. officials. The nationalist press criticized the government's inaction, and five hundred students marched in the streets of Mexico City, protesting American racism, President Franklin Roosevelt, and Ezequiel Padilla, the head of the Mexican foreign ministry.[2]

The zoot suit style did not spark a riot in Mexico—although there were reports of a few men beaten and stripped of their drapes—but it did contribute to an ongoing debate about the meaning of Mexican identity, or *Mexicanidad*. Even as they decried white Americans' violence in Los Angeles, newspapers distanced themselves from the *pachucos,* who were not seen as authentic Mexicans. Covering the riot, *La Prensa*'s headline summarized the problem: "Without Being Truly Mexicans, They Are an Embarrassment to Our Republic." This article was unusual for perceiving the *pachuco* as a degenerate racial mixture; more commonly writers cast such youths as existing between two worlds, the children of working-class, uneducated migrants, too Americanized to be Mexican. For Mexicans, historian Richard Griswold del Castillo argues, the zoot suit riots made Mexican American ethnic culture visible, and it was a distressing sight.[3]

After the war, renowned writer Octavio Paz would open *The Labyrinth of Solitude,* his meditation on Mexican identity, with a consideration of "The *Pachuco* and Other Extremes." Paz saw the *pachuco* up close when he lived in Los Angeles from 1943 to 1945. He was at once mesmerized and repulsed. To Paz, the *pachuco* had "lost his whole inheritance" as a Mexican, and yet he had not been accepted by American society. His "grotesque dandyism"—a disguise that "both hides him and points him out"—was not a protest against social injustice but rather a demonstration of willfulness and difference. Changing "ordinary apparel into art" conveyed mixed messages of aggression and nihilism, vitality and desire. In the United States, "everyone agrees in finding something hybrid about him, something disturbing and fascinating," wrote Paz, but to Mexicans, the *pachuco* could only be seen as an extreme deviation. Paz articulated anxieties that had circulated among Mexican intellectuals and leaders about the nature of national identity and their country's troubling cultural encounters with the United States.[4]

Nevertheless, the zoot-suited *pachuco* as a cultural hybrid became a popular figure in Mexico during the war years and afterward. Called *tarzanes*—presumably after the movie image of Tarzan, whose long hair they copied—some young Mexican men dressed in pegged pants and drape jackets and spoke *pochismo*, Anglicized Spanish or "Gringo lingo," as a form of hip slang. The most famous of these was Germán Valdéz. Valdéz was raised in the border city of Ciudad Juárez and toured northern Mexico and the southwestern United States as a performer in the late 1930s and early 1940s. In 1943, he turned himself from a little known actor and singer into a national sensation when he created the comic character Tin Tan. Valdéz celebrated the border-crossing, code-switching, fashion-conscious *pachuco* by further exaggerating his theatrical style; he had been influenced by Cab Calloway's larger-than-life image as well as the growing notoriety of Mexican American youth after the zoot suit riot. Tin Tan appeared in a purple velvet zoot suit, hat with a long feather, a long watch chain, and ballooning trousers pegged at the ankles; according to *Time* magazine, his performances mixed "crazy versions of mariachi tunes, Russian melodies, Italian arias[,] but mostly he just spouts pocho like so much fast doubletalk." Despite condemnations from Mexican nationalist elites, who abhorred the invasion of U.S. popular culture, Tin Tan drew enthusiastic crowds and became a major radio and film star.[5]

To the north, some Canadian youth discovered the drape shape in news reports, in popular magazines and films, and from visitors and their own travels. As in Mexico, the Los Angeles riot had the effect of promoting the extreme style even as it provoked condemnations from Canadian officials. In Montreal, many believed zoot suiters to be Francophones who adopted the outfits to reinforce their sense of cultural difference. However, English-speaking youths, often of working-class

Figure 26. Germán Valdéz as the Mexican *pachuco* "Tin Tan," in a publicity shot by Simón Flechine, known as Semo.

©(329514). CONACULTA. INAH-SINAFO-FN-Mexico.

background and Italian or Jewish descent, also wore the style in Montreal and other Canadian cities. Similar to zoot suiters in the United States, these Canadian youths were typically identified as extraordinary dancers or as members of gangs or cliques who frequented local cafes, dance halls, and other nightspots. Whatever their backgrounds, they were viewed as outsiders who had not embraced the wartime call for social cohesion and sacrifice. In the summer of 1944, zoot suiters and Canadian servicemen clashed in Montreal and Vancouver, following the pattern of the Los Angeles riot. In the dance halls of Verdun, a suburb of Montreal, sailors "politely ordered" young women and men wearing conventional clothes to leave, and then proceeded to battle and undress those in zoot suits. Their fashion assessments were not always right, as one journalist reported: many patrons "wearing pre-war suits, pre-W.P.T.B. [Wartime Prices and Trade Board]-regulated suits, were mistaken for zooters and set upon by the mob." Montreal's chief counselor, A. E. Goyette, called zoot suiters "*fifis*"—"pansies"—"who were exempted from the army or who weren't called up." Confounding country and manhood, they raised the ire of those in the armed forces.[6]

A particularly interesting case of the zoot suit's diffusion and local significance occurred in Trinidad. In 1941, the British government gave the United States permission to build an extensive military base on its colony. The American occupation, as it came to be known, not only offered high-paying jobs but also introduced American-style consumption and leisure to Trinidadians, who had long endured rural poverty and colonial dependency. White civilian contractors and black soldiers likely brought the zoot suit to Trinidad, explains historian Harvey Neptune. Screenings of the film *Stormy Weather* (1943), with its zoot-suited musicians and dancers, spread its image across the island. Young men known as "saga boys"—perhaps so named as a corruption of "swagger"—quickly embraced the zoot suit and made it part of their way of life in the war years. Some were simply followers of fashion, but others were gamblers or members of small gangs. In either case, Neptune explains, the zoot suit conveyed a new sense of social and economic independence: Saga boys used the extreme American style as a way to repudiate the British authorities' demands on male colonial subjects for "humility, discipline, and respectability." Other Caribbean islands were used as bases for training U.S. and British forces, which may explain why some Bahamian migrants were already wearing zoot suits when they arrived in the United States to work. Afro-Cubans also wore the style, and were teased as urban dandies; José Portuondo's 1944 poem, "Zoot-Suit Fruit," pokes fun at one fashion plate's "two-tone shoe" and "bright new suit / all speckle' and blue."[7]

By following the zoot suit in Canada, Mexico, and the Caribbean, we can see how this fashion spread along several distinct relays of transmission. Certainly American popular music and film contributed heavily to the promotion of the zoot suit in the Western hemisphere. But just as significant were the many interpersonal encounters that enabled men to see the fashion firsthand. Longstanding patterns of regional migration between Mexico and the southwestern United States facilitated the rapid movement of the *pachuco* style on both sides of the border; zoot suits found their way into Canada, Trinidad, and the Bahamas in large part because of the presence of U.S. Americans, especially the personnel involved in the war effort. In Canada and Mexico, news reporting on the Los Angeles riot carried additional weight, linking extreme clothing with the social tensions and politics of the war; as was the case in the United States, this coverage also exposed many to the style.

In other places, images from American mass media, not face-to-face encounters, spread the zoot suit. Black South Africans absorbed American fashions through motion pictures, including those featuring all-black casts. In the early 1940s, theaters in Johannesburg and other urban centers not only showed American gangster movies and film noir but also featured such films as *Stormy Weather* and *Cabin in the Sky* (1943). These became highly popular with black audiences and offered a powerful example for South African youth, who picked up the sense of buoyancy, danger, and sophistication in this suit of clothes. Recent urban migrants and dandified men known as "clevers" had already begun to develop a new male stylishness as early as the 1930s; they sometimes formed youth gangs that were seen as a source of criminal activity and social tension. In the mid-1940s, a growing number of black South African city-dwellers began to imitate the specific look of the zoot suiters and gangsters who appeared on the screen.[8]

Wearing long American-style jackets, bright shirts, narrow-bottomed trousers, and snap-brim hats, these men became known as *tsotsis*. The term may have derived from "zoot" or from "ho tsotsa" ("to sharpen"), referring either to the narrowing of trousers or generally to looking sharp. Bearing a resemblance to Harlem's sharpies and zoot suiters, *tsotsis* spoke their own slang, hung out on street corners, and sometimes engaged in petty crime and gang activity. Typically, *tsotsis* or their families had migrated from rural areas only to experience a constricted job market and harsh racial segregation. Still, they had become acclimated to urban life and commercialized leisure, including dance halls, movie theaters, and "shebeens," illegal bars that sometimes took the names of popular films, including *The Thirty-Nine Steps* and *Cabin in the Sky*. *Tsotsis'* stylishness newly declared their allegiance to an identity as urban, streetwise youths, now distanced far from the "well-mannered, well-brought up God fearing country kid." It also marked a sense of separation and difference from their parents' authority and traditions. Strikingly, historian Clive Glaser observes, "parents still expected their teenage sons to wear shorts in the 1940s," making the long stove-pipe trousers an added affront. This sense of a generational identity marked by historic breaks with tradition was articulated in part through American mythology and styles. As Stanley Motjuwadi, a writer who followed this phenomenon, wrote, "Anything American was something to imitate." This America was Hollywood's version, and the imitation a fusion inspired by white, vaguely ethnic gangsters and dazzling African American performers.[9]

Controversies over *tsotsis* erupted in print as early as the mid-1940s. The *Bantu World*, a Johannesburg newspaper for the black middle class, ran numerous letters from readers about these young men and their style. A number scorned the "budding 'men of tomorrow'" as criminals, ne'er-do-wells, and moral failures. Others emphasized the need to improve education, provide job opportunities, and end the pass laws to make the figure of the *tsotsi* less appealing. At the same time, Glaser notes, the observations of readers pointed to a distinctive group experience and culture, marked by men's extreme clothing, gang affiliation, female companionship, and the pursuit of pleasure. W. N. Nzima noted how fashion had taken hold more generally among black urban youth: it was not only criminals but also most students who wore *tsotsi* pants or "bottoms," as they were sometimes called. Walter M. B. Nhiapo warned not to make too much of the symbolism of fashion. "It is a fallacy that certain clothes signify corruption or degradation of the spirit," he observed. "Their clothing is not worse than that of other people, nor is it a symbol of the real man. And their dressing . . . is but a barometer of the tastes, not their innerselves [*sic*]." These moderate views did not prevail: By the early 1950s, "tsotsiism" had come to be seen as a political threat and an intractable social problem.[10]

Variations of the zoot suit also became assimilated into the lives of youths in Europe during and after the war. Many had already become attuned to American popular culture in the interwar years. American jazz musicians and entertainers, including many African Americans, went on European tours right up to the eve of World War II, popularizing contemporary American styles. Local performers quickly imitated their music, clothing, dance steps, and gestures, offering cabaret acts and musical reviews with such themes as "Miss America" or "Tarzan." By the mid-1930s, a "jazz youth subculture," as historian Anton Tantner calls it, appeared all over Europe. Like their American counterparts, these young people loved swing music and dance, congregated in nightspots and on the streets, and gathered in homes to listen to jazz records. The brisk export trade in Hollywood films also broadcast the "American drape" and exaggerated features of the late 1930s—in gangsters' double-breasted suits, long frock coats in Westerns and Civil War dramas, and the urbane male style of romantic comedies. Few of these highlighted zoot suits, but such films as *Stagecoach* (1939) and *The Roaring Twenties* (1939), highly popular abroad, influenced young men's attire even as they nourished a fantasy of America as a land of cowboys and mobsters.[11]

As their nations prepared for war, German "swing boys," Czech "*potápki*," Austrian "*schlurfs*," and French "*zazous*" all embraced extreme styles. Although the details of their clothing varied, these young men tended to wear long, draped jackets, colorful ties, and long hair. Some wore wide trousers, others narrow drainpipe pants. They did not slavishly imitate an American look: In Hamburg, a commercial port oriented to the North Atlantic, swing boys were drawn as much to British haberdashery as to American styles, wearing tailored suits, trench coats, and silk scarves, and carrying umbrellas. Influenced by the newsreels of 1938, which repeatedly portrayed Neville Chamberlain during the Sudetenland crisis, they gestured to the ideal of the English gentleman at the moment of English appeasement. In France, singer Johnny Hess made the song "Je Suis Swing" a popular hit in 1939, and its chorus—"zazou, zazou"—is credited with inspiring the eponymous Parisian youth fad. As described by the journal *L'Oeuvre,* the *zazou* dressed in a "soft, tiny brown hat, striped shirt collar . . . gaudy tie with an ultra tight knot . . . long jacket covering most of the buttocks, trousers short, narrow at the bottom and loose at the knees, quite high turn-ups [cuffs], white socks, suede shoes with quadruple soles." Even in the midst of the war, according to historian Rodger Potocki, the "Polish underground press reported on Warsaw youths who sported 'long, loose suit-jackets, hanging almost to the knees . . . [and] tight trousers.'"[12]

Few Americans abroad during the war years actually wore zoot suits and most, of course, were in uniform. In England, U.S. civilians and off-duty soldiers were more likely to wear moderate "American drapes," but even those styles sparked criticism. Subjected to strict textile limitations and "utility" clothes for the duration, British civilians viewed American menswear as oversized, loose, and gaudy, somewhat like the Yanks themselves. The zoot suit arrived in England worn by African American and West Indian seamen on supply ships that docked at British ports. The extreme American style made a vivid impression on some: "Zoot suits

are all reet, old chap," wrote the black activist and intellectual George
Padmore, who served as a war correspondent from London for African
American newspapers in 1943. The American look particularly attracted
young working-class men, although military mobilization and rationing
made it tricky for them to adopt the style until after the war.[13]

American soldiers abroad also found occasions to poke fun at the
home-front style, which might have been seen by locals. In Italy, for
example, GIs staged a variety show with a "snappy-suited Italian all
dolled up" in a zoot suit. Postwar references to the zoot suit in Italy,
in such films as *Peccato Che Sia Una Canaglia* ("Too Bad She's Bad"),
Alessandro Blasetti's 1954 screwball tale of thieves, suggest that the fashion had become a familiar one, associated with American hustlers and
black-market traders.[14]

American government and private relief programs may have spread
the style as well. Roosevelt's Lend-Lease policy, initially a maneuver to
supply war materiel to those fighting the Axis, contained shipments of
consumer goods, including clothing. The British Board of Trade claimed
that "large stocks of Zoot suits left on the hands of American manufacturers since Pearl Harbor" had been dispatched to England and remade
into clothing for children who had endured the Blitz, thus turning an
unpatriotic style into victory clothes. Whatever the truth of this story,
quantities of men's wool overcoats, suits, and pants were sent to the
Allies. Although there is no clear evidence that extreme styles had been
"deported" for violating the textile limitation orders, as the press account suggests, something akin to the zoot suit may have found its way
to men in Great Britain and other countries through these shipments.
For Polish intellectual Aleksander Wat, Lend-Lease offered "countless
trainloads of gifts," including men's clothing. Like many in eastern Poland after the 1939 Russian invasion, Wat had been forcibly resettled in
Soviet Central Asia. Going to warehouses in Kazakhstan filled with Lend-
Lease goods, he chose "a wonderful suit, better than anything I'd had
before, a beautiful tan material," and "paraded around Alma-Ata in that
wonderful suit."[15]

Whether seen in the movies, in cabarets, on the streets, or in relief packages, the drape of men's conventional suits from the late 1930s to the early 1940s combined with the occasional visibility of extreme fashion to create, in the minds of many, a sense of American style that could be adopted and adapted by youths around the world. The cut of a jacket, snap of a hat, and syncopated stroll were visible in different ways and rapidly refashioned by young people. As in the United States, generational experiences and social disparities shaped the meaning of such styles. As important were the distinct social and political circumstances young people encountered in the 1940s and early 1950s.

Even before war enveloped Europe, what started as a youthful expression of difference and as a marker of class and generational identity increasingly took on political overtones. "Swing boys" found ways around restrictions imposed by the Nazi authorities, who wanted to create a new German youth dedicated to work and the state. Despite official condemnation of the "degenerate" music of African Americans and Jews, the ban on American jazz was porous: jazz aficionados smuggled records across the border, renamed American songs to deceive censors, and tuned in distant radio stations abroad. Nazi newsreels and propaganda condemned American culture as materialistic and depraved but ironically publicized the very styles they denounced. At the same time, Joseph Goebbels's film policy allowed some American films to be shown in German theaters before the U.S. entrance into the war; young audiences copied the dance steps they saw in such films as *Broadway Melody of 1936* and *Born to Dance* (1936). The "swing youth" were from wealthier and professional class backgrounds and went further than other young people in their dislike of Nazi regimentation; for example they refused to join the Hitler Youth and counted on the social status of their parents to protect them. The Nazi regime increasingly found them an affront to their authority and moved to suppress them, which in turn led the swing youth to grow more political. By the early 1940s, Nazi authorities had rounded up and imprisoned swing boys and their female counterparts.[16]

The *zazou* phenomenon similarly changed, as the *New York Times* reported in 1942, "from a seemingly innocent faddist movement into an openly Nazi-baiting organization." Some *zazous*, like those who had fled Paris for Cannes, denied they intended anything by their choice of style: "We have nothing to do with the war, nothing at all. We are the Zazous, the Zazous!" But their clothes, music, and attitudes were a rebuke to the message of moral regeneration and respectability articulated by the Vichy regime, and came to be seen as a protest against the war and German control. At first they simply continued to congregate in cabarets and gave quick improvisational performances, proclaiming themselves *zazous* in the metro. Like the German swing boys, the French *zazous* carried furled umbrellas as a witty jab against the Occupation authorities, a subtle symbol of their alignment with the Allies.[17]

As the occupation deepened, *zazous* moved to more overt opposition. When Jews in France were required to place a yellow Star of David on their clothing, some zazous began to wear yellow handkerchiefs in their breast pockets and even sewed Stars of David on their own clothes with "swing" printed in the middle. The official reaction to *zazous* was harsh, with scathing criticism from the press beginning in 1942 and violent efforts to suppress their outré fashion. Collaborationist groups chased *zazous* and cut their long hair. Such styles were a "victory of democratic besottedness and Jewish degeneracy," wrote one French collaborationist, "the product of twenty years of Anglo-Saxon snobbery on the part of the decadents." A growing number were arrested in bars and cafes and sent to German labor camps.[18]

Still, the idea of the *zazou* continued to percolate on the stage and in song. "There are *Zazous* in my neighborhood," Andrex (André Jaubert) sang in 1944. "I'm half there myself." His humorous song was sharply political, apparently attacking Nazi racism as it affirmed the unity of humankind—a unity based on free spirit:

So far on earth a man could be
White or black, or red, or yellow and that is all

But another race is emerging
It's the *zazous*, it's the *zazous*.

By the end of the war, the zoot suit had become interwoven with notions
of Americanness, a hybrid of Hollywood and Harlem, and the outsized
presence of the wartime victor and liberator. As the Allies neared Paris
in August 1944, a war correspondent for an African American newspaper
exclaimed, "French youth in search of some appropriate expression of
anticipated liberation has turned to the American Negro way of doing
things by wearing zoot suits and jitterbugging."[19]

In countries devastated by loss, destruction, shortages, and political
repression, many youths took up extreme clothing as an aesthetic to live
by. These styles referenced an idealized America that oddly mingled GIs,
gangsters, and sharpies as its quintessential representatives. At the same
time, young European men added accoutrements and embellishments
that diverged from the drape jackets and pegged pants that had made
their fantastic appearance in Harlem, Los Angeles, and elsewhere in the
United States. Differing from place to place, these styles were hybrids:
They followed local fads for drainpipe pants or wide trouser legs, they
ranged from highly tailored to loose and draped, and their trimmings
varied, from painted ties to striped socks. These fashions, and their
American inspiration, became a hallmark for young people in the midst
of war and its aftermath, as they threaded their way through the social,
economic, political, and familial wreckage of this time. As in the United
States, such styles were also linked, in the minds of authorities and commentators, with a worldwide sense of youthful unrest, discontent, degeneracy, and delinquency.

After the war, many British working-class youths adopted the
"American drape," seeing power, panache, and self-assertion in this foreign style. Among them were "spivs"—shiftless men who engaged in
black marketeering and petty criminal activity. They wore oversized apparel more structured than the zoot suit, similar to the style of film
gangsters, along with startling painted neckties. Also embracing extreme

Figure 27. Andrex (André Jaubert) sang provocatively about *zazous* during the German occupation of France during World War II. *Y'a des Zazous* sheet music, 1943.

styles were the growing numbers of West Indian immigrants to England after the war. Social anxieties about the fate of postwar Britain—directed at American influence, the increasing presence of blacks, and upstart working-class youths—zeroed in on such clothing. Cartoons condemned spivs as antisocial figures, while Jamaican migrants were dismissed as "'Zootable' imports."[20]

Savile Row tailors made a conscious decision to challenge American styling in 1950 by reviving an Edwardian look for men, initially for the upper class. Much to everyone's surprise, marginalized working-class youths embraced a highly exaggerated, theatrical version of the Edwardian suit in the early 1950s. Known as "teddy boys," these men announced their public presence with a stylized parody of the social elites, wearing "curiously mixed costumes" made by plebeian tailors in South and East London. In their long coats with velvet collars, waistcoats, stovepipe trousers, and cowboy ties, American journalist Peter D. Whitney observed, "they have made a strange trans-Atlantic shotgun wedding of styles, grafting the fastidious Edwardian onto the flamboyant American zoot suit." Some were simply fashion-conscious youths, while others were members of criminal gangs.[21]

Although he did not address the hybrid style of the teddy boys, noted fashion historian James Laver perceptively discussed the differences in young men's style at this time, in a series of essays on "clothes and the welfare state." Laver read menswear as an expression of worldview, an aesthetic commentary on the past, present, and future. Unlike the "New Edwardians," whose clothes were a "discreet but definite protest against every aspect of modernity from motor-cars to income tax," young men who had embraced the postwar world "adopted American modes, the sinister hat of the Chicago gangster, the exaggerated shoulders of the would-be tough guy." These distinct styles reflected class differences as well as ideals of manliness; English tailoring "deliberately soft-pedal[ed] the note of masculinity," while American clothes emphasized it. At the same time, he observed that American inspiration took different paths among men in England. Laver contrasted the look of the "home-grown spiv" to that of the black Americans and West Indians he saw in England, whose draped American style—large sloping shoulders, very long and loose jackets, and legs that "seem to dwindle away into nothing"—facilitated a loose-limbed walk and magnetic presence. To Laver, their fashion awareness was profound. "If the top of the trousers sometimes shows in the opening of the coat that is not carelessness but *style*," he marveled. "They have *been through* European clothes, and come out on the other side, into a world of freedom and fantasy."[22]

Through the 1950s, British youths would create an elaborate array of extreme styles associated with peer groups and gangs, and tied to distinctions of class, status, and race. As Steve Chibnall observes, however, an "embryonic teenage culture and style" appeared "five full years before its discovery by pressmen and academics in the Teddy Boy panic."[23] In the war's wake, this new sense of generation and identity would be irrevocably shaped by American clothing, music, and affect.

Given the important role and cultural influence of the United States in postwar England, the lingering hold of the zoot suit there may be understandable. More curious is the spread of this style among youth in the Soviet Union and Eastern bloc countries after World War II. As Frederick Starr has shown, the wartime alliance with the United States opened the USSR to American films featuring swing music, new dance steps, and unusual clothing styles. The 1941 motion picture *Sun Valley Serenade*, with its lively version of "Chattanooga Choo Choo" by Glenn Miller's orchestra, Dorothy Dandridge, and the Nicholas Brothers, lifted spirits in wartime Russia; incongruously, Red Army bands played the song when their troops occupied Krakow and Warsaw. After the war, Soviet audiences could see "trophy films" removed from Germany; these were mostly German titles but included such American films as *The Roaring Twenties*. Strangely, as the Cold War quickly took hold and contemporary American cultural exports again were restricted, the American films that were available helped diffuse a prewar American male look in postwar Russia.[24]

In the months after the war, especially in Berlin, Soviet officials, military officers, and ordinary soldiers fraternized with their American counterparts, newly arrived journalists, and other visitors from the United

States. They obtained copies of *Life* and *Time* magazines, traded for garments and jazz records on the black market, and received items of clothing as gifts from Westerners. Some of the *frontniki*—the revered veterans of the war—returned home with a new sense of style. As historian Mark Edele observes, they were "among the first men to stress clothes and outer appearance" in the Soviet Union. Too young to go to war, admiring adolescents eagerly imitated their looks.[25]

These young men were called *stiliagi*, translated into English as "style chasers" or "style hunters." The first public notice of the strange young men came in 1949, when D. Belyaev published a satirical piece in *Krokodil*, describing a young man at a student dance who "looked incredibly absurd: the back of his jacket was bright orange, while the sleeves and lapels were green; I hadn't seen such broad canary-green trousers since the days of the renowned bell-bottoms." Such self-conscious airs and stylishness rendered him effeminate to Belyaev, who remarked that "the most fashionable lady in Paris would have envied his perm and manicure." Retailing hipster's slang, jazz rhythms, and Western fashions, the *stiliagi* were ignorant of classic Russian music and dance. "The most important part of their style is not to resemble normal people," the satirist averred.[26]

This was not a zoot-suit imitator, *New York Times* Moscow correspondent Harrison Salisbury was quick to point out, but rather a style devotee with "a Russian personality of his own." According to Edele, *stiliagi* created "adaptations of adaptations, peculiarly Sovietized forms of originally Western models," an "alternative form of manliness" and self-fashioning that drew upon an imagined West. They ordered long drape jackets and narrow pants from tailors or even made these themselves. Cowboy shirts and loud ties, often painted with monkeys or cactuses—a detail seemingly inspired by Tarzan films and Westerns—accessorized their suits. They wore long hair in what was called the Tarzan fashion, used English phrases or their own invented slang, listened to prewar jazz records, danced "the atomic style, the Hamburg style, and Canadian style," and even walked an allegedly Western walk. "They do not seem to rock slightly from side to side as many

In the hall there is laughter and the phonograph plays cheerfully,
The students are spiritedly doing the Krakow dance.
But one unhappy fellow stands on the side,
A representative of those incorrigible stilyagi.
He cannot understand the charm of the folk dance,
The modesty of the girls' dresses does not please his eyes.
He cannot enjoy himself in recreation
Among the simple and happy youngsters—among us!
Among us there is no place for vulgar tastes and modes.

Figure 28. A Soviet newspaper's caricature and denunciation of *stiliagi*.
New York Times, January 11, 1953.

Russian men . . . but pitch slightly forward," wrote one observer, and they gave the impression "that they can deal with any situation, that nothing would surprise them."[27]

Western fashions continued to percolate into the Soviet Union in the late 1940s and 1950s, but what seems to have been as important as their place of origin was the very concept of style itself. In a departure from the earlier aesthetic of socialist realism that had insisted on the "identity of art and life," art historian Susan Reid explains, "style began to acquire broad cultural importance in practice," apparent not only in the fine arts but also in a popular phenomenon like the *stiliagi*. The post-Stalin "thaw" of the mid-1950s, when Premier Nikita Khrushchev partially loosened state repression, released political prisoners, and permitted cultural exchange with the West, furthered the *stiliagi* phenomenon. "*Stiliaga* culture," writes Juliane Fürst, "floated on top of a general culture of pleasure-seeking." By this time, however, the fashions had begun to change. Earlier, *stiliagi* frequented large hotels in Moscow and Leningrad to scrutinize foreign visitors' looks, but after the mid-1950s, International Youth Festivals and the presence of American students brought new Western styles to the attention of young Russians, including blue jeans and rock and roll.[28]

The *stiliagi* were a puzzling challenge to Soviet officials. Although neither political dissenters nor common criminals, they deviated from the ideal of Socialist youth. "Pioneers of the unofficial culture," historian James von Geldern calls them: They preferred the pleasures of nightlife, sensuality, and costume to sanctioned youth activity, but their apparently apolitical hedonism was nevertheless construed as a challenge to the state. *Stiliagi* came from different backgrounds, and included many working-class men. Prominent among them, however, were the "gilded youth," the children of Party leaders and middle-class bureaucrats, who had access to education, leisure, consumer goods, and a degree of protection accorded by their parents' rank.[29]

The primary strategy for dealing with *stiliagi*, then, was public ridicule and denunciation. The Communist Party launched a campaign to promote proper lifestyles and guidance for Soviet youth in 1953; historian Miriam Dobson argues that they did so as a way to deflect attention from the rising crime rate that had resulted from Khrushchev's large-scale release of prisoners from the gulags. This had the effect of highlighting the activities of non-criminal *stiliagi*. The newspaper *Komsomolskaya Pravda* repeatedly chided the fashion-seeker as an unsightly and amoral individualist, someone out of the American Wild West: "He dresses in a loud fashion. He has a lush hair-do. His stride is 'unscrewed.' In public places he conducts himself impertinently, trying to show himself a 'desperado' who doesn't give a damn about anything." They also attacked "girl *stiliagi*" for wearing makeup, dressing provocatively, and styling their hair like foreign movie stars. Caricatures of *stiliagi* were a common feature of the satirical magazine *Krokodil*, and composer Lev Oshanin wrote a musical parody that became popular in Moscow in 1955. Although these efforts may have dissuaded some, they were just as likely to have the opposite effect; as Fürst observes, "Nowhere did one learn better how to dress as a *stiliaga* than in the post-Stalinist press." Public mockery was backed by the more threatening approach of the Communist Youth League, whose members denounced *stiliagi*, reported them to teachers or work supervisors, and at times resorted to violence. *Komsomolskaya Pravda* reported that "league patrols had been nabbing youths in extreme attire, cutting off their long hair and ripping off their cowboy shirts," and it urged them to take less drastic measures. Still, there was an ongoing debate about whether *stiliagi* should be lumped together with more serious forms of youth misbehavior.[30]

Eastern European countries all had their own version of zoot-suited youth, from the Hungarian *jampec* to the Polish *bikiniarze* or "bikini boys." The identification of distinctive youth cultures was not new: the word *jampec* had been used as early as 1928 to label idle, foppish youths. It came to have a more specific meaning after World War II, describing young men who loved jazz and adopted extreme style—tight pants, checked jackets, loud ties, and shiny shoes with thick soles. Generally of working-class origin, *jampec* had been children during the war, and had developed survival skills and an attitude of independence. They bought jazz records and clothes on the black market; as one noted, "It was a big thing that you could buy it on the side." Their style and toughness became legendary. "In the fifties, if a young boy decided to enter the wild side, the *jampec* was at hand ready-made," sociologist Ferenc Hammer observes.[31]

As the neologism *bikiniarze* suggests, these postwar Polish youths had a specific persona that derived from their consumption of Western culture—or at least a culture they understood as Western. In Poland, despite the Communist takeover after the war, a governmental policy of moderation was maintained until 1948, which, according to historian Rodger Potocki, "made the *bikiniarze* possible." The American embassy circulated copies of *Time* and *Life*, Western "trophy films" appeared in movie theaters, and Poles could hear jazz at American-founded YMCAs and on the U.S. Armed Forces Radio Network. Most important in the immediate postwar period was the arrival of Western goods through the black market and humanitarian organizations like CARE, United Nations Relief and Rehabilitation Administration (UNRRA), and Polish-American aid societies. Secondhand clothing from abroad supplied 75 percent of Poles' clothing needs right after the war. Notes Potocki, "It became known as *ciuchy* [duds] and from it came the garb of the *bikiniarze*." Later, diplomats, visiting athletes and musicians, and merchant sailors brought foreign clothes into the country, even as the government tried to limit their availability by imposing high import duties and suppressing the black market. The "attire of a bygone era," worn out of necessity, played into notions of an imagined West and a nostalgia for the interwar period, the time of the second Polish republic, before the succession of fascist and Communist occupiers. Bikini boys punctuated their suited look with colorful socks and distinctive ties, sometimes pinning American cigarette labels onto them or painting them with bikini-clad women, atomic bombs, or palm trees. In 1955, however, when the Fifth World Youth Festival was held in Warsaw and young Poles witnessed firsthand the sea change in youth attire, they threw away their zoot suits.[32]

What did these styles mean? If historians of the Soviet Union have differentiated style-chasers from political dissenters, the line is less clear in the case of Eastern Europe. In Poland, the bikini boys made their presence felt on the streets, in theaters, and in other public places. In contrast to the saboteurs and partisans engaging in hit-and-run attacks on Russian officials, journalist Thomas Harris observed in 1953, these were "the most subtle resisters"; they "burlesque Communist propaganda against the United States" by dressing in zoot suits, red socks, and painted ties. Leopold Tyrmand, an anti-regime writer and editor, embraced the look of the *bikiniarze*, especially the socks. Agnieszka Oziecka, who wrote a song about the phenomenon in the mid-1950s, recalled that for Tyrmand "the red or striped socks . . . were not only socks. They were a challenge and an appeal, they were a charter of human rights. These socks spoke for the right to be different, or even to be silly." Tyrmand called it "the right to one's own taste." Similarly in Yugoslavia, clothing inspired by Western styles took on political meanings. In his memoir, Serbian writer Borislav Pekić described the long, broad-shouldered jackets and narrow pants worn by his generation. They frequented the American Reading Room in Belgrade for its books and recordings, only to be beaten up by thuggish members of SKOJ, the Union of Communist Youth of Yugoslavia, who patrolled the streets around the library.[33]

As in the Soviet Union, Communist officials in Eastern Europe in the 1950s faced the dilemma of trying to control the behavior of "gilded youth," the privileged children of Party officials, as well as young men among the working class who had picked up unconventional styles. They derided those who embraced Western-oriented clothing and culture, criticizing them as "hooligans," a category that included antisocial and criminal behavior. As Karl Brown has found, official Hungarian criticism of the *jampec* was extensive beginning in 1952. Communist Party newspapers called for a crackdown against youths who "portray the dismal picture of imitating the American gangster's misanthropic spirit, moral decay and spiritual degeneration." Such propaganda campaigns against

Western fashion came at a time of serious food and clothing shortages. Budapest department stores created display windows that featured mannequins in zoot suits posed with apes and placards that stated, "We don't sell capitalistic fashions in this store." Feature films appeared with the *jampec* as a law-breaker, and some working-class dance halls banned zoot suits.[34]

State-run motion picture units in Poland made newsreels that mocked bikini boys' "decadent western fashions." The distinctive voice of actor Andrzej Lapicki narrated one such film whose title was, loosely translated, "the cameraman spied on you":

> It's nice to dress up as a bum, to block the entrance to the trolley and laugh at the conductor who asks you to buy a ticket. Let others bore themselves in schools and beat records in new construction. . . . Is there anything as beautiful as a tie with naked girls à la Hollywood? Low-tops with five-centimeter-thick white rubber soles, "Sing-Sing" socks [i.e. striped], are further attributes of men's fashion. Hats with rims as big as pancakes are proof of a subtle soul and sensitivity to beauty. *Bikiniarz*, *dzoler*, hooligan: the names differ but the type is the same! It is not enough to ignore them, you have to ridicule them and drive them away!

The accompanying film footage, with a sprightly jazz tune playing in the background, likely undercut this message. The newsreel showed cheerful workers from the Rosa Luxemburg factory engaged in calisthenics and sports, "propagating physical fitness among the workers" and "taking an active role in the fight to fulfill production plans."[35] But the bikini boys seemed to be the ones having the most fun, as the camera shot them traveling the city, enjoying street life, playing cards, dancing, and horsing around.

Authorities worried that these styles were the "secret weapon" of the West. Observed a Romanian government spokesman, "jitterbugging, boogie-woogie, Bikiniism . . . and hooliganism are features of the ethics of American imperialism designed to destroy the creative intelligence of our youth." Some noted, however, that the drab Soviet-style culture could not compete with the enticements of American entertainment. As a Budapest newspaper lamented, "One cannot replace boogie-woogie by sour music." Still, the official attacks on these styles, linked to criticisms of the United States and the West, were less an example of overt repression than an effort to define and contour Communist culture, and to bring young people into its fold.[36]

The extreme style of the zoot suit, with its outré proportions and eccentricity, caught the imagination of young men around the world. This is remarkable, given its origins in Harlem among poor but fashion-conscious African American youth in the late 1930s. Hollywood helped spread the style, although not in any organized way. *Cabin in the Sky* and *Stormy Weather*, which so influenced the attire of South African *tsotsis* and Trinidadian saga boys, were atypical films for 1943. Beyond such images, the style circulated outside the normal channels of distribution for consumer goods—glimpsed on American civilians, appearing on the black market, stuffed into relief packages. The spread of the zoot suit shows how rapidly and successfully a style could take hold when it seemed to embody the sense of generational identity and affiliation sharpened by the war and its aftermath. Yet wherever zoot suits appeared, controversy followed—among British administrators reasserting the colonial dependence of Trinidadians, Mexican intellectuals pondering authentic national identity, South African officials concerned about unruly urban black youth, or Communist leaders trying to advance anti-Western, anti-capitalist sentiments. These controversies often educated youths in the mysteries of fashion, but they also clarified what was at stake in embracing it. Thus the aesthetic of an extreme style that incorporated elements of Western clothing conveyed a range of meanings. For people like Tyrmand, a fashion statement could be consciously oppositional, if not in the explicit way of a speech or text. For others, its meaning was more subtle, a declaration of individuality, modishness, and peer group identity, set against family expectations, a drab environment, poverty, and the requirements imposed on everyday life by authoritarian regimes. Into the mid-1950s, there were young men whose style retained the traces of the wartime zoot suit, referencing an America of the imagination, an aspect of their self-fashioning.

AFTERMATH

E ven as new clothing styles prevailed among postwar American youth, the zoot suit did not vanish. Into the 1950s and beyond, ordinary Hispanic, African American, and white working-class men continued to wear variations of drape jackets and pegged pants. What had been a controversial outfit during the war years now went largely unremarked. Yet the zoot suit retained an unusual symbolic charge that was reignited by the radical politics of the 1960s and 1970s. The "Chicano power" movement revived the *pachuco* as a heroic and mythological figure, dressed in zoot-suited splendor. Activists and academics attributed new meanings to the style: What social scientists of the 1940s had assayed as a sign of social deviance and psychological disorder transmuted into an emblem of resistance and an oppositional subculture. The zoot suiter became an early ancestor in a genealogy of politicized style and youth subcultures since the mid-twentieth century.

★   ★   ★

The figure and style of the zoot suit continued to catch the eye of many young black men after World War II. Watching Harlem's Easter parade in 1946, columnist Dan Burley commented on the "zoot suits, reet pleats, glad rags, sharp tops and ready Mr. Freddy combinations in all sizes," and quoted singer Pearl Bailey, "90 percent of us dressed wrong but were in the right town." He saw in the parade of Easter fashion something more: black people responding to racial discrimination and violence with laughter and stylishness, "the grandest display of glory, glamour, and revival of life." *Time* magazine reported that young Baltimoreans known as "drapes" lit up dances dressed in long, loose jackets and pegged pants. The city had banned members of this group from recreation centers if their cuffs were too tight, with one official explaining that "extreme dress leads to poor behavior." Protesting the ban, the young men denied they were zoot suiters, whom they identified with draft dodgers and street-corner bums. "A drape is a human, like anybody else," came the response. "It's just sharp dressing." By 1950, African American fashion arbiters declared the extreme style in decline; as the *Atlanta Daily World* declared, "Zoot suits are out for men."[1] Nevertheless, the drape suit never disappeared from African American communities. It continues to appear in shop windows in Philadelphia, for example, in downtown commercial districts and neighborhood clothing stores; on an evening stroll, in Sunday church, and in dance halls, African American men of a certain age still dress down to the bricks in vivid colors, stylish oversized jackets, and pegged pants. For them, the zoot suit remains a living aesthetic tradition, the epitome of cool, a source of pleasure gained in wearing a style that continues to turn heads.

Strikingly, many young, white working-class men, especially from Southern and Eastern European ethnic backgrounds, wore vestiges of the zoot suit through the 1950s. Pegged pants in particular spread widely among high school boys, as historian William Graebner has documented for Buffalo, New York. The press saw little distinctive in the style by then and paid scant attention to white working-class youths wearing it. *Life* ran a feature in 1954 on the new "high style" among teens that included pegged pants; their interest may have been sparked by the more visible teddy boy phenomenon in England. Instead, it was the newer fads among middle-class teens and a fixation with the style of juvenile delinquency that garnered the most public attention—jeans, T-shirts, leather jackets. Those who grew up in cities in the 1950s, however—in Philadelphia, New York, and Detroit—remember the appeal of the zoot suit, and how it persisted well after its heyday. The style still conveyed an aura of the cool hipster, necessary wear among certain cliques or for going out at night; it remained a flashpoint for parents who associated it negatively with African Americans and juvenile delinquents.[2] Yet by the 1960s, it was gone.

For Mexican Americans, the zoot suit summoned a deeper set of meanings, originally forged in the aftermath of the Los Angeles riot. The style had lived on in popular memory, passed from older siblings and relatives to youngsters who eagerly glamorized *pachucos.* One Mexican American, born in 1938 and interviewed fifty-one years later, had come of age in the barrio of East Los Angeles in the 1950s. Some of his uncles were *pachucos,* he recalled, and when he was a boy, one of them had taken him into the Los Angeles riot and a fight with the Ku Klux Klan. "I was lucky to be able to see that, that part," he observed. "My generation was the last one to dress sort of like the *pachucos.*" Songs and stories featuring the *pachuco* life appeared after the war. Songwriter and performer Lalo Guerrero wrote "El Pachuco" intending to poke fun at the phenomenon, and had even developed proficiency in *caló* to do so. As anthropologist George Carpenter Barker observed, "instead of discouraging the *pachucos,* the song had the effect of dramatizing and popularizing their life in the eyes of other Spanish-speaking people." Recordings of *pachuco* songs sold briskly and could be heard on jukeboxes throughout the Southwest. In Tucson, Barker noted, "when the song 'Pachuco Boogie' first appeared in the machine at the Jukeland concession on West Congress street, a crowd of boys stood around it for hours at a time."[3]

For many, *pachuquismo* constituted a stage in men's lives, and when they married and settled into working-class jobs after the war, they gave up extreme styles, slang, and street life. Still, elements of *pachuco* style continued long after the 1940s. *Vato locos* and *cholos* wore "baggies," high-waisted pants with deep pleats reminiscent of those of zoot suiters. Men who customized old cars into "low riders," with adjustable suspensions and elaborately painted exteriors, also passed on the image of the *pachuco,* in murals recalling the 1930s and 1940s; one car called "The

Gangster of Love" featured gangland scenes of Al Capone and John Dillinger along with depictions of zoot suiters. Anthropologist Brenda Bright, investigating the world of low riders, has described how "generations of clothing . . . become the territory of memory 'vested' with signs of conflict, resistance, and necessary manhood."[4]

To whatever extent the zoot suit continued to be worn after the war, by the 1960s and 1970s, its aesthetic had become a cultivated memory, spurred by the politics of radical social change. In the wake of the civil rights and Chicano nationalist movements of these years, activists, artists, and scholars believed that the development of a cultural domain independent of Anglo society was a critical element in political liberation. In keeping with the time, they looked to the past for archetypes of defiance and autonomy, ranging from indigenous Aztec warriors and the Virgin of Guadalupe to modern images of revolutionary Mexico. And so they embraced the *pachuco* as an example of ethnic assertion and Chicano power, with his dress, language, and music early strategies of resistance to discrimination, invisibility, and assimilation. Chicano artists and writers honored the *pachuco* as a mythic figure while scholars in the new field of Chicano studies began to revisit the history of the Sleepy Lagoon murder case and the zoot suit riots. Their efforts to reassess the *pachuco* and place him within a contemporary narrative of resistance occurred simultaneously with a new veneration of the "zoot suit life" among Mexican Americans in the 1970s. Exemplifying this trend was the publication of *Low Rider* magazine beginning in 1976, which, in addition to carrying articles on current Chicano culture, featured reminiscences and photographs of those who had been *pachucos* in the 1940s. Reporting on the renewed interest in the zoot suit, the *Los Angeles Times* noted that "the revival has turned into big business."[5]

What had been a local phenomenon among southwestern Chicanos entered into national consciousness through Luis Valdez's 1978 play *Zoot Suit*, which not only revived the style of the 1940s but retold the story of *pachucos* in wartime Los Angeles. Valdez was a founder of El Teatro Campesino in 1965, an ensemble troupe that gathered to support the organizing efforts of the United Farm Workers union and radicalize Chicano consciousness. It combined a sharp-edged political style, reminiscent of Bertolt Brecht and the New Deal's Federal Theatre Project, with Mexican popular performance traditions—the *carpa* or "tent show," with its mix of acts, theatricality, and humor. Although Valdez had created zoot-suited characters as early as 1970, he made their lives the central focus of *Zoot Suit*, which retold the story of the Sleepy Lagoon murder case and the Los Angeles riot. Valdez portrayed the wartime *pachuco* as part of a hidden history, "a skeleton in the closet" to later generations of Mexican Americans. To bring it to light, he drew on archives and contemporaneous newspaper coverage that recorded the lives of Mexican Americans and their experience of discrimination, injustice, and violence on the home front. The lead character, Henry Reyna, was based on one of the actual defendants in the case and portrayed as a youth seeking his sense of self and destiny. Valdez also created an archetypal figure, El Pachuco, dressed to the nines and full of attitude, to play Henry's alter ego and commentator on the action. "The Pachuco style was an act in life / and his language a new creation," he proclaims. "His will to be was an awesome force / eluding documentation." When rioters beat El Pachuco and strip him of his elegant drapes, he arises in a loincloth, looming large as a symbol of Aztec defiance and sacrifice.[6]

The elevation of the zoot-suited *pachuco* contributed to a new Chicano pride even as it generated controversy. Many Latino and Latina residents who had never attended live theater flocked to *Zoot Suit* when it ran in Los Angeles, and a national audience learned about the history of Mexican Americans in the 1940s, probably for the first time, when the play was made into a film in 1981. But Valdez's effort to "bring a new consciousness into being" also touched a nerve. Eight Sleepy Lagoon defendants sued him for invasion of privacy in 1979, a case settled out of court; the men had kept their involvement a secret, even from their families.[7]

Although Valdez's play was the most widely recognized effort, many artists and writers in the last third of the twentieth century turned to the *pachuco* as a symbol of Chicano cultural nationalism. In the 1990 touring exhibition, "CARA: Chicano Art, Resistance and Affirmation"—praised as path-breaking for its subject matter and scope—at least fifteen major works depicted *pachucos*. Still, the adulation of *pachuquismo* did not sit well with all Chicano intellectuals and activists. When *Zoot Suit* first appeared, historian Richard A. Garcia criticized Valdez for "romanticiz-[ing] the *pachuco* beyond historical recognition"; the effort to join the wartime *pachuco* to the Chicano movement of the 1960s and 1970s was "a forced marriage at best." By the 1990s, feminist critics charged that too many artistic works reinforced and essentialized the hyper-masculine character of the Chicano movement and sidelined attention to women's activism and community building.[8]

The reclamation of the zoot-suited *pachuco* reflected a larger intellectual development after 1960, when style, popular culture, and consumption—particularly among youth—were collectively reappraised for their social and political meanings. An earlier generation of social scientists had viewed extreme fashion as emblematic of youths' maladjustment and social deviance; their development of the concept of subculture after World War II initially described patterns of belief and behavior that were often labeled deviant, abnormal, and outside the mainstream of society. By the 1960s and 1970s, many social analysts on the left perceived the adoption of such styles as a creative act of identity formation and a quasi-political refusal of social norms. Historians and anthropologists turned to the micropolitics of style and gesture to explore everyday protest and subtle contestation over power. For those with an historical bent, the zoot suit—an article of clothing that sparked a riot—fit perfectly into this analytical frame as an early instance of "style warfare."

The practice of reading style for its social and political meaning became not just a dominant strain of academic cultural studies but also a routine mode of popular interpretation. Fashion magazines speak knowingly of "deconstructing" style for what it communicates about identity and social status. Today many subcultural styles are readily understood to be intrinsically political, particularly when, as in the case of punk and hip hop, they are associated with youth who seem ideologically, socioeconomically, and psychologically outside the mainstream. The long black coats and accessories of two young men who went on a killing spree at Columbine High School in 1999 provoked anxious discussions of Goth culture. A 2007 Puerto Rican Day Parade in New York City resulted in mass arrests of the Latin Kings for wearing black and yellow, the colors of this street gang; a profusion of interpretations of such fashion coding followed, with police officers claiming that the situation determined their intent, a sociologist declaring they "show[ed] resistance and autonomy," and the Latin Kings themselves asserting it was "a matter of cultural pride and identity."[9]

The scholarly investigation of style politics blossomed, ironically, even as the zoot suit made another appearance, this time as postmodern retro-fashion. The last decade of the twentieth century witnessed zoot-suit fashion shows, a neo-swing dance craze, and the Cherry Poppin' Daddies' hit song, "Zoot Suit Riot." Clothing manufacturers like Suavecito Apparel Company, El Pachuco Zoot Suits, and Siegel's Clothing Superstore found a market for elaborate drapes online, offering colors and tailoring more lush and outré than that available in the 1940s.[10] A spate of historical dramas made in the 1990s, including *Malcolm X* (1992), *American Me* (1992), and *Swing Kids* (1993), featured the style. It also appeared in cartoons, music videos, and comedies, most famously in *The Mask* (1994), when Jim Carrey's mild-mannered character changed into a wild, green-faced zoot suiter. Evocative of Tex Avery's famous *Wolf* cartoons of the World War II era, this was the zoot suit of the imagination, an explosive mixture of desire, bravado, and id. The 1940s are the source of such recent images, but they come to us drained of historical meaning, let alone ideas of protest and resistance. Instead, they are items from the storehouse of American popular culture, embraced ironically and worn as pastiche. Long after its heyday, the zoot suit appears time and again, resurrected first as a piece of cultural heritage and then as an image available for commercial recycling.

After the zoot suit burst onto the scene in the early 1940s, it took two trajectories. Initially, it was grounded in the particular history of the war years—in the changing configurations of ethnic and racial minorities, the new opportunities for work and leisure, a government clampdown on textiles and clothing styles, and a press and popular culture attuned to these changes. This volatile mixture, concentrated on an extreme style of dress, exploded in Los Angeles in June 1943. Careful attention to this history as it unfolded—the creation and circulation of the drape shape, its assimilation into the youth culture of jitterbug and swing, and the local conditions that transformed a harmless fashion into a sinister one—reveals a cultural process that defies generalizations about the politics of this style, particularly for the youths who had adopted drapes as their uniform.

The other trajectory moved rapidly away from those who wore drapes to those who would interpret them—a profusion of journalists, ministers, reformers, public officials, and academics. Fashion had long been subject to social and political interpretation, and by the early twentieth century youth clothing trends already offered a field day for commentary; there were even nascent fashion theorists investigating the social and psychological meaning of style. But the arrival of the zoot suit, seemingly out of nowhere, was a turning point in the interpretation of clothing. It would be the first in a long line of fads and styles that would be compulsively assessed for their meaning. The ascendancy of the social and behavioral sciences in the war years rendered the drape shape a ready-made object of analysis, revealing everything from psychological damage and social deviance to political protest and resistance. The growing attention paid to the meaning of symbols—in art criticism, semiotics, and anthropology—contributed to these interpretations.

These exercises are significant in themselves for what they tell us about the intellectual and political climate of different eras. The view of the zoot suit as a gesture of resistance among Mexican Americans and other young people of color, emerging in the 1960s and continuing to the present day, is a meaningful one. It no doubt characterized the views of at least some zoot-suited men. But this designation may tell us as much or more about the activists, poets, and historians producing it: as a felt need in recent decades to read everyday life foremost as an expression of power relations and to subordinate cultural and aesthetic considerations to oppositional politics, at a time when the large-scale, collective expression of such views has diminished. Still, the zoot suit, with its many mutations in the United States and abroad, continues to defy fixed meanings. Its riddle lies in the very specificity of its history and in the constant proliferation of meanings generated by an extreme suit of clothes.

NOTES

The following abbreviations are used in the notes:

American Journal of Sociology	*AJS*
Atlanta Daily World	*ADW*
Baltimore Afro American	*Afro*
California Eagle	*Eagle*
Chicago Defender	*Defender*
Chicago Tribune	*Chi.Trib.*
Hartford Courant	*HC*
Los Angeles Examiner	*Examiner*
Los Angeles Times	*LAT*
Men's Apparel Reporter	*MAR*
New York Amsterdam News	*NYAN*
New York Times	*NYT*
Philadelphia Tribune	*Phila.Trib.*
Pittsburgh Courier	*Courier*
Wall Street Journal	*WSJ*
War Production Board	WPB
Washington Post	*WP*

Introduction

1. Frank Walton, *Thread of Victory* (New York: Fairchild Publishing, 1945), 124; Ralph Ellison, "Editorial Comment," *Negro Quarterly* (Winter–Spring, 1943): 301; Octavio Paz, "The Pachuco and Other Extremes," in *The Labyrinth of Solitude: Life and Thought in Mexico*, trans. Lysander Kemp (New York: Grove Press, 1961), 14.

2. Luis Valdez, *Zoot Suit and Other Plays* (Houston: Arte Publico Press, 1992), 25.

3. See, for example, Shane White and Graham J. White, *Stylin': African American Expressive Culture from Its Beginnings to the Zoot Suit* (Ithaca, N.Y.: Cornell University Press, 1998); Robin D. G. Kelley, "The Riddle of the Zoot: Malcolm Little and Black

Cultural Politics During World War II," in *Race Rebels: Culture, Politics, and the Black Working Class* (New York: Free Press, 1994), 161–82; Bruce M. Tyler, "Black Jive and White Repression," *Journal of Ethnic Studies* 16 (1989): 31–66; Douglas Henry Daniels, "Los Angeles Zoot: Race 'Riot,' the Pachuco, and Black Music Culture," *Journal of African American History* 87 (Winter 2002): 98–118.

4. Early publications include Mauricio Mazón, *The Zoot-Suit Riots: The Psychology of Symbolic Annihilation* (Austin: University of Texas Press, 1984); Stuart Cosgrove, "The Zoot-Suit and Style Warfare," *History Workshop Journal* 18 (1984): 77–91. Among recent works, see Eduardo Obregón Pagán, *Murder at the Sleepy Lagoon: Zoot Suits, Race, and Riot in Wartime LA* (Chapel Hill: University of North Carolina Press, 2003); Luis Alvarez, *The Power of the Zoot: Youth Culture and Resistance During World War II* (Berkeley: University of California Press, 2008); Catherine S. Ramírez, *The Woman in the Zoot Suit: Gender, Nationalism, and the Cultural Politics of Memory* (Durham, N.C.: Duke University Press, 2009). For dissertations, see Susan Marie Green, "Zoot Suiters: Past and Present" (Ph.D. diss., University of Minnesota, 1997); David Alfonso-Jose Rojas, "The Making of Zoot Suiters in Early 1940s Mexican Los Angeles" (Ph.D. diss., University of California, Berkeley, 2001); James Terence Sparrow, "Fighting over the American Soldier: Moral Economy and National Citizenship in World War II" (Ph.D. diss., Brown University, 2002); Elizabeth Rachel Escobedo, "Mexican American Home Front: The Politics of Gender, Culture, and Community in World War II Los Angeles" (Ph.D. diss., University of Washington, 2004). Solomon James Jones, "The Government Riots of Los Angeles, June 1943" (M.A. thesis, University of California—Los Angeles, 1969), was an influential, if unpublished, work.

5. See the useful analyses in Rogers Brubaker and Frederick Cooper, "Beyond 'Identity,' " *Theory and Society* 29 (February 2000): 1–47; Jocelyn A. Hollander and Rachel L. Einwohner, "Conceptualizing Resistance," *Sociological Forum* 19 (December 2004): 533–54; Mary Bucholtz, "Youth and Cultural Practice," *Annual Review of Anthropology* 31 (2002): 525–52.

6. Chris Jenks, *Subculture: The Fragmentation of the Social* (London: Sage Publications, 2005); Garth S. Jowett, Ian C. Jarvie, and Kathryn H. Fuller, *Children and the Movies: Media Influence and the Payne Fund Controversy* (Cambridge: Cambridge University Press, 1996); James Gilbert, *A Cycle of Outrage: America's Reaction to the Juvenile Delinquent in the 1950s* (New York: Oxford University Press, 1986), chap. 2; Grace Palladino, *Teenagers: An American History* (New York: Basic Books, 1996), 48–94.

7. On the history of the concept of subculture, see F. Dubet, "Subculture, Sociology of," *International Encyclopedia of the Social and Behavioral Sciences* (Amsterdam: Elsevier, 2004), 15,245–47; Jenks, *Subculture*; Ken Gelder and Sarah Thornton, eds., *The Subcultures Reader* (London: Routledge, 1997).

8. Ellison, "Editorial Comment," 301. The Birmingham School's early treatment of culture and style appears in Stuart Hall and Tony Jefferson, eds., *Resistance Through Rituals* (London: Hutchinson, 1976). On the development of this perspective, see Dennis L. Dworkin, *Cultural Marxism in Postwar Britain: History, the New Left, and the*

Origins of Cultural Studies (Durham, N.C.: Duke University Press, 1997); David Harris, *From Class Struggle to the Politics of Pleasure: The Effects of Gramscianism on Cultural Studies* (London: Routledge, 1992), 72–95.

9. Dick Hebdige, *Subculture: The Meaning of Style* (London: Methuen, 1979), quotations on 18, 100. Although Hebdige revised his argument somewhat in *Hiding in the Light* (London: Routledge, 1988), 35, *Subculture* remains the canonical work.

10. For pioneering cultural studies of gender and race, see Angela McRobbie, *Feminism and Youth Culture: From "Jackie" to "Just Seventeen"* (London: Unwin Hyman, 1991); Paul Gilroy, *"There Ain't No Black in the Union Jack": The Cultural Politics of Race and Nation* (London: Hutchinson, 1987).

11. Cosgrove, "The Zoot-Suit and Style Warfare," 77–91, quotation on 89. See also Steve Chibnall, "Whistle and Zoot: The Changing Meaning of a Suit of Clothes," *History Workshop* 20 (Autumn 1985): 56–81.

12. George Lipsitz, *Rainbow at Midnight: Labor and Culture in the 1940s* (Urbana: University of Illinois Press, 1994), 84; Kelley, "Riddle of the Zoot," 163; Alvarez, *Power of the Zoot*, 8.

13. On the African American tradition of style and cultural performance, see, e.g., White and White, *Stylin'*; Lawrence Levine, *Black Culture and Black Consciousness: Afro-American Folk Thought from Slavery to Freedom* (New York: Oxford University Press, 1977); W. T. Lhamon, *Raising Cain: Blackface Performance from Jim Crow to Hip Hop* (Cambridge, Mass.: Harvard University Press, 1998). See also Roger D. Abrahams, *Everyday Life: A Poetics of Vernacular Practice* (Philadelphia: University of Pennsylvania Press, 2005). On everyday resistance, see James C. Scott, *Domination and the Arts of Resistance: Hidden Transcripts* (New Haven, Conn.: Yale University Press, 1990); Kelley, *Race Rebels*. For a critique of Scott and Kelley, see Michael George Hanchard, *Party/Politics: Horizons in Black Political Thought* (New York: Oxford University Press, 2006), 55–67.

14. See, for example, Pagán, *Murder at the Sleepy Lagoon*; Alvarez, *The Power of the Zoot*; Ramírez, *The Woman in the Zoot Suit*; and "Zoot Suit Riots," *American Experience*, PBS documentary, 2001, and website (www.pbs.org/wgbh/amex/zoot/).

15. Jenks, *Subculture*, 10.

16. Alfred Barela to Judge Arthur S. Guerin, May 21, 1943, box 15, folder 16, "Delinquency, reports on 1938–1943," Manuel Ruiz Papers, Stanford University. Barela's letter is quoted in, among other studies, George Sanchez, *Becoming Mexican American: Ethnicity, Culture, and Identity in Chicano Los Angeles, 1900–1945* (New York: Oxford University Press, 1995), 253; Anthony F. Macias, "Bringing Music to the People," *American Quarterly* 56 (September 2004): 695; Alvarez, *Power of the Zoot*, 1–2, 166; Edward J. Escobar, *Race, Police, and the Making of a Political Identity: Mexican Americans and the Los Angeles Police Department, 1900–1945* (Berkeley: University of California Press, 1999), 232.

17. Malcolm X, *The Autobiography of Malcolm X*, with the assistance of Alex Haley (1964; New York: Ballantine Books, 1992), see especially 64–65. Kelley, "Riddle of the Zoot," 163, 166.

18. David Muggleton, *Inside Subculture: The Postmodern Meaning of Style* (Oxford: Berg, 2000); Sarah Thornton, *Club Cultures: Music, Media, and Subcultural Capital* (Middletown, Conn.: Wesleyan University Press, 1996); David Muggleton and Rupert Weinzierl, eds., *The Post-Subcultures Reader* (Oxford: Berg, 2003); Andy Bennett and Keith Kahn-Harris, *After Subculture: Critical Studies in Contemporary Youth Culture* (New York: Palgrave Macmillan, 2004). See also, from the perspective of a fashion historian, Valerie Steele, *Fifty Years of Fashion* (New Haven, Conn.: Yale University Press, 1998), 4–5.

19. See, e.g., Alvarez, *Power of the Zoot*, 5, 139. For a nuanced portrait of multiethnic youth culture, see Allison Varzally, *Making a Non-White America: Californians Coloring Outside Ethnic Lines, 1925–1955* (Berkeley: University of California Press, 2008).

20. Thornton, *Club Cultures*, 162.

21. Ian Hunter, "Aesthetics and Cultural Studies," in *Cultural Studies*, ed. Lawrence Grossberg, Cary Nelson, and Paula A. Treichler (New York: Routledge, 1991), 348–49.

Chapter 1. Making the Suit Zoot

1. "Here's What All the Excitement's About," *PM*, June 13, 1943, 17. Eugene Kinkead and Russell Maloney, "Zoot Lore," Talk of the Town, *New Yorker*, June 19, 1943, 14–15, New Yorker Digital Edition.

2. Walter White to *NYT*, June 11 1943 (unpublished letter), General Office Files, Part 7, Anti-lynching campaign, 1916–1950, Series A, Anti-lynching investigative files, 1912–1953, reel 29, Papers of the NAACP (Frederick, Md.: University Publications of America, 1987). "Zoot Suit Charivari," A Line O' Type or Two, *Chi.Trib.*, June 14, 1943, 12, ProQuest Historical Newspapers; see also "Zoot Suits No Longer Replete with Mystery," *Chi.Trib.*, August 15, 1943, B18.

3. See David Kuchta, *The Three-Piece Suit and Modern Masculinity; England, 1550–1850* (Berkeley: University of California Press, 2002); Michael Zakim, *Ready-Made Democracy: A History of Men's Dress in the American Republic, 1760–1860* (Chicago: University of Chicago Press, 2003); Anne Hollander, *Sex and Suits* (New York: Knopf, 1994). See also Diana Crane, *Fashion and Its Social Agendas: Class, Gender, and Identity in Clothing* (Chicago: University of Chicago Press, 2000).

4. Thomas Carlyle, *Sartor Resartus: The Life and Opinions of Herr Teufelsdrockh. The Works of Thomas Carlyle*, vol. 12 (1831; New York: Peter Fenelon Collier, 1897), 205–6, Google Books.

5. Shane White and Graham J. White, *Stylin': African American Expressive Culture from Its Beginnings to the Zoot Suit* (Ithaca, N.Y.: Cornell University Press, 1998); W. T. Lhamon, *Raising Cain: Blackface Performance from Jim Crow to Hip Hop* (Cambridge, Mass.: Harvard University Press, 1998). See also Roger D. Abrahams, *Everyday Life: A Poetics of Vernacular Practice* (Philadelphia: University of Pennsylvania Press, 2005).

6. G. Bruce Boyer, "The Cut of Men's Clothes, 1930–1940," in *Fashion Is the News: Apparel Arts*, vol. 1, ed. Giannino Malossi (Turin: Gruppo GFT, 1989), 20–26, quotation on 23. See also Rob Schorman, *Selling Style: Clothing and Social Change at the Turn of the Century* (Philadelphia: University of Pennsylvania Press, 2003), 18–44; Farid Chenoune, *A History of Men's Fashion*, trans. Deke Dusinberre (Paris: Flammarion, 1996), 181; Otis Ferguson, "What the Well Dressed Man Will Bear," *New Republic*, July 12, 1939, 281–83.

7. For a comment on Flynn's "zoot suit" style, see Dave Kehr, "His Wicked, Wicked Ways Go West," *NYT*, August 25, 2008, E1.

8. Duke of Windsor, *A Family Album*, quoted in Chenoune, *History of Men's Fashion*, 169. On Gingrich, see Kenon Breazele, "In Spite of Women: *Esquire* Magazine and the Construction of the Male Consumer," *Signs* 20 (Autumn 1994): 1–22; Bill Osgerby, "A Pedigree of the Consuming Male: Masculinity, Consumption and the American 'Leisure Class,'" in *Masculinity and Men's Lifestyle Magazines*, ed. Bethan Benwell (Oxford: Blackwell, 2003), 57–86.

9. "Activewear Accents Economy," *MAR* 12 (February 1943): 69. "Retailing Goes to War," *MAR* 11 (April 1942), 39. See also "Sportswear Goes to Work," *MAR* 12 (January 1943): 101; "Sportswear Is Your Oyster," *MAR* 11 (November 1941): 64–65; Henry L. Jackson, "West Coast Contribution," *MAR* 12 (January 1943): 73. On the rise of the California men's sportswear industry, see William R. Scott, "California Casual: Lifestyle Marketing and Men's Leisurewear, 1930–1960," in *Producing Fashion: Commerce, Culture, and Consumers*, ed. Regina Blaszczyk (Philadelphia: University of Pennsylvania Press, 2007), 169–86.

10. JoAnn Olian, ed., *Everyday Fashions of the Forties, as Pictured in Sears Catalogs* (New York: Dover Publications, 1992), 14. Henry L. Jackson, "Princeton House Party," *MAR* 11 (June 1941): 55.

11. "Here's What All the Excitement's About," 17. Cf. Shank's, *NYAN*, March 2, 1932, 13, ProQuest Historical Newspapers; Westin-Shank, *NYAN*, March 24, 1934, 10; J. C. Curtis, *NYAN*, April 4, 1936, 14; Westin, *NYAN*, March 27, 1937, 2; Savon Clothes, *NYAN*, Dec. 17, 1938, 12; Hatter Bill, *NYAN*, November 26, 1938, 18. For identification of these fashions with Harlem, see "Fashion Flashes," *ADW*, January 28, 1937, 5, ProQuest Historical Newspapers; "'Jitterbug' Pants Have Style Grip on Harlemites," *ADW*, March 14, 1941, 2. The cowboy hat style may have originated in Detroit; see Dan Burley, "Back Door Stuff," *NYAN*, October 3, 1942, 16. See also White and White, *Stylin'*, 248–54.

12. "Trouble in Los Angeles," *NYT*, June 13, 1943, E2, ProQuest Historical Newspapers; "Elks Rendezvous New Show Classy," *NYAN*, October 30, 1943, B7. Kinkead and Maloney, "Zoot Lore," 14.

13. Cheryl Lynn Greenberg, *"Or Does It Explode?" Black Harlem in the Great Depression* (New York: Oxford University Press, 1991), chap. 5.

14. Marty Clausen, "Growing Up Musically in Chicago," Jazz Institute of Chicago

(http://www.jazzinchicago.org/educates/journal/articles/growing-musically-chicago). For an oral history of Fox Brothers, see Carolyn Eastwood, *Near West Side Stories: Struggles for Community in Chicago's Maxwell Street Neighborhood* (Chicago: Lake Claremont Press, 2002), 67–86. Robert McG. Thomas, Jr., "Harold Fox, Who Took Credit for the Zoot Suit, Dies at 86," *NYT*, August 1, 1996, D23.

15. Eldon Roark, *Memphis Bragabouts, Characters I Have Met* (New York: McGraw-Hill, 1945), 78–79.

16. Frank L. Walton, *Thread of Victory* (New York: Fairchild Publishing, 1945), 130. "Here's What All the Excitement's About," 17.

17. Meyer Berger, "Zoot Suit Originated in Georgia; Bus Boy Ordered First One in '40," *NYT*, June 11, 1943, 21; Johnny Vardeman, "Zoot Suit Order from Local Store Put Gainesville Man in Spotlight," *Gainesville Times*, October 8, 2006. I am grateful to Mr. Vardeman for finding and interviewing octogenarian Clyde Duncan Rakestraw, as he is now known; according to Rakestraw, he was a bellhop at the local hotel, not a busboy. Thanks also to Steve Gurr, Northeast Georgia History Center, for information about wartime Gainesville. See also "Camera Go Round," *MAR* 10 (February 1941): 78. J. V. D. Carlyle, "The Psychological Implications of the Zoot Suit," *MAR* 13 (July 1943): 36.

18. Roark, *Memphis Bragabouts*, 78; Philip L. Elkus, "Zoot Suit Required Cutting and Cajoling," Letter to the Editor, *NYT*, August 4, 1996, section 4, 14; Earl Brown and Russell Maloney, "Down to the Bricks," Talk of the Town, *New Yorker*, April 12, 1941, 14–15.

19. RJ Smith, *The Great Black Way: L.A. in the 1940s and the Lost African American Renaissance* (New York: Public Affairs, 2006), 21.

20. Kermisch's, *Afro*, October 14, 1939, 24; Solomon's, *Afro*, June 8, 1940, 22; April 18, 1942, 21. Malcolm X, *The Autobiography of Malcolm X*, with the assistance of Alex Haley (1965; New York: Ballantine Books, 1992), 61–62. "Reading the Riddle," A Line O' Type or Two, *Chi.Trib.*, June 24, 1943, 16.

21. Brown and Maloney, "Down to the Bricks," 15; Solomon's, *Afro*, September 13, 1941, 26. On dry cleaners, see Bruce Tyler, "Black Jive and White Repression," *Journal of Ethnic Studies* 16, no. 4 (1989): 38.

22. "Zoot Suit Catalog Arrives in Clearwater," *St. Petersburg Times*, June 13, 1943, 21. For mail order ads, see, e.g., *Courier*, January 17, 1942, 16–17; November 7, 1942, 16, ProQuest Historical Newspapers.

23. Malcolm X, *Autobiography*, 61; Eastwood, *Near West Side Stories*, 75; Barney, *Afro*, February 24, 1945, 23.

24. "Drape Shape," *Newsweek* 20 (September 7, 1942): 48–49; Faith Ringgold, *We Flew Over the Bridge: The Memoirs of Faith Ringgold* (New York: Little, Brown, 1995), 19.

25. Walton, *Thread of Victory*, 124; Emory S. Bogardus, "Gangs of Mexican-American Youth," *Sociology and Social Research* 28 (September–October 1943): 55–56.

26. "Jitterbugs Mad at Axis Now, Cause War Takes Away Their 'Zoot' Suits,"

Defender, September 12, 1942, 3; "Here's What All the Excitement's About," 17; Eastwood, *Near West Side Stories,* 79. For the early styling, see "Camera Go Round," 78; photographs in the hardcover edition of *The Autobiography of Malcolm X* (New York: Grove Press, 1965). See also "Drape Shape," 48–49; Walter Davenport, "Swing It, Swing Shift!" *Colliers* (August 22, 1942): 28; "Zoot Suit War Grows: Army and Navy Act," *Chi.Trib.,* June 9, 1943, 1; Earlbrook Clothes ad, *Phila.Trib.,* September 22, 1942, 14, ProQuest Historical Newspapers.

27. Ernest R. Hilgard to Carroll Burton, "History of the development of requirements for Apparel and House furnishings," November 10, 1944; G. R. MacDonald to Arthur W. Whiteside, "Reasons to Avoid Rationing," May 18, 1943, 546.09 Clothing and Knit Goods—Rationing, Policy Documentation File, RG 179, Records of the WPB, National Archives, College Park, Maryland. Charles E. Egan, "WPB Plan Opposes Clothes Rationing," *NYT,* May 21, 1943, 21. On wartime textile conservation, see Walton, *Thread of Victory;* Rachel Pearl Maines, "Textiles for Defense: Emergency Policy for Textiles and Apparel in the Twentieth Century" (Ph.D. diss., Carnegie-Mellon University, 1983). The WPB records are very incomplete and contain little internal or external correspondence on the zoot suit.

28. "Verbatim Transcript of Proceedings, Informal Conference, Men's and Boys' Clothing Industry," January 8, 1942, 54, Select Document File: Textiles, Clothing and Knit Goods; G. R. MacDonald to Arthur W. Whiteside, "Suggestions to be explored to match consumer demand with production." May 18, 1943, 3, 546.09, Clothing and Knit Goods—Rationing, Policy Documentation File, RG 179, WPB. Frank L. Walton, *Thread of Victory,* 111.

29. "Industry Advisory Committee Meeting, Men's and Boys' Clothing, August 25, 1942," 2, 546.105 Men's Apparel—Industry Advisory Committee Meetings, Policy Documentation File, RG 179, WPB. Compliance studies include: "Summary of Compliance Survey Covering Manufacturers of Wool Clothing for Men and Boys, Under General Conservation Order M-73a Issued March 2, 1942 and Amended April 27, 1942, Report of the Survey Section, Field Investigation by the Wage and Hour Division, U.S. Department of Labor, Period Under Investigation, June 1942"; "Notes used at meeting with Cong. Boren, November 30, 1945. P.F. Maguire"; Janet Dublon to Charles E. Noyes, "Men's Wool Suits—Past and Anticipated Production," June 15, 1945, all in Select Document File, Textiles, Clothing and Knit Goods, RG 179, WPB. See also Maines, "Textiles for Defense," 99–102, 180.

30. Gaston de Vigne, "Now We Think," *Phila.Trib.,* April 4, 1942, 1.

31. Joe Shephard, "AFRO Reporter Hepped on Cats' Plans for Stashing," *Afro,* September 12, 1942, 11.

32. Helene Champlain, "One-Button-Roll Job Arrives to Mollify D.C. Zoot Suiters," *WP,* October 12, 1943, B1. "Agency Is Planning to Put Stop to Waste of Fabric by Fad," *WP,* September 4, 1942, B1; "Zoot Suit, Juke Coat Face WPB Crackdown to End Waste of Cloth," *WSJ,* September 4, 1942, 2; "'Zoot Suit' Models Rouse Ire of WPB," *NYT,* September 4, 1942, 26.

33. "WPB Bars 'Zoot Suit' Made in Any Material," *NYT*, September 12, 1942, 8. Frank L. Walton to A. I. Henderson, memorandum, September 7, 1942, Office of Procedures, Work Folders L 219–L 240: Folder L-224, Men and Boys Clothing, RG 179, WPB. See also Frank L. Walton, *Thread of Victory*, 125.

34. "Agency Is Planning to Put Stop to Waste of Fabric," B1. G. H. McCowan to James J. Short, "For the Clearance Committee, October 21, 1942; Subject: Clothing for Men and Boys," memo dated October 19, 1942, General Records, Orders, Regulations, Directives and Related Papers of the WPB and Civilian Production Administration ("Recording Secretary's File"), 1941–47, L-219 to L-226, RG 179, WPB.

35. "Yon Clink Nods to Bootleggers of Zoot Suits, Gussets or Not," *WP*, September 3, 1942, 1. "City Council Goes Nuts," *Eagle,* June 10, 1943, 1, also June 17, 1943, 1; "Ban on Freak Suits Studied by Councilmen," *LAT*, June 10, 1943, p. A, ProQuest Historical Newspapers.

36. "Agency Is Planning to Put Stop to Waste of Fabric," B1; "Yon Clink Nods," 1. For the injunction against a clothing store in Los Angeles, see "Zoot-Suiters Call Truce, Disorders Ebb," *WP*, June 13, 1943, M12. New York, Philadelphia, Chicago, and Washington newspapers reported no local injunctions or prosecutions. See also "Zoot Suits and Service Stripes: Race Tension Behind the Riots," *Newsweek,* June 21, 1943, 40.

37. Richman's, *Chi.Trib.*, October 22, 1942, 7; Horsfall's, *Courant*, August 16, 1942, 2.

38. M. S. Verner, Jr. to Morton J. Baum, October 5, 1944, General Records, Orders, Regulations, Directives, and Related Papers of the WPB and Civilian Production Administration ("Recording Secretary's File"), 1941–47, L-219 to L-226, RG 179, WPB.

39. Berger, "Zoot Suit Originated in Georgia," 21. Cartoon in *MAR* 12 (January 1943): 47.

40. Walton, *Thread of Victory,* 126–127; *Charleston Daily Mail,* June 20, 1943, 3, Access Newspaper Archive, newspaperarchive.com.

41. National Clothing Stores, *Courier*, October 10, 1942, 17; Elmer Liepman, *Afro*, March 27, 1942, 27; Northwestern Loan Office, *Afro*, April 4, 1942, 30; Kermisch's, *Afro,* March 14, 1942, 24; King Clothing Company, *Defender*, October 9, 1943, 7.

42. "WPB Lists Curbs from A Clear to Z," *NYT*, June 3, 1943, 7.

43. "Easter Sales Show Heavy Increases," *WP*, April 23, 1943, B4; "Topics of the Times," *NYT*, April 8, 1944, 12. "WPB Approves Zoot Suits," *WP*, October 17, 1944, 1.

Chapter 2. Going to Extremes

1. Earl Brown and Russell Maloney, "Down to the Bricks," Talk of the Town, *New Yorker,* April 12, 1941, 14–15, New Yorker Digital Edition; "Agency Is Planning to Put Stop to Waste of Fabric by Fad," *WP*, September 4, 1942, B1; Holly Alford, "The Zoot

Suit: Its History and Influence," *Fashion Theory* 8 (2004): 232. See also Dan Burley, "Portrait of a Hepcat Getting 'Sharp,'" Back Door Stuff, *NYAN*, September 18, 1943, 22; "Drape Shape," *Newsweek* 20 (September 7, 1942): 48–49.

2. "Duke Ellington and Henry Armstrong Introduced the Famous 'Zoot' Suit," *Defender*, November 14, 1942, 20. Julius J. Adams, "Who Was First Zoot-Suiter? Was It the Duke of Windsor?" *NYAN*, May 29, 1943, 11. See also Shane White and Graham J. White, *Stylin': African American Expressive Culture from Its Beginnings to the Zoot Suit* (Ithaca, N.Y.: Cornell University Press, 1998), 248–62.

3. Meyer Berger, "Zoot Suit Originated in Georgia; Bus Boy Ordered First One in '40," *NYT*, June 11, 1943, 21. See also "Here's What All the Excitement's About," *PM*, June 13, 1943, 17; Jack Saunders, "I Love a Parade," *Phila.Trib.*, October 24, 1942, 11. The belief that Gable was the inspiration for the style may be seen in Ol Harrington's cartoon, "Dark Laughter," *Phila.Trib.*, September 6, 1941, 11. On the design of Rhett Butler's costumes, see *Gone with the Wind* Online Exhibit, Harry Ransom Center, University of Texas at Austin, (www.hrc.utexas.edu/exhibitions/web/gwtw/wardrobe/rhett/rhett.html). Historian Adam Green discusses the irony of the style in *Selling the Race: Culture, Community, and Black Chicago, 1940–1955* (Chicago: University of Chicago Press, 2007), 241.

4. "Lucius Beebe Sets a Style," *Life*, January 16, 1939, cover, 40; "Men's Fashions," *NYAN*, April 13, 1940, 15.

5. *LAT* quoted in Linda España-Maram, *Creating Masculinity in Los Angeles's Little Manila: Working-Class Filipinos and Popular Culture, 1920s–1950s* (New York: Columbia University Press, 2006), 150. España-Maram discusses the McIntosh suit and zoot suits in the context of Filipino leisure culture. On traditional dress, see Mina Roces, "Gender, Nation and the Politics of Dress in Twentieth-Century Philippines," *Gender and History* 17 (August 2009): 354–77. See also Walter Davenport, "Swing It, Swing Shift!" *Colliers* (August 22, 1942): 24; "Zoot Suit War Grows: Army and Navy Act," *Chi.Trib.*, January 9, 1943, 1; Emory S. Bogarus, "Gangs of Mexican-American Youth," *Sociology and Social Research* 28 (September–October 1943): 55.

6. Menjou quoted in Patricia Grady, "Hollywood on the Potomac," *WP*, 26 October 1942, B6. Arenas quoted in "Zoot Suit Riots," *American Experience*, PBS/WGBH, website, http://www.pbs.org/wgbh/amex/zoot/eng_sfeature/sf_zoot_text.html. See also Luis Alvarez, *The Power of the Zoot: Youth Culture and Resistance During World War II* (Berkeley: University of California Press, 2008); Eduardo Obregón Pagán, *Murder at the Sleepy Lagoon: Zoot Suits, Race, and Riot in Wartime L.A.* (Chapel Hill: University of North Carolina Press, 2003).

7. Laura L. Cummings, "Cloth-Wrapped People, Trouble, and Power: Pachuco Culture in the Greater Southwest," *Journal of the Southwest* 45 (2003): 329–48; George Carpenter Barker, *Pachuco: An American-Spanish Argot and Its Social Functions in Tucson, Arizona* (Tucson: University of Arizona Press, 1950; rev. ed. 1974), 21–23. Pagán, *Murder at the Sleepy Lagoon*, 39.

8. Jess Guitiérrez, "Interview: César Chávez," *Lowrider*, October 1980, 42; Lalo

Guerrero and Sherilyn Meece Metes, *Lalo: My Life and Music* (Tucson: University of Arizona Press, 2002), 94–102, quotation on 98.

9. "Zoot Suit, Juke Coat Face WPB Crackdown to End Waste of Cloth," *WSJ*, September 4, 1942, 2; Malcolm X, *The Autobiography of Malcolm X*, with the assistance of Alex Haley (1964; New York: Ballantine Books, 1992), 62; Carolyn Eastwood, *Near West Side Stories: Struggles for Community in Chicago's Maxwell Street Neighborhood* (Chicago: Lake Claremont Press, 2002), 81. See also Eric Lott, "Double V, Double Time: Bebop's Politics of Style," *Callaloo* 36 (Summer 1998): 600; " 'Zoot Suit' Models Rouse Ire of WPB," *NYT*, September 4, 1942, 26.

10. Bruce Tyler, "Black Jive and White Repression," *Journal of Ethnic Studies* 16, no. 4 (1989): 34; Carey McWilliams, *North from Mexico: The Spanish-Speaking People of the United States* (Philadelphia: J. B. Lippincott Co., 1949), 242; Malcolm X, *Autobiography*, 60; Carl Dunbar Lawrence, "Lace Up Your Boots and Dig This Jive!" *NYAN*, March 2, 1940, 21. See also Joel Dinerstein, *Swinging the Machine: Modernity, Technology, and African American Culture Between the World Wars* (Amherst: University of Massachusetts Press, 2003), 265; Gena Caponi-Tabery, "Jump for Joy: The Jump Trope in African America, 1937–1941," *Prospects* 24 (October 1999): 521–74; David W. Stowe, *Swing Changes: Big-Band Jazz in New Deal America* (Cambridge, Mass.: Harvard University Press, 1994); Lewis A. Erenberg, *Swingin' the Dream: Big Band Jazz and the Rebirth of American Culture* (Chicago: University of Chicago Press, 1998). For "killer-diller" and other jive, see Cab Calloway's *Hepster's Dictionary*, 1944 edition reprinted in Cab Calloway and Bryant Rollins, *Of Minnie the Moocher and Me* (New York: Thomas Crowell, 1976), online version http://cabcalloway.cc/jive_dictionary .htm; Scott Saul, *Freedom Is, Freedom Ain't: Jazz and the Making of the Sixties* (Cambridge, Mass.: Harvard University Press, 2003), 32–35.

11. See, e.g., Chad Heap, *Slumming: Sexual and Racial Encounters in American Nightlife, 1885–1940* (Chicago: University of Chicago Press, 2009); RJ Smith, *The Great Black Way: L.A. in the 1940s and the Lost African American Renaissance* (New York: Public Affairs, 2006).

12. España-Maram, *Creating Masculinity in Los Angeles's Little Manila*, 132; Mc-Williams, *North from Mexico*, 242.

13. On Kikuchi's interviews, see Charlotte Brooks, "In the Twilight Zone Between Black and White: Japanese-American Resettlement and Community in Chicago, 1942–1945," *Journal of American History* 86 (March 2000): 1682–83. Ayako Noguchi, "Behavior and Unconventional Dress of Denver Nisei 'Zoot Suit' Boys Decried," *Denson Tribune*, vol. 1, no. 32 (June 16, 1943): 5, Densho Digital Archives (archive.densho .org). Paul R. Spickard, "Not Just the Quiet People: The Nisei Underclass," *Pacific Historical Review* 68 (1999): 78–94.

14. For the fullest development of this position, see Alvarez, *Power of the Zoot*; Pagán, *Murder at the Sleepy Lagoon*.

15. Arenas quoted in "Zoot Suit Riots." Julian Nava quoted in William Overend,

"The '43 Zoot Suit Riots Reexamined," *LAT*, May 9, 1978, G5. On John Kinloch, see Smith, *The Great Black Way*, 21. For black college students, see Gordon Parks, "Daytona Beach, Florida. Bethune-Cookman College, 'Zoot suits'" (January 1943), Library of Congress, Prints and Photographs Division, FSA-OWI Collection [LC-USW3-014839-E]. For images of *Nisei* in modified zoot suits, see "Young Japanese Hold Dance," May 21, 1943, JARDA-6–16; Francis Stewart, "A view at a dance given at Camp #2 to celebrate the Harvest Festival," November 26, 1942, WRA no. D-690, in JARDA: Japanese American Relocation Digital Archives, Calisphere, University of California, www.calisphere.universityofcalifornia.edu/jarda/.

16. *MAR* 11 (June 1941): 98. My thanks to James H. Madison, Indiana University (June 14, 2004 email) and Beth E. Oljace, Anderson (Ind.) Public Library (August 17, 2007 email), for information about Anderson.

17. Henry McLemore, "The Lighter Side," *LAT*, February 6, 1942, 10; Walter Davenport, "Swing It, Swing Shift!" *Colliers* (August 22, 1942): 24–30, quotation on 30; Lloyd Lewis, "Revenge on Chicago," *NYT*, March 14, 1943, XI.

18. "Leveling Men's Fashions," *Prescott Evening Courier*, March 2, 1943; Henry Jackson, "Gilt and Goulash," *MAR* 11 (June 1941): 29. See also *MAR* 11 (December 1941): 21; 12 (March 1943): 63; 12 (April 1943): 93; "New Rich, New Poor," *Time*, May 4, 1942, 16. Frank M. Davis, "A 'Cake-Eater' Looks at the 'Zoot Suiters'; Both Fine," *Afro*, June 12, 1943, 14. On the consumer in the war years, see Meg Jacobs, *Pocketbook Politics: Economic Citizenship in Twentieth-Century America* (Princeton, N.J.: Princeton University Press, 2005), 179–220; Lizabeth Cohen, *A Consumers' Republic: The Politics of Mass Consumption* (New York: Knopf, 2003), 62–109.

19. On white zoot suiters, see Eastwood, *Near West Side Stories*, 75, 77; Ralph Banay, "A Psychiatrist Looks at the Zoot Suit," *Probation* 22 (February 1944): 82; Jean Craighead, "New Boogie Woogie Dance Steps with Strange Names, Born of Night Life," *WP*, December 18, 1943, B3; "Here's What All the Excitement's About," *PM* June 13, 1943, 17; *Alton Evening Telegraph*, October 17, 1942, 4, Access Newspapers Archive (access.newspaperarchive.com). On the Harry James concert, see Bosley Crowther, "Hounds of Spring," *NYT*, May 2, 1943, X3. For one teacher's response, see Samuel G. Gulbert, "Schools vs. Frank Sinatra and Zoot Suits," *Journal of Education* 127 (May 1944): 153–55.

20. "Rugcutters Find Harlem 'Heaven,'" *NYAN*, April 8, 1939, 20; *Los Angeles Sentinel*, June 29, 1939, 1; Erenberg, *Swingin' the Dream*, xv, 55; Orlando Suero, "Jive, as a Hep-Cat Hears It," *NYT*, 9 May 1943, X5. On jive, see Scott Saul, *Freedom Is, Freedom Ain't*, 35–44.

21. On Cab Calloway, see *Of Minnie the Moocher and Me*. On Washington dances, Frank L. Walton, *Thread of Victory* (New York: Fairchild Publishing, 1945), 125; "Zoot Suit Pockets Prize," *WP*, August 29, 1942, B1; "Agency Is Planning to Put Stop to Waste of Fabric by Fad," *WP*, September 4, 1942, B1. Farm Security Administration photographers took numerous shots of dancers in drape jackets and pegged pants. See

Esther Bubley, "Washington, D.C. Jitterbugs at an Elk's Club dance, the 'cleanest dance in town' April 1943" [LC-USW3–023090-E DLC], John Ferrell, "Washington, D.C. Soldier inspecting a couple of 'zoot suits' at the Uline Arena during Woody Herman's Orchestra engagement there," June 1942 [LC-USF34–011543-D DLC], Library of Congress, Prints and Photographs Division, FSA-OWI Collection. On the interracial music scene, see Erenberg, *Swingin' the Dream*; Alvarez, *Power of the Zoot*, chap. 4.

22. For bands in Anderson, "Count Basie Praises Press for Its Work," *Defender*, April 12, 1941, 21; Beth Oljace to author, email August 14, 2007. FSA photographs include Russell Lee, "Jitterbug Contest," March 1942 [LC-USF 34–072189-D], Marjory Collins, "Zoot Suits and Jitterbugs," November 1942 [LC-USW3–010936-D]; Arthur Siegal, "Jitterbug Dance at Scrap Salvage Rally," fall 1942 [LC-USW3–016198], all in Library of Congress, Prints and Photographs Division, FSA-OWI Photograph Collection. On migrant men, see Tyler, "Black Jive and White Repression," 38; Malcolm X, *Autobiography*, 62.

23. "Focus: Zoot Suit Revisited" interview/call-in radio show with author, WILL-AM, Illinois Public Media, University of Illinois, Urbana-Champaign, Oct 25, 2005, will.illinois.edu/focus/interview/focus051025a/.

24. Malcolm X, *Autobiography*, 47. Maxine Leeds Craig, *Ain't I a Beauty Queen? Black Women, Beauty, and the Politics of Race* (New York: Oxford University Press, 2002), 112. See also Tyler, "Black Jive and White Repression," 38–41; Robin D. G. Kelley, "The Riddle of the Zoot: Malcolm Little and Black Cultural Politics During World War II," in *Race Rebels: Culture, Politics, and the Black Working Class* (New York: Free Press, 1994), 161–82; White and White, *Stylin'*.

25. Banay, "Psychiatrist Looks at the Zoot Suit," 83. Manuel Delgado, "Zoot Suiter: Drawing," ca 1943 or 1944, box 4, folder 2, Sleepy Lagoon Defense Committee Records (Collection 107), Department of Special Collections, Charles E. Young Research Library, UCLA, Los Angeles. For an excellent discussion, see Pagán, *Murder at the Sleepy Lagoon*, 124–25. On Mexican American caricaturists, see McWilliams, *North from Mexico*, 230.

26. Wallace Stegner and the Editors of *Look*, *One Nation* (Boston: Houghton Mifflin, 1946), 133. On the fad for writing on clothes, see Kelly Schrum, *Some Wore Bobby Sox: The Emergence of Teenage Girls' Culture, 1920–1945* (New York: Palgrave Macmillan, 2004), 45.

27. José "Chepe" Ruiz letter to Alice Greenfield, May 18, 1944, box 4, folder 2, Sleepy Lagoon Defense Committee Records; for the full text, see Online Archive of California, http://www.oac.cdlib.org/ark:/13030/hb7w1011h7/?brand=oac4. His conviction was later overturned.

28. Malcolm X, *Autobiography*, photographs in hardcover edition (New York: Grove Press, 1965); Spike Lee, dir., *Malcolm X*, 40 Acres & A Mule Filmworks/Warner Brothers Pictures, 1992. "Mexican American Youth Detained for Questioning," *Los*

Angeles Daily News, ca. 1942 (uclamss_1387_b60_28789–3), *Los Angeles Daily News* Negatives Collection, Department of Special Collections, Charles E. Young Research Library, UCLA; this and similar photographs may be found at the Online Archive of California, http://www.oac.cdlib.org/.

29. Rudy Leyvas quoted in Overend, "The '43 Zoot Suit Riots Reexamined," G6. Rollanza quoted in España-Maram, *Creating Masculinity in Los Angeles's Little Manila*, 140–41. On East and West Coast styles, see Pagán, *Murder at the Sleepy Lagoon*, 107–15.

30. "The Watch Tower," *Eagle*, January 27, 1941, quoted in Smith, *Great Black Way*, 32; Arenas quoted in "Zoot Suit Riots"; Frances Esquibel Tywoniak and Mario T. Garcia, *Migrant Daughter: Coming of Age as a Mexican American Woman* (Berkeley: University of California Press, 2000), 81.

31. Carlos Espinoza quoted in "Zoot Suit Riots." Margarita Salazar McSweyn interview in Sherna Berger Gluck, *Rosie the Riveter Revisited: Women, the War, and Social Change* (Boston: G. K. Hall, 1987), 84–85. Spickard, "Not Just the Quiet People," 83; Noguchi, "Behavior and Unconventional Dress of Denver Nisei 'Zoot Suit' Boys Decried."

32. Barker, *Pachuco*, 29; Jacques E. Levy, *César Chávez: Autobiography of La Causa* (1975; Minneapolis: University of Minnesota Press, 2007), 82–83; Nava quoted in Overend, "The '43 Zoot Suit Riots Reexamined," G5; Timothy Turner, "Zoot Suits Still Parade Here Despite O.P.A. Ban," *LAT*, March 22, 1943, A8. See also Guitiérrez, "Interview: César Chávez."

33. Levy, *César Chávez*, 83; McSweyn interview in Gluck, *Rosie the Riveter Revisited*, 84–85.

34. McLemore, "Lighter Side." On the imperative for women to wear pants, see U.S. Women's Bureau, *Safety Clothing for Women in Industry*, Special Bulletin No. 3 (Washington, D.C.: Government Printing Office, 1941), Historical Government Publications from World War II, Southern Methodist University, http://digitalcollections .smu.edu/u?/hgp,467.

35. For insightful discussions of Mexican American women, see Catherine S. Ramírez, "Crimes of Fashion: The Pachuca and Chicana Style Politics," *Meridians* 2 (2002): 1–35; Catherine S. Ramírez, *The Woman in the Zoot Suit: Gender, Nationalism, and the Cultural Politics of Memory* (Durham, N.C.: Duke University Press, 2009); Elizabeth R. Escobedo, "The Pachuca Panic: Sexual and Cultural Battlegrounds in World War II Los Angeles," *Western Historical Quarterly* 38 (Summer 2007): 133–56; Elizabeth R. Escobedo, "Mexican American Home Front: The Politics of Gender, Culture, and Community in World War II Los Angeles," chap. 3 (Ph.D. diss., University of Washington, 2004). See also Rosa Linda Fregosa, "Home Girls, Cholas, and Pachucas in Cinema," *California History* (Fall 1995): 317–18; Cummings, "Cloth-Wrapped People," 342.

36. Elizabeth Lapovsky Kennedy and Madeline D. Davis, *Boots of Leather, Slippers*

of Gold: The History of a Lesbian Community (New York: Routledge, 1993), 151, 56. "Gets Tough in Café, Cops Discover 'He' Is a Female," *Defender,* March 21, 1942, 9; "Girls Fined for Wearing 'What White Girls Wear,'" *Defender,* January 24, 1942, 1.

Chapter 3. Into the Public Eye

1. "Camera Go Round," *MAR* 10 (February 1941): 78; Meyer Berger, "Zoot Suit Originated in Georgia; Bus Boy Ordered First One in '40," *NYT,* June 11, 1943, 21. Earl Brown and Russell Maloney, "Down to the Bricks," *New Yorker,* April 12, 1941, 14–15, New Yorker Digital Edition.

2. Bill Chase, "Phooey on Fashions!" *NYAN,* August 31, 1940, 11; "It's a Fake! No Crepe on Drapes on Beale St.," *ADW,* January 10, 1941, 1.

3. Gordon Parks, "Daytona Beach, Florida. Bethune-Cookman College, 'Zoot suits'" (January 1943), Library of Congress, Prints and Photographs Division, FSA-OWI Collection [LC-USW3–014839-E]. Raymond Steth, *Evolution of Swing* (mezzotint, n.d.); Claude Clark, *In the Groove* and *Jumpin' Jive* (lithographs, n.d.), in WPA Collection, Free Library of Philadelphia, Print and Picture Collection. Erin Park Cohn, "Imprinting Race: The Philadelphia Fine Print Workshop of the WPA Federal Art Project and the Visual Politics of Race," paper presented at the American Studies Annual Meeting, October 2007. My thanks to Erin Park Cohn for sharing these images and information about them with me.

4. For an example, see Jay Jackson, "So What?" *Defender,* July 19, 1941, 15. Ted Shearer, "Around Harlem," *NYAN,* October 10, 1942, 7; February 14, 1942, 12. For an overview, see Bruce Tyler, "Zoot-Suit Culture and the Black Press," *Journal of American Culture* 17, no. 2 (Summer 1994): 21–33.

5. Jay Jackson, "So What?" *Defender,* February 15, 1941, 15; May 10, 1941, 15; November 27, 1943, 15; July 19, 1941, 15; February 7, 1942, 15.

6. Abbé Wallace Service, "Guiding Light on Your Human Relation Problems," *ADW,* January 4, 1943, 3. Dan Burley, "This Is on the Trifling Husbands," Back Door Stuff, *NYAN,* June 3, 1944, 10.

7. Dan Burley, Back Door Stuff, *NYAN,* April 5, 1941, 13; October 3, 1942, 16; September 18, 1943, 22; October 9, 1943, 20. Herman Hill, "Hill's Side," *Courier,* May 15, 1943, 17. "I Go to Market," *Defender,* June 15, 1940, 13; "Men's Fashions," *NYAN,* April 13, 1940, 15.

8. "On the Reel," *ADW,* February 26, 1944, 3. "'Zoot Suit' Philosophy of Life Must Go, A. L. Holsey Tells Memphis Citizens," *ADW,* February 5, 1943, 6. Editorial, *ADW,* March 17, 1943, 6; Roy Leeland Hopkins, "Toppin' the Town," *Courier,* June 12, 1943, 17.

9. Adam Green, *Selling the Race: Culture, Community, and Black Chicago, 1940–1955* (Chicago: University of Chicago Press, 2006), 8. "Tells Negroes How They Can Secure Defense Jobs," *NYAN,* March 13, 1943, 20; "Zoot Suits with Drape Shapes,"

ADW, September 25, 1942, 5. George Neely, "How Bright Is Harlem's Future? Reader Says It's in Jeopardy," *NYAN*, May 29, 1943, 11. "Three Zoot-Suited Brothers Face Sentence After 30 Thefts," *NYAN*, December 26, 1942, 18.

10. Joseph D. Bibb, "What's Hurting Us?" *Courier*, January 30, 1943, 13. "Behavior Pattern Scored at Meeting," *Courier*, June 5, 1943, 13. Wilbur C. Douglass, "'Are We Asking Too Much, Too Soon?' Reader Asks," *Courier* April 3, 1943, 23. "Uncle Toms: Young and Old," *Courier*, February 27, 1943, 6. For a discussion of this editorial cartoon, see Bruce Tyler, "Black Jive and White Repression," *Journal of Ethnic Studies* 16, no. 4 (1989): 36–37. On the wartime black press, see Patrick S. Washburn, *The African American Newspaper: Voices of Freedom* (Evanston, Ill.: Northwestern University Press, 2006), 143–79.

11. *Down Beat*, March, 15, 1942, 12; Dizzy Gillespie with Al Fraser, *To Be or Not . . . to Bop* (1979; Minneapolis: University of Minnesota Press, 2009), 279; Johnny Otis, *Listen to the Lambs*, foreword by George Lipsitz (1968; Minneapolis: University of Minnesota Press, 2009), 94–95. On the zoot suit among musicians and in popular culture, see Susan Marie Green's thorough research in "Zoot Suiters: Past and Present" (Ph.D. diss., University of Minnesota, 1997).

12. Gena Caponi-Tabery, *Jump for Joy: Jazz, Basketball, and Black Culture in 1930s America* (Amherst: University of Massachusetts Press, 2008), 175–86; RJ Smith, *The Great Black Way: L.A. in the 1940s and the Lost African American Renaissance* (New York: Public Affairs, 2006), 33–35; Michael Denning, *The Cultural Front: The Laboring of American Culture in the Twentieth Century* (London: Verso, 1998), 309–19. On Pot, Pan, and Skillet's tour, see *Afro*, March 17, 1942, 10; *Down Beat*, March 15, 1942, 12; April 1, 1942, p. 4; Rhumboogie ad, *Southeast Economist* [Chicago], October 8, 1942, 6.

13. Ray Gilbert and Bob O'Brien, "A Zoot Suit (for My Sunday Gal)," Greene-Revel, Inc., 1941. "Record Briefs," *WP*, March 1, 1942, L3. On the similarity between "Made to Order" and "A Zoot Suit," see Richard Bambach and Sjef Hoefsmit postings, Duke Ellington Music Society, International DEMS Bulletin, 14/1, August–November 2002, http://www.depanorama.net/dems/02dems2b.htm (accessed August 16, 2010).

14. Henry McLemore, The Lighter Side, *LAT*, January 29, 1942, 6; February 6, 1942, 10.

15. Walter Davenport, "Swing It, Swing Shift!" *Colliers* 110 (August 22, 1942): 24; "Drape Shape," *Newsweek* 20 (September 7, 1942): 48–49.

16. "'Zoot Suit' Models Rouse Ire of WPB," *NYT*, September 4, 1942, 26. "Zoot Suits of Any Material Ruled Out by WPB as Waste," *WP*, September 12, 1942, 3.

17. "Zoot Suits of Any Material Ruled Out by WPB"; Joe Shephard, "AFRO Reporter Hepped on Cats' Plans for Stashing," *Afro*, September 12, 1942, 11; "Zoot Suit, Juke Coat Face WPB Crackdown to End Waste of Cloth," *WSJ*, September 4, 1942, 2. See also Helene Champlain, "One-Button-Roll Job Arrives to Mollify D.C. Zoot

Suiters," *WP*, October 12, 1942, B1; "Death Sentence Imposed on Zoot Suits by WPB," *WSJ*, October 28, 1942, 5; "A Killer Diller," *Courant*, October 29, 1944, E1; "How You Look in a Zoot Suit" photographs for *Philadelphia Inquirer*, September 5, 1942, in Zoot Suits, box 213, Fashions, Newsphotograph Collections, Temple University Urban Archives. "Zoot Suits," *Life*, September 21, 1942, 44–45.

18. "Dave Boone's Homespun News Slants," *Courant*, October 28, 1942, 5. Lichty, "Grin and Bear It," *LAT*, September 2, 1942, 22. "Speaking of Zoot Suits," *LAT*, September 16, 1942, A4; "Zoot Uniform!" *LAT*, May 24, 1943, A4. See also "Tojo's Zoot Suit," *LAT*, May 31, 1943, 13.

19. Carmen Lombardo and Pat Innisfree, "Since He Traded His Zoot Suit for a Uniform," Irving Berlin, Inc., 1942. *Spirit of '43*, Walt Disney Productions, 1943. The cartoon can be viewed on Internet Archive: http://www.archive.org/details/TheSpirit of43_56. Jerry Mason, "For Man of the Month We Nominate . . .," *LAT*, March 3, 1943, G6; Edwin Schalbert, "Drama," *LAT*, June 15, 1943, 23. On Disney's wartime films, see Steven Watts, *The Magic Kingdom: Walt Disney and the American Way of Life* (Boston: Houghton Mifflin, 1997), 228–42.

20. "Agency Is Planning to Put Stop to Waste of Fabric by Fad," *WP*, August 4, 1942, B1; "Hank the Prank," letter to the editor, *WP*, September 8, 1942, 14; "Zoot Suit Fad Not Bad, Says Gillette," *WP*, September 7, 1942, B1.

21. Hedda Hopper, "Looking at Hollywood," *Chi.Trib.*, June 25, 1942, 18; Hedda Hopper, "Hopes Soon to 'Bounce' Into Opera," *WP*, March 4, 1943, B8. See also Associated Press photograph, "Zoot gangsters are portrayed by actors in a movie," Los Angeles, March 4, 1943 (ID 430304066), AP Images, APimages.com.

22. *Swing Wedding*, dir. Hugh Harman, MGM, 1937. *Coal Black and de Sebben Dwarfs*, dir. Bob Clampett, Leon Schlesinger Studios/Warner Bros., 1943. The cartoon is available on Internet Archive, http://www.archive.org/details/CoalBlackAndDeSebben Dwarfs1943. See the interesting discussion by Terry Lindvall and Ben Fraser, "Darker Shades of Animation: African-American Images in the Warner Bros. Cartoon," in *Reading the Rabbit: Explorations in Warner Bros. Animation*, ed. Kevin S. Sandler (New Brunswick, N.J.: Rutgers University Press, 1998), 121–36.

23. *Star Spangled Rhythm*, dir. George Marshall, Paramount Productions, 1942; *Cabin in the Sky*, dir. Vincent Minnelli, MGM, 1943. McManus quoted in Billy Rowe, "Says Hollywood Made a Promise It Hasn't Kept," *Courier*, March 6, 1943, 21. Charlotte Charity, "Billy Rowe Told Film Producers Willing to Help," *Courier*, April 3, 1943, 20. See also Jack Saunders, "I Love a Parade," *Phila.Trib.*, May 22, 1943, 11.

24. *A Zoot Suit with a Reet Pleat*, dir. Josef Berne, RCM Productions, 1942. On Soundies, see Maurice Terenzio et al., *The Soundies Distribution Corporation of America: A History and Filmography of their "Jukebox" Musical Films of the 1940s* (Jefferson, N.C.: McFarland, 1991).

25. Delta Rhythm Boys, *Jack, You're Playing the Game*, dir. William Forest Crouch, Soundies, 1941; see http://www.youtube.com/watch?v=v34n_6TrfsM. I am

grateful to Susan Delson for referring me to this and other Soundies featuring zoot suiters.

26. *Stormy Weather*, dir. Andrew L. Stone, Twentieth Century Fox Film Corporation, 1943.

27. "Zoot Suit (For My Sunday Gal)," sheet music in author's possession. Eric Lott, *Love and Theft: Blackface Minstrelsy and the American Working Class* (New York: Oxford University Press, 1993).

28. *Ghost Catchers*, dir. Edward F. Cline, Universal Pictures, 1944; for the swing exorcism, see: http://www.youtube.com/watch?v=l6CrXrj01GA. *Red Hot Riding Hood*, dir. Tex Avery, MGM, 1943; *Swing Shift Cinderella*, dir. Tex Avery, MGM, 1945; *The Zoot Cat*, dir. Joseph Barbera and William Hanna, MGM, 1944. On the reaction of the NAACP to such films, see Thomas Cripps, *Making Movies Black: The Hollywood Message Movie from WWII to the Civil Rights Era* (New York: Oxford University Press, 1993), 196–97.

29. On the zoot fad, see "Ringside Table with Mary Harris," *WP*, October 9, 1942, B12; John Chapman, "Miss Cornell Brilliant in 'Lovers and Friends,'" *Chi.Trib.*, December 5, 1943, D4; "Boys Club Holds Egg-Decorating Contest," *WP*, April 25, 1943, M8. On the zoot-suit photograph, see "Wallace Disagrees with Award in News Photographic Exhibit," *WP*, June 25, 1943, 11. On the Harry James concertgoers, see Bosley Crowther, "Hounds of Spring," *NYT*, May 2, 1943, X3; Roy Gibbons, "Hepcats Purr as Jive Jams Times Square," *Chi.Trib.*, April 27, 1943, 16.

30. Malvina Lindsay, "American Tradition," *WP*, November 26, 1942, B2. Lucy Greenbaum, "Fighters with a Boogie Beat," *NYT*, December 27, 1942, SM10. Andrew Sisters, "Boogie Woogie Bugle Boy," music and lyrics by Don Ray and Hughie Prince, Decca, 1941. See also Emily C. Davis, "To Swing Off to War," *Science News Letter*, July 15, 1939, 42–43.

31. Robert David Abrahams, "Zoot-Suit Kid," *Saturday Evening Post* 215 (April 24, 1943): 90.

32. Sol Holt, "Students in War Effort," letter to the editor, *NYT*, January 5, 1943, 18. Maureen Daly, "Easy Does It!" *Chi.Trib.*, October 25, 1942, E7. "And the Home of the Brave, Extension of Remarks of Hon. F. Edward Hebert," June 15, 1943, Appendix to the Congressional Record, 89 Cong. Rec A 3000–1, 1943, HeinOnline.

33. Sterling A. Brown, "Georgia Sketches," *Phylon* 5 (1945): 225–31. See also Donald Jones, "Sterling Brown Defends Wearers of 'Zoot Suits'" *Afro*, October 31, 1942, 6.

34. For cartoons, see Gustav Lundberg, *This Week Magazine*, November 1, 1942, reproduced in Frank Walton, *Thread of Victory* (New York: Fairchild Publications, 1945), 132; E. Simms Campbell, "Sketches," *Courier*, October 10, 1942, 13. "Negro Soldiers Deportment Shown as 'Tops,'" *NYAN*, November 21, 1942, 13; "Sergeant's Uniform Frowned on by Army," *Courant*, November 24, 1942, 4; "Army & Navy—Material: Uniforms Will be Worn So," *Time*, December 7, 1942, http://www.time.com/

time/magazine/article/0,9171,774019,00.html); "Featuring 'G.I.' Zoot Suit?" *NYAN*, July 10, 1943, 16.

35. "With America's Fighters," *Chi.Trib.*, December 5, 1943, NW1; "Southwest Side Soldiers in Odd Jobs in England," *Chi.Trib.*, December 19, 1943, SW4. For more information on the WASPs, see "Fly Girls," *American Experience*, PBS/WGBH, 1991, and website: http://www.pbs.org/wgbh/amex/flygirls/index.html, where the text of the song is available. "Two German Spies in Rome Trapped by Hep-Cat Talk," *NYT*, October 8, 1944, 26.

36. Jack Jacobs, "Yank Writes Home," letter to the editor, *WP*, December 16, 1942, 14; "Ringside Table with Mary Harris," *WP*, September 9, 1942, B9. John Ferrell, "Washington, D.C. Soldier inspecting a couple of 'zoot suits' at the Uline Arena during Woody Herman's Orchestra engagement there," June 1942, Library of Congress, Prints and Photographs Division, FSA-OWI Photographs [LC-USF34–011543-D DLC].

37. Al Capp, *Li'l Abner*, United Features Syndicate, 1943; the "Zoot-Suit Yokum" story ran in the *Los Angeles Times* from April 11, 1943, to May 23, 1943. It is reprinted in Mauricio Mazón, *The Zoot-Suit Riots: The Psychology of Symbolic Annihilation* (Austin: University of Texas Press, 1984), 39–51. Cf. Ole Harrington cartoon, *People's Voice*, March 21, 1942, 6.

38. Mazón, *The Zoot-Suit Riots*, 31–53, quotations on 33, 53.

39. "Victim Found Dying," *Phila.Trib.*, October 10, 1942, 1; "Youth, 16, Draped in Zoot Suit, Held for Attack on Mt. Vernon Girl, After Dance," *NYAN*, November 28, 1942, 5; "Negro Cook Charged with Train Murder," *WP*, February 2, 1943, 11. On wartime gang violence and crime, see Eric C. Schneider, *Vampires, Dragons, and Egyptian Kings: Youth Gangs in Postwar New York* (Princeton, N.J.: Princeton University Press, 1999), 51–77.

40. "Jitterbug Handicapped by Zoot Suit Loss," *WP*, March 19, 1943, 5. "Zoot Pants (Off) Cost Snoozing Owner $10 Fine," *Chi.Trib.*, June 9, 1943, 14. "City News in Brief," *WP*, April 17, 1943, 8; "Bandits in Zoot Suits Get $50," *Chi.Trib.*, November 23, 1942, 9. "Window Breaker Makes Off with Zoot Trousers," *WP*, September 7, 1942, B1; "Horrors! They'll Even Steal Them," *WP*, September 12, 1942, B1.

41. "'Show Off' Killers Whimper in Court," *NYT*, October 4, 1942, 47; "'Zoot Suit' Killer was Peacemaker," *NYT*, November 18, 1942, 27; "Zoot-Suit Killers Get 50-Year Terms," *NYT*, December 4, 1942, 27. "Death Penalty to Be Asked for Jitterbug Killers of Teacher," *LAT*, October 4, 1942, 12.

Chapter 4. From Rags to Riot

1. "Los Angeles Zoot War Called 'Near Anarchy,'" *WP*, June 11, 1943, 1. Eduardo Obregón Pagán presents an excellent reconstruction of the riot in *Murder at the Sleepy Lagoon: Zoot Suits, Race, and Riot in Wartime L.A.* (Chapel Hill: University of North Carolina Press, 2003). See also Luis Alvarez, *The Power of the Zoot: Youth Culture and Resistance During World War II* (Berkeley: University of California Press, 2008).

2. Carey McWilliams, *North from Mexico: The Spanish-Speaking People of the United States*. (Philadelphia: J. B. Lippincott, 1949), 241–42; Studs Terkel, *"The Good War": An Oral History of World War Two* (New York: New Press, 1984), 146. On Los Angeles in the World War II years, see Kevin Starr, *Embattled Dreams: California in War and Peace, 1940–1950* (New York: Oxford University Press, 2003); Kevin Allen Leonard, *The Battle for Los Angeles: Racial Ideology and World War II* (Albuquerque: University of New Mexico Press, 2006). See also Maggie Rivas-Rodriguez, ed. *Mexican Americans and World War II* (Austin: University of Texas Press, 2005); Scott Kurashigo, *The Shifting Grounds of Race: Black and Japanese Americans in the Making of Multiethnic Los Angeles* (Princeton, N.J.: Princeton University Press, 2007); U.S. Army Western Defense Command and Fourth Army, *Japanese Evacuation from the West Coast, 1942, Final Report* (Washington, D.C.: Government Printing Office, 1943), 79.

3. George J. Sánchez, *Becoming Mexican American: Ethnicity, Culture, and Identity in Chicano Los Angeles, 1900–1945* (New York: Oxford University Press, 1993); Pagán, *Murder at the Sleepy Lagoon*; Luis Alvarez, *The Power of the Zoot*; David G. Gutiérrez, *Walls and Mirrors: Mexican Americans, Mexican Immigrants and the Politics of Ethnicity* (Berkeley: University of California Press, 1995); Michael Nevin Willard, "Urbanization as Culture: Youth and Race in Postwar Los Angeles" (Ph.D. diss., University of Minnesota, 2001), 88–99.

4. Edward J. Escobar, *Race, Police, and the Making of a Political Identity: Mexican Americans and the Los Angeles Police Department, 1900–1945* (Berkeley: University of California Press, 1999). For the definitive reconstruction of these events, see Pagán, *Murder at the Sleepy Lagoon.*

5. "Navy-Battered Zoot Suiters Jailed by Police," *Examiner*, June 7, 1943, pt. 2, 1; "Zoot Suit War Grows: Army and Navy Act," *Chi.Trib.*, June 9, 1943, 1; Pagán, *Murder at the Sleepy Lagoon,* 160. On shore leaves, see Records of the Commandant's Office, Eleventh Naval District, General Correspondence, 1924–1955, folder P8–5 (Zoot Suit Gang, 1943), RG 181, Records of Shore Establishments and Naval Districts, National Archives and Records Administration Pacific Region, Laguna Niguel.

6. Walter Davenport, "Swing It, Swing Shift!" *Colliers* 110 (August 22, 1942): 24. Chester B. Himes, *If He Hollers Let Him Go* (Thunder's Mouth Press/Persea Books, 1986); for an analysis, see Lynn M. Itagaki, "Transgressing Race and Community in Chester Himes's 'If He Hollers Let Him Go,'" *African American Review* 37 (Spring 2003): 65–80, JSTOR.

7. Guy Nunn to [Stephen] Dimitroff, April 11, 1967, Series 4, box 2, folder 46, Ron Lopez Sleepy Lagoon Research Papers, Collection 6, Chicano Studies Research Center, University of California Los Angeles. On the problem of the second generation, see Sánchez, *Becoming Mexican American*; Gutiérrez, *Walls and Mirrors*. On Anglo perceptions, see Phoebe Kropp, *California Vieja: Culture and Memory in a Modern American Place* (Berkeley: University of California Press, 2006).

8. Joint Fact-Finding Committee on Un-American Activities in California, " 'Zoot-Suit' Riots in Southern California," *Report* (Assembly of the State of California, Excerpts from Assembly Journal of April 16, 1945), 160–63, quotations on 161,

163. See also "Trial of Mexican Youths Used as Axis Propaganda," *LAT*, November 24, 1942, 1.

9. Citizens' Committee for the Defense of Mexican American Youth, *The Sleepy Lagoon Case* (Los Angeles: Citizens Committee, 1942), 21; "Hair Style Used in Identification of Hoodlums, Suspects Must Not Change Haircut, Judge Rules," *Examiner*, October 27, 1942, reprinted in "Zoot Suit Riots," *American Experience*, PBS/WGBH, website, http://www.pbs.org/wgbh/amex/zoot/eng_sfeature/sf_press_text_02.html; Pagán, *Murder at the Sleepy Lagoon*, 96–97.

10. Nick Williams quoted in William Overend, "The '43 Zoot Suit Riots Re-Examined," *LAT*, May 9, 1978, G6. McWilliams, *North from Mexico*, 237–78; Grand Jury (Los Angeles County), "Report of Special Committee on Problems of Mexican Youth of the 1942 Grand Jury of Los Angeles County" (December 22, 1942), 43, Sleepy Lagoon Defense Committee Records, (Collection 107), Special Collections, Charles E. Young Research Library, UCLA; "Trial of Mexican Youths Used as Axis Propaganda," *LAT*, November 24, 1942, 1. Ralph H. Turner and Samuel J. Surace, "Zoot-Suiters and Mexicans: Symbols in Crowd Behavior," *AJS* 62 (July 1956): 14–20, offers a content analysis of the *Los Angeles Times*, its increasingly negative references to Mexicans, and the linkage of criminality and the zoot suit.

11. For a contemporaneous discussion, see Carey McWilliams, "The Zoot-Suit Riots," *New Republic*, June 21, 1943, 818–20.

12. Pagán, *Murder at the Sleepy Lagoon*, 39.

13. Youth Committee for the Defense of Mexican American Youth to Vice-President Henry A. Wallace, n.d., Series 1, box 1, folder 60, Ron Lopez Papers. Alfred Barela to Judge Arthur Guerin, May 21, 1943, quoted in Sánchez, *Becoming Mexican American*, 235. Rudy Sanchez and the young man at the Waxman meeting are quoted in Pagán, *Murder at the Sleepy Lagoon*, 171, 179; Pagán places them in the context of the riot, 167–87; Al S. Waxman, "Column Left," *Eastside Journal*, June 9, 1943, 1. Allison Varzally is the only historian to identify Sanchez as a sailor, in *Making a Non-White America: Californians Coloring Outside Ethnic Lines, 1925–1955* (Berkeley: University of California Press, 2008), 163–64. See also statement by Dan G. Acosta discussed in Escobar, *Race, Police, and the Making of a Political Identity*, 237–38.

14. "Dorsey High Principal Wants No 'Zoot Suits,'" *Eagle*, June 3, 1943, 1.

15. Kevin Allen Leonard, *The Battle for Los Angeles*, 173–74; Allison Varzally, *Making a Non-White America*, 164. "Dorsey High Principal Wants No 'Zoot Suits,'"; Alice Greenfield, "Trip to Folsom and San Quentin, Nov. 7–13, 1943," November 15, 1943, box 3, folder 3, Sleepy Lagoon Defense Committee Records.

16. Lee Shippey, "Lee Side o'L.A.," *LAT*, April 2, 1942, A4.

17. Robert A. Hill, comp. and ed., *The FBI's RACON: Racial Conditions in the United States During World War II* (Boston: Northeastern University Press, 1995), 378. Captain J. F. Reed testimony, "'Zoot-Suit' Riots in Southern California," *Joint Fact-Finding Committee on Un-American Activities in California Report*, 163. Mrs. Fred

Holley to Ed Gossett, June 4, 1943; Ed Gossett to Hon. Frank Knox, June 7, 1943; D. W. Bagley to Honorable Ed Gossett, July 2, 1943, Records of the Commandant's Office, Eleventh Naval District, folder P8–5 (Zoot Suit Gang, 1943). See also Constance Clotfelter, letter to the editor, *Time*, July 12, 1943, http://www.time.com/time/magazine/article/0,9171,766802-2,00.html. On the role of rumor on the homefront, see Marilynn S. Johnson, "Gender, Race, and Rumours: Re-examining the 1943 Race Riots," *Gender and History* 10 (August 1998): 252–77; the classic study is Howard Odum, *Race and Rumors of Race: The American South in the Early Forties* (1943; Baltimore: Johns Hopkins University Press, 1997).

18. Lawrence E. Davies, "Army Takes a Hand in Zoot Suit Frays," *NYT*, June 12, 1943, 28. On "de-bagging," see "Zoot Suit Charivari," Line O'Type or Two, *Chi.Trib.*, June 14, 1943, 12. On the practice of stripping clothing, see, e.g., Paul A. Gilje, "The Baltimore Riots of 1812 and the Breakdown of the Anglo-American Mob Tradition," *Journal of Social History* 13 (Summer 1980): 555; Andy Wood, "Fear, Hatred, and the Hidden Injuries of Class in Early Modern England," *Journal of Social History* 39 (2006): 803–26. On the psychological conflict between servicemen and zoot suiters, see Mauricio Mazón, *The Zoot-Suit Riots: The Psychology of Symbolic Annihilation* (Austin: University of Texas Press, 1984). For an analysis of military rituals, see Carol Burke, *Camp All-American, Hanoi Jane, and the High-and-Tight: Gender, Folklore, and Changing Military Culture* (Boston: Beacon Press, 2004).

19. Rudy Leyvas quoted in Overend, "The '43 Zoot Suit Riots Revisited," G6. "Magistrate 'Unfrocks' Pair of Zoot-Suiters," *LAT*, March 7, 1943, A1. Rita Michaels, "On January 13, 1943 the Axis radio beamed . . .," April 30, 1943, 4, publicity fragment, box 1, folder 12, reel 1, Sleepy Lagoon Defense Committee Records; Carey McWilliams quoted in Joint Fact-Finding Committee on Un-American Activities in California, *Report to California Legislature* (Senate, California Legislature, 57th session, 1943), 203. On degrees of violence, see also Pagán, *Murder at the Sleepy Lagoon*, 185.

20. John Robert Badger, "Inside Story of Coast Zoot Suit Riots Told by Defender Reporter," *Defender*, June 19, 1943, 20; "Los Angeles Council Bans Zoot-Suits to Curb Rioting," *PM*, June 10, 1943, 3; "Loses Pants in 'Zoot War,'" *NYAN*, June 26, 1943, 3.

21. "'Zoot Suit' Fracas Hits San Diego," *Defender*, June 19, 1943, 20.

22. Peter Furst, "Press Blamed for Spread of Zoot Suit Riots," *PM*, June 10, 1943, clipping in General Office Files, Part 7, Anti-lynching campaign, 1916–1950, Series A, Anti-lynching investigative files, 1912–1953, reel 29, Papers of the NAACP (Frederick, Md.: University Publications of America, 1987). "Zoot Suiters Learn Lesson in Fights with Servicemen," *LAT*, June 7, 1943, A1. Lawrence Lamar, "'Zoot Wars' Based on Racial Hatreds," *NYAN*, June 17, 1943, 1. Harry Levette, "Negroes Involved as 'Zoot Suit' Rioting Grips Los Angeles, Calif.," *ADW*, June 13, 1943, 1.

23. Edward C. McDonagh, "Status Levels of Mexicans," *Sociology and Social Research* 33 (July–August 1949): 452.

24. Lawrence E. Davies, "Los Angeles Group Insists Riot Halt," *NYT*, June 13, 1943, 30; "Zoot-Suit Fighting Spreads on Coast," *NYT*, June 10, 1943, 23. "Screwball Serenade: Council Forbids Zoot Suits!" *Eagle*, June 10, 1943, 1; "Ban on Freak Suits Studied by Councilmen," *LAT*, June 10, 1943, A.

25. Thomas L. Griffith, Jr. to Walter White, June 9, 1943, 2, General Office Files, Part 7, Series A, reel 29, NAACP Papers. McWilliams, *North from Mexico*, 250, estimated that not more than one-half of the victims wore zoot suits. "Portent of Storm," *Christian Century* 60 (June 23, 1943): 735.

26. Lawrence E. Davies, "Zoot Suits Become Issue on Coast," *NYT*, June 13, 1943, E10; "Who Is Really Stirring Up the Racial Prejudice?" *LAT*, June 15, 1943, A4.

27. Davies, "Zoot Suits Become Issue"; see also "Press Blamed for Spread of Zoot Suit Riots," *PM*, June 10, 1943. Timothy G. Turner, "Significance of Zoot-Suit Gangsters," *LAT*, January 14, 1943, A4; Timothy Turner, "Zoot Suits Still Parade Here Despite O.P.A. Ban," *LAT*, March 22, 1943, A8. "Flags on Maps Outline Web of 100 Gangs," *Examiner*, June 9, 1943, 9. Leonard, *Battle for Los Angeles*, 168–74.

28. "Unconditional Surrender," *LAT*, June 8, 1943, 1; for military language, see "Navy-Battered Zoot Suiters Jailed by Police," *Examiner*, June 7, 1943, pt. 2, 1. *Herald Express* quoted in Beatrice Griffith, *American Me* (Boston: Houghton Mifflin, 1948), 26. "Zoot Suiters Learn Lesson in Fights with Servicemen," *LAT*, June 7, 1943, A11. The comic imagery may be seen in "Girl Injured in Attack by Cholita Trio," *Examiner*, June 11, 1943, 12; "Downtown Crowds Storm Streets in Zoot Suiter Hunt," *Examiner*, June 8, 1943, 1. For photographs of Rodriguez, see "Navy-Battered Zoot Suiters Jailed by Police."

29. "Telephone conversation between Admiral Bagley and Captain Heim at 1035, June 11, 1943," 2, Records of the Commandant's Office, Eleventh Naval District, folder P8–5 (Zoot Suit Gang, 1943), RG 181.

30. Lawrence E. Davies, "Seek Basic Causes of Zoot Suit Fray," *NYT*, June 11, 1943, 21; Carey McWilliams, "The Zoot-Suit Riots," 819. "Camera Sees Wild Riot Nite," *Eagle*, June 10, 1943, 3A; Furst, "Press Blamed for Spread of Zoot Suit Riots."

31. "Mexican-American Girls Meet in Protest," *Eastside Journal*, June 16, 1943, 5; McWilliams, *North from Mexico*, 257–58; Beatrice Griffith, *American Me*, 321–22. For a superb discussion, see Catherine S. Ramírez, *The Woman in the Zoot Suit: Gender, Nationalism, and the Cultural Politics of Memory* (Durham, N.C.: Duke University Press, 2009), 43–46.

32. Marcia Winn, "Front Views and Profiles: Angels at Bay," *Chi.Trib.*, June 17, 1943, 22.

33. Charles C. Dail, Councilman, San Diego, to Rear Admiral David W. Bagley, June 10, 1943, Records of the Commandant's Office, Eleventh Naval District, folder P8–5 (Zoot Suit Gang, 1943), RG 181; Mozell C. Hill, "Basic Racial Attitudes Toward Whites in the Oklahoma All-Negro Community," *AJS*, 49 (May 1944): 522.

34. McWilliams, *North from Mexico*, 250; "Ban on Freak Suits Studied by Councilmen"; Lalo Guerrero and Sherilyn Meece Metes, *Lalo: My Life and Music* (Tucson: University of Arizona Press, 2002), 98. Griffith, *American Me,* 26–27.

35. "A Challenge," *Mexican Voice*, 1943, 2 (folder 37); Paul Coronel, "The Pachuco Problem," *Mexican Voice*, 1943, 3 (folder 52), in series 1, Ron Lopez Papers. "Mother Tears Up Zoot Suit of Boy Wounded in Clash," *LAT*, June 11, 1943, A; "Brass Knuckles Found on Woman 'Zoot Suiter,'" *LAT*, June 10, 1943, A. For an insightful discussion of the political ramifications of the riot, see Escobar, *Race, Police, and the Making of a Political Identity*; on the role of gender, see Ramírez, *The Woman in the Zoot Suit.*

36. "State Group Probes Zoot Suit Rioting," *Hollywood Citizen News*, June 14, 1943. "Zoot-Suiters Call Truce, Disorders Ebb," *WP*, June 13, 1943, M12. "The Zoot-Suiters Give Their Blood," *PM*, July 7, 1943. "Mexico Seeks Damage Grants in Zoot Rioting," *Chi.Trib.*, June 16, 1943, 19.

37. "Zoot Suiters Call Truce"; "State Group Probes Zoot Suit Rioting."

38. "Krupa Musicians Beaten in Subway," *WP*, June 11, 1943, 12. See also *Philadelphia Evening Bulletin* clippings: "Sailors Beat Two in Krupa Band," June 10, 1943; "4 Are Beaten Here over Zoot Suits," June 12, 1943; "Zoot Suit Rioting Flares in Detroit," June 12, 1943, all in "Zoot Suit" file, George D. McDowell Philadelphia Evening Bulletin News Clipping Collection, Urban Archives, Temple University Library. "Sailors Attack Richmond Zooter," *Examiner*, June 11, 1943, 12. "Baltimore Acts to Break Up Zoot Gang," *Chi.Trib.*, June 10, 1943, 9.

Chapter 5. Reading the Riddle

1. "Report on Coast Riots," *NYT,* June 28, 1943, 23; "Damon Runyon Says Axis Elements May Back Zoot Suit War," *Miami Herald*, June 13, 1943. "'Zoot-Suit' Riots in Southern California," Joint Fact-Finding Committee on Un-American Activities in California, *Report* (Assembly of the State of California, April 16, 1945), 160. For the view that the riot was fomented by a racist "Pacific First" movement, see Marion Bachrach, "The Truth About Los Angeles," *New Masses*, July 6, 1943, 12–13.

2. Carey McWilliams, *North from Mexico: The Spanish-Speaking People of the United States* (Philadelphia: J. B. Lippincott Co., 1949), 250; "Watts Pastor Blames Riots on Fifth Column," *LAT,* June 11, 1943, A; "Remarks of Hon. John E. Rankin of Mississippi in the House of Representatives, Tuesday, June 15, 1943," Appendix to the Congressional Record, 89 Cong. Rec. (1943), A3083.

3. "Zoot Suit," *WP*, June 11, 1943, 10; "Reading the Riddle," A Line O' Type or Two, *Chi.Trib.*, June 24, 1943, 16; Fritz Redl, "Zoot Suits: An Interpretation," *Survey Midmonthly* 76 (October 1943): 259; S. I. Hayakawa, "Second Thoughts," *Defender*, June 19, 1943, 15. See also H. I. Phillips, "The Once Over," *WP*, June 17, 1943, 16.

4. "Funny Bone," *WP*, August 13, 1943, 10; "Jitters and Zooters," A Line O' Type or Two, *Chi.Trib.*, June 16, 1943, 18; Joseph D. Bibb, "Study in Conduct," *Courier*, July 10, 1943, 13. On Alexander, see "Girl Injured in Attack by Cholita Trio," *Examiner*, June 11, 1943, 12. On Fisk researchers, "Ends Study of Racial Factors in Pittsburgh," *Courier*, March 30, 1946, 29. See also "Clothes and the Gang," A Line O' Type or Two, *Chi.Trib.*, July 10, 1943, 1; "Zoot Suits and Service Stripes: Race Tensions Behind the Riot," *Newsweek*, June 21, 1943, 38.

5. See Ellen Herman, *Romance of American Psychology: Political Culture in the Age of Experts* (Berkeley: University of California Press, 1995); Regna Darnell, *Invisible Genealogies: A History of American Anthropology* (Lincoln: University of Nebraska Press, 2001).

6. "'Zoot-Suit' Riots in Southern California," 164. See Edward J. Escobar, *Race, Police, and the Making of a Political Identity: Mexican Americans and the Los Angeles Police Department, 1900–1945* (Berkeley: University of California Press, 1999); Kevin Allen Leonard, *The Battle for Los Angeles: Racial Ideology and World War II* (Albuquerque: University of New Mexico Press, 2006); Eduardo Obregón Pagán, *Murder at the Sleepy Lagoon: Zoot Suits, Race, and Riot in Wartime LA* (Chapel Hill: University of North Carolina Press, 2003).

7. Edward Duran Ayres, Foreign Relations Bureau, "Statistics" (1942), Sleepy Lagoon Defense Committee Records, Department of Special Collections, Charles E. Young Research Library, UCLA; the text is reprinted at http://content.cdlib.org/ark:/13030/hb6m3nb79m/. Lawrence E. Davies, "Zoot Suits Become Issue on Coast," *NYT*, June 13, 1943, E10. On Duran's statement, see Leonard, *Battle for Los Angeles*, 91–93.

8. "Zoot Suit War Grows: Army and Navy Act," *Chi.Trib.*, June 9, 1943, 1. Julian Hartt, "Zoot-Suiters Again on Prowl as Navy Holds Back Sailors," *WP*, June 9, 1943, 1. Cf. Edward Alsworth Ross, "The Present Problems of Social Psychology," *AJS* 10 (1905): 456–72.

9. "Findings and Recommendation of the Grand Jury of Los Angeles for 1943," Series 1, box 1, folder 64, Ron Lopez Sleepy Lagoon Research Papers (Collection 6), Chicano Studies Research Center, UCLA. Kenny quoted in Lawrence E. Davies, "Seek Basic Causes of Zoot Suit Fray," *NYT*, June 11, 1943, 21. "Full Detailed Text of Kenny Body's Report," *Eagle*, June 17, 1943, 5A; "Kinloch's Corner," *Eagle*, June 17, 1943, 1B. On the Sleepy Lagoon defendants, see "The Neutral Corner," *The News* [San Quentin, California], November 25, 1943, rpt. Sleepy Lagoon Defense Committee, in General Office Files, Part 7, Anti-lynching campaign, 1916–1950, Series A, Anti-lynching Investigative Files, 1912–1953, reel 29, Papers of the NAACP (Frederick, Md.: University Publications of America, 1987); Sleepy Lagoon Defense Committee, *The Sleepy Lagoon Case* (Los Angeles, 1943).

10. "Portent of Storm," *Christian Century*, June 23, 1943, 735. Chester B. Himes, "Zoot Riots Are Race Riots," *Crisis* 50 (July 1943): 200. "The Zoot Suit Riots," *Chi. Trib.*, June 10, 1943, 14. "Mrs. Roosevelt Links Zoot War to Race Unrest," *Chi.Trib.*, June 17, 1943, 16; cf. "Mrs. FDR's Version of 'Zoot' Trouble," *NYAN*, June 26, 1943,

10. See also Jacob I. Zeitlin, "What Makes Race Riots Possible?" *New Republic* 109 (October 18, 1943): 522.

11. Myrdal quoted in Lee D. Baker, *From Savage to Negro: Anthropology and the Construction of Race* (Berkeley: University of California Press, 1998), 181. See also Daryl Michael Scott, *Contempt and Pity: Social Policy and the Image of the Damaged Black Psyche, 1880–1996* (Chapel Hill: University of North Carolina Pres, 1997); Marlon B. Ross, *Manning the Race: Reforming Black Men in the Jim Crow Era* (New York: New York University Press, 2004), 145–91. Leonard, in *Battle for Los Angeles*, argues that the zoot suit riot ultimately turned many away from a belief in the biological basis of race toward anthropological perspectives.

12. Robert Sutherland, *Color, Class, and Personality* (Washington, D.C.: American Council on Education, 1942), 38. W. Lloyd Warner, et al., *Color and Human Nature: Negro Personality Development in a Northern City* (Washington, D.C.: American Council on Education, 1941); James H. S. Bossard and Eleanor S. Boll, eds., *Adolescents in Wartime, Annals of the American Academy of Political and Social Science*, vol. 236 (Philadelphia, 1944). James B. McKee, *Sociology and the Race Problem: The Failure of a Perspective* (Champaign: University of Illinois Press, 1993), chap. 5; James B. Gilbert, *A Cycle of Outrage: America's Reaction to the Juvenile Delinquent in the 1950s* (New York: Oxford University Press, 1986), chap. 2.

13. Agnes E. Meyer, "Zoot-Suiters—A New Youth Movement," *WP*, June 13, 1943, B1; "Zoot-Suit Epidemic," *Science News Letter*, June 19, 1943, 388. Harold L. Rausch, "Fritz Redl (1902–1988)," *American Psychologist* 47 (September 1992): 1143. "'Zoot' Danger Termed Grave," *Charleston Daily Mail*, June 17, 1943, 4, Access Newspaper Archive, access.newspaperarchive.com. "Doctors Analyze Zoot Suiters," *Philadelphia Evening Bulletin*, June 28, 1943, N.E., "Zoot Suit" file, George D. McDowell Philadelphia Evening Bulletin News Clipping Collection, Urban Archives, Temple University Library.

14. Fritz Redl, "Zoot Suits: An Interpretation," *Survey Midmonthly* 76 (October 1943): 259–62.

15. On Catton, see "Tells What Ails Minds of Zooters," *ADW*, June 13, 1943, 1. Ralph Banay, "A Psychiatrist Looks at the Zoot Suit," *Probation* 22 (February 1944): 81–85, quotations on 84, 85. Bert Kemmerer, "Delinquent Parents Blamed for Mistakes of Teen-Agers," *WP*, July 20, 1943, 1; "Fresno Police Press Drive to Halt Crimes," *Chi.Trib.*, September 20, 1945, 15.

16. Ernest R. Mowrer, "War and Family Solidarity and Stability," *Annals of the American Academy of Political and Social Science* 229 (September 1943): 101. Emory S. Bogardus, "Gangs of Mexican-American Youth," *Sociology and Social Research* 28 (September–October 1943): 55–66, quotation on 66.

17. Kenneth B. Clark and James Barker, "The Zoot Effect in Personality: A Race Riot Participant," *Journal of Abnormal and Social Psychology* 40 (1945): 143–48, quotations on 147, 143, 144. Eric Lott calls this article an "early attempt to read a subculture," in "Double V, Double-Time: Bebop's Politics of Style," *Callaloo* 36 (Summer

1988): 597–98. For a discussion of Clark's concept of "zoot personality," see Damon Freeman, "Kenneth B. Clark and the Problem of Power," *Problems of Prejudice* 42 (September 2008): 413–37, especially 417–19 (accessed April 16, 2009); also Scott, *Contempt and Pity.*

18. Clark and Barker, "Zoot Effect," 148.

19. Clark and Barker, "Zoot Effect," 146, 143.

20. Horace R. Cayton, "Exhibitionism," *Courier*, June 26, 1943, 13. Cayton later emphasized the importance of sex as a factor leading to the riot, specifically the interest of white sailors in Mexican women; see "Riot Causes," *Courier*, September 25, 1943, 13. Cayton's path-breaking study, co-authored with St. Clair Drake, is *Black Metropolis: A Study of Negro Life in a Northern City* (1945; Chicago: University of Chicago Press, 1993).

21. Lawrence D. Reddick quoted in Albert Deutsch, "Zoot Suiters: Do Clothes Make the Criminal?" *PM*, June 14, 1943, 11. L. D. Reddick, "Foreword," *Journal of Educational Sociology* 17 (January 1944): 257–60, quotation on 260.

22. Samuel Willard Crompton, "Hayakawa, S. I.," American National Biography Online Feb. 2000 (http://www.anb.org/articles/07/07-00676.html; accessed August 8, 2009).

23. S. I. Hayakawa, "Second Thoughts," *Defender*, June 19, 1943, 15; June 26, 1943. Hayakawa reflected on these columns in S. I. Hayakawa and Margedant Peters Hayakawa, "From Semantics to the U.S. Senate," an oral history conducted in 1989 by Julie Gordon Shearer, Regional Oral History Office, Bancroft Library, University of California, Berkeley, 1994, 139–146 (http://content.cdlib.org/view?docId = hb5q2-nb40v&query = &brand = calisphere) .

24. Meyer, "Zoot-Suiters—A New Youth Movement," B1. Westbrook Pegler, "Fair Enough," *LAT,* May 25, 1943, A. Bill Gottlieb, "Don't Blame Swing Music for Sins of Modern Youth," *WP*, July 25, 1943, L1. On the "culture and personality" school, see George W. Stocking, ed., *Malinowski, Rivers, Benedict and Others: Essays on Culture and Personality* (Madison: University of Wisconsin Press, 1986); Joanne Meyerowitz, " 'How Common Culture Shapes the Separate Lives': Sexuality, Race, and Mid-Twentieth Century Social Constructionist Thought," *Journal of American History* 96 (March 2010): 1057–84.

25. Bill Gottlieb, "Swing Sessions," *WP*, July 4, 1943, L2. Lillian Gray, "Zoot-Suit Youth, or What Happened to Juan Garcia," *Childhood Education* 23 (October 1946): 68. Walter White to *New York Times,* June 11, 1943, NAACP General Office Files, Part 7, Series A, reel 29, NAACP Papers.

26. J. V. D. Carlyle, "The Psychological Implications of the Zoot Suit," *MAR* 11 (July 1943): 36.

27. (Pvt.) Kenneth King, letter to the editor, *Time*, July 12, 1943, 8. For Tellez's photograph, see "Zoot-Suit Fighting Spreads on Coast," *NYT*, June 10, 1943, 23. See also "Perplexed," letter to the editor, *WP*, June 25, 1943, 8.

28. Theresa H. Russell, letter to the editor, *WP*, June 17, 1943, 16; Malvina Lindzay, "In Defense of 'Lowbrows,' " *WP*, Sept 16, 1943, B4; William C. Lee, letter to the

editor, *WP*, July 14, 1943, 12; Joseph Bougere, "Zoot Suits and Prejudice," letter to the editor, *Chi.Trib.*, June 16, 1943, 18.

29. Harold Gemmell and William N. Rosenberger, letter to the editor, *Newsweek*, September 6, 1943, 4. William D. Eastlake, letter to the editor, *Time*, July 5, 1943 (http://www.time.com/time/magazine/article/0,9171,802763,00.html). See also Fred J. Young, "Zoot Suit Riots," letter to the editor, *Courant*, June 25, 1943, 12.

30. J. A. Rogers, "Rogers Says," *Courier*, June 26, 1943, 7; "Warning to Zoot Suiters," *Defender*, June 19, 1943, 11; Marjorie McKenzie, "Pursuit of Democracy," *Courier*, June 10, 1944, 6; Langston Hughes, "Here to Yonder," *Defender*, June 19, 1943, 14. See also Joseph D. Bibb, "Rainbows," *Courier*, June 19, 1943, 13; Bibb, "Hanging Out," *Courier*, April 10, 1943, 13; Chester B. Hines, "Zoot Riots Are Race Riots."

31. Ed Peterson, "Interesting Comment on Zoot Suit Syle," *NYAN*, June 26, 1943, 10. Pvt. Clifton Searles, "Fighting for a Double Victory," *Defender*, July 3, 1943, 14; Frances M. Seeberg, "'I Want You to Write to Me': The Papers of Anna Eleanor Roosevelt," *Prologue*, Summer 1987, Franklin D. Roosevelt Presidential Library and Museum, http://docs.fdrlibrary.marist.edu/erprolog.html. V.V. to Walter White, July 15, 1943, General Office Files, Part 7, Series A, reel 29, NAACP Papers.

32. George I. Sánchez, "Pachucos in the Making," *Common Ground* 4 (Autumn 1943): 13–20, quotation on 20; Bogardus, "Gangs of Mexican-American Youth." This early sociological research includes Manuel Gamio, *Mexican Immigration to the United States: A Study of Human Migration and Adjustment* (Chicago: University of Chicago Press, 1930); for a discussion of Gamio and similar intellectuals, see George J. Sánchez, *Becoming Mexican American: Ethnicity, Culture and Identity in Chicano Los Angeles, 1900–1945* (New York: Oxford University Press, 1993), chap. 5.

33. Thomas J. McCarthy, "Report from Los Angeles," *Commonweal* (June 25, 1943): 243–44; Wallace Stegner and the Editors of *Look*, *One Nation* (Boston: Houghton Mifflin, 1945), 95–140, quotation on 119; *The World Today*, CBS Radio Network, June 15, 1943, June 16, 1943, MR-2624, MR-2625, Milo Ryan Phonoarchive Collection, RG 200 MR, Motion Picture, Sound, and Video Section, National Archives, College Park. For an excellent history of these contradictions, see Phoebe Kropp, *California Vieja: Culture and Memory in a Modern American Place* (Berkeley: University of California Press, 2006).

34. "Testimony of Carey McWilliams, Papers Read in Meeting Held October 8, 1942, Called by Special Mexican Relations Committee of the Los Angeles County Grand Jury," 2, Series 1, box 2, folder 2, Ron Lopez Sleepy Lagoon Research Papers. McWilliams, "Los Angeles' Pachuco Gangs," *New Republic*, January 18, 1943, 76–77; McWilliams, "The Zoot-Suit Riots," *New Republic*, June 21, 1943, 818–20; McWilliams, *North from Mexico*, 241–42. See also Peter Richardson, *American Prophet: The Life and Work of Carey McWilliams* (Ann Arbor: University of Michigan Press, 2005).

35. Alice Greenfield, "The Wearing of the 'Drape' Is No Sign of Delinquency," *Daily World*, May 21, 1945, clipping; "Mexicans called their new home 'Maravilla'—at

First," *Daily World*, n.d., clipping, oversize box 5, Alice Greenfield McGrath Papers (Collection 1490), Department of Special Collections, Charles E. Young Research Library, UCLA.

36. Ruth D. Tuck, "Behind the Zoot Suit Riots," *Survey Graphic* 32 (August 1943): 313–16, 335–36, quotations on 314–15. See also Ruth D. Tuck, *Not with the Fist: Mexican-Americans in a Southwest City* (New York: Harcourt, Brace, 1946).

37. Beatrice Griffith, "In the Flow of Time," *Common Ground* (Autumn 1948), reprinted in Beatrice Griffith, *American Me* (Boston: Houghton Mifflin, 1948), 3–14. See also Griffith, "Who Are the Pachucos?" *Pacific Spectator* 1 (1947): 352.

38. Griffith, *American Me*, 44.

39. Ralph H. Turner and Samuel J. Surace, "Zoot-Suiters and Mexicans: Symbols in Crowd Behavior," *AJS* 62 (July 1956): 14–20; T. W. Adorno et al., *The Authoritarian Personality* (New York: Harper & Row 1950), 106, 142–43, 147; Haldeen Braddy, "The *Pachucos* and Their Argot," *Southern Folklore Quarterly* 24 (December 1960): 259–60. For other postwar studies, see Edward C. McDonagh, "Status Levels of Mexicans," *Sociology and Social Research* 33 (July–August 1949): 447–59; George Carpenter Barker, *Pachuco: An American-Spanish Argot and Its Social Functions in Tucson, Arizona* (1950; Tucson: University of Arizona Press, 1974). See also Martin Roiser and Carla Willig, "The Strange Death of the Authoritarian Personality: 50 Years of Psychological and Political Debate," *History of the Human Sciences* 15 (2002): 71–96.

40. "Dan Burley's Back Door Stuff," *NYAN*, January 25, 1947, 19.

Chapter 6. Zooting Around the World

1. Agnes E. Meyer, "Zoot-Suiters—A New Youth Movement," *WP*, June 13, 1943, B1.

2. Richard Griswold del Castillo, "The Los Angeles 'Zoot Suit Riots' Revisited: Mexican and Latin American Perspectives," *Mexican Studies/Estudios Mexicanos* 16 (Summer 2000): 367–91. For U.S. coverage, see "Pachuco Troubles," *The Inter-American* 2 (August 1943): 5; "Students in Mexico City Shout Zoot Suit Riot Protests," *Chi.Trib.*, June 26, 1943, 6; "Mexicans Hold Little Rancor for Zoot Riots," *Chi.Trib.*, July 1, 1943, 6.

3. Griswold del Castillo, "Los Angeles 'Zoot Suit Riots' Revisited."

4. Octavio Paz, "The Pachuco and Other Extremes," in *The Labyrinth of Solitude: Life and Thought in Mexico*, trans. Lysander Kemp (New York: Grove Press, 1961). Jesús Chavarría, "A Brief Inquiry into Octavio Paz' *Laberinto* of *Mexicanidad*," *The Americas* 27 (April 1971): 381–88 (JSTOR).

5. "Authentic Pachuco," *Time*, July 10, 1944, http://www.time.com/time/magazine/article/0,9171,791506,00.html. Joseph Jones, "Pochismo," *American Speech* 20 (October 1945): 235. Javier Durán, "Nation and Translation: The *Pachuco* in Mexican Popular Culture: Germán Valdéz's Tin Tan," *Journal of the Midwest Modern Language Association* 35: 2 (Autumn 2002): 41–49; Carlos Monsiváis, "Tin Tan: The Pachuco," in *Mexican Postcards*, ed. and trans. John Kraniauskas (London: Verso, 1997), 106–18.

6. "Nombreux blessés dans les bagarres entre 'zoot-suiters,' soldats, marins, policiers," *La Patrie*, June 5, 1944, 7; "Les fabricants de zoot suits seront poursuivis," *La Patrie*, June 6, 1944, 22, Digital Collection, Bibliothèque et Archives Nationales du Québec, http://collections.banq.qc.ca/ark:/52327/1056029#; thanks to Greg Robinson for these articles from Montreal newspapers, and to Heather Murray for translating them. On the riot, see Serge Marc Durflinger, "The Montreal and Verdun Zoot-Suit Disturbances of June 1944: Language Conflict, a Problem of Civil Military Relations, or Youthful Over-Exuberance?" Canadian Museum of Civilization, http://www.civilization.ca/cmc/index_e.aspx?DetailID = 227, originally published in Serge Bernier, ed., *L'impact de la Deuxième Guerre mondiale sur les sociétés canadienne et québécoise*, Université du Québec à Montréal et la Direction Histoire et patrimoine de la Défense nationale, Ottawa, 1998, 7–21. On Vancouver zoot-suiters, see Michael G. Young, "The History of Vancouver Youth Gangs, 1900–1985" (M.A. thesis, Simon Fraser University, 1993), http://ir.lib.sfu.ca/bitstream/1892/7173/1/b15282892.pdf.

7. Harvey R. Neptune, *Caliban and the Yankees: Trinidad and the United States Occupation* (Chapel Hill: University of North Carolina Press, 2007), 105–28. On the Bahamian farmhands, see "42 Farm Hands Flown to Miami from Bahamas," *Chi.Trib.*, April 12, 1943, 10; "Bahamians Arrive," *Life*, April 26, 1943, 24–25. Macha Rosenthal, "Notes on Some Afro-Cuban Translations," *Phylon* 6 (1945): 272.

8. For a superb discussion, see Clive Glaser, *Bo-Tsotsi: The Youth Gangs of Soweto, 1935–1976* (Portsmouth, N.H.: Heinemann, 2000), 37, 47–77. See also Rob Nixon, *Homelands, Harlem and Hollywood: South African Culture and the World Beyond* (New York: Routledge, 1994), 11–41.

9. Glaser, *Bo-Tsotsi*, 51. See also Louis Molamu, *Tsotsi-taal: A Dictionary of the Language of Sophiatown* (Pretoria: University of South Africa, 2003), 22–23; Morley Cassidy, "Zoot Suiters Spark Crime Among African Juveniles," *Philadelphia Evening Bulletin*, May 21, 1953, Zoot Suit folder, George D. McDowell Philadelphia Evening Bulletin News Clipping Collection, Urban Archives, Temple University Libraries.

10. J.N.D. letter, April 7, 1945. 9; Mr. W. N. Nzima, June 17, 1945, 9; Walter M. B. Nhiapo, July 7, 1945, 9, all in "Readers Forum," *Bantu World* (Johannesburg); the series of letters ran from April to July 1945. On the political threat, see Glaser, *Bo-Tsotsi*, 34.

11. Anton Tantner, "Jazz Youth Subcultures in Nazi Europe," in *ISHA Journal: Publication Series of the International Students of History Association* (February 1994): 22–28, http://mailbox.univie.ac.at/Anton.Tantner/publikationen/Tantner_Jazz YouthSubcultures_ISHAJournal1994-2.pdf. Ralph Willett, "Hot Swing and the Dissolute Life: Youth, Style, and Popular Music in Europe, 1939–49," *Popular Music* 8 (May 1989): 157–63; William A. Shack, *Harlem in Montmartre: A Paris Jazz Story between the Great Wars* (Berkeley: University of California Press, 2001); Rodger P. Potocki, Jr., "The Life and Times of Poland's 'Bikini Boys,'" *Polish Review* 39 (1994): 273.

12. Tantner, "Jazz Youth Subcultures"; Michael H. Kater, *Different Drummers: Jazz in the Culture of Nazi Germany* (New York: Oxford University Press, 1992), 101–

10. *L'Oeuvre*, 1942, quoted in Dominique Veillon, *Fashion Under the Occupation* (Oxford: Berg, 2002), 134; see also Jean-Claude Loiseau, *Les Zazous* (Paris: Le Sagittaire, 1977). For Johnny Hess's performance of "Je Suis Swing," see http://www.youtube.com/watch?v=5LF0NxSvnRY. Potocki, "Life and Times of Poland's 'Bikini Boys,'" 284.

13. George Padmore, "Zoot Suits Are All Reet, Old Chap," *Courier*, November 20, 1943, 5; Padmore, "Zoot Suits Converted to Aid Blitzed Britishers," *Defender*, November 20, 1943, 1, 4. Willett, "Hot Swing and the Dissolute Life," 162; Steve Chibnall, "Whistle and Zoot: The Changing Meaning of a Suit of Clothes," *History Workshop Journal* 20 (Autumn 1985): 56–81.

14. "Italian Zoot Suit," *WP*, February 20, 1944, M1.

15. Padmore, "Zoot Suits Are All Reet"; "Clothing for Britain," *NYT*, October 17, 1943, SM 37. Aleksander Wat, *My Century*, quoted in Potocki, "The Life and Times of Poland's 'Bikini Boys,'" 340.

16. Tantner, "Jazz Youth Subcultures in Nazi Europe"; Kater, *Different Drummers*; Jon Savage, *Teenage: The Creation of Youth Culture* (New York: Viking, 2007), 375–90.

17. [No title], *NYT*, June 19, 1942, 4. "Letter from Cannes," *New Yorker*, October 21, 1944, 55. Veillon, *Fashion Under the Occupation*, 134–38; Shack, *Harlem in Montmartre*, 116–23. Loiseau, *Les Zazous*; Savage, *Teenage*, 383–89.

18. Collaborationist quoted in W. D. Halls, *The Youth of Vichy France* (Oxford: Clarendon Press, 1981), 178. "Parisian Zoot Suiters Sent to Nazi Labor Camps," *Chi.Trib.*, April 10, 1944, 1. For an excellent discussion of the *zazous*' protests, see Sophie B. Roberts, "A Case for Dissidence in Occupied Paris: The Zazous, Youth Dissidence and the Yellow Star Campaign in Occupied Paris (1942)," *French History* 24, no. 1 (June 2010): 82–103 (fh.oxfordjournals.org, accessed August 21, 2010).

19. Andrex, "Y'a des Zazous," words and music by Raymond Vincy and H. Martinet (Paris: Éditions Réunies, 1943), sheet music in author's possession; "Jitterbug Craze Hits France as Allies Near Paris," *ADW*, August 20, 1944, 1. See also Shack, *Harlem in Montmartre*, 123; Larry Portis, *French Frenzies: A Social History of Pop Music in France* (College Station, Tex.: Virtualbookworm.com, 2004), 104–5.

20. See Chibnall's excellent discussion in "Whistle and Zoot," 63–71.

21. Peter D. Whitney, "Commons Demands Police Curbs on Hoodlum 'Edwardian' Bands," *NYT*, May 7, 1954, 6. See also Whitney, "Britain's Zoot Suiters—The Edwardians," *NYT*, June 6, 1954, SM 17, 53–55; George Sokolsky, "These Days," *WP*, May 26, 1955, 17; "Edwardians and Their Crimes," *Chi.Trib.*, November 15, 1954, 5. On British youth styles of the 1950s, see T. R. Fyvel, "Fashion and Revolt" [1963], in *The Subcultures Reader*, ed. Ken Gelder and Sarah Thornton (London: Routledge, 1997), 388–92; Stuart Hall and Tony Jefferson, eds., *Resistance Through Rituals* (London: Hutchinson, 1976); Dick Hebdige, *Subculture: The Meaning of Style* (London: Methuen, 1979).

22. James Laver, "The New Edwardians," *Punch*, February 25, 1953, 269; "A Touch of Colour," *Punch*, April 22, 1953, 487.

23. Chibnall, "Whistle and Zoot," 70.

24. S. Frederick Starr, *Red and Hot: The Fate of Jazz in the Soviet Union, 1917–1991* (1983; New York: Limelight Editions, 1994), 235–43. See also Kristen Joy Roth-Ey, "Mass Media and the Remaking of Soviet Culture, 1950s–1960s" (Ph.D. diss., Princeton University, 2003), for a discussion of trophy films (106–16) and *stiliagi* (46–98).

25. Mark Edele, "Strange Young Men in Stalin's Moscow: The Birth and Life of the Stiliagi, 1945–1953," *Jahrbücher für Geschichte Osteuropas* 50 (2002): 37–61. Juliane Fürst, "The Arrival of Spring? Changes and Continuities in Soviet Youth Culture and Policy Between Stalin and Khrushchev," in *The Dilemmas of De-Stalinization: Negotiating Cultural and Social Change in the Khrushchev Era*, ed. Polly Jones (New York: Routledge, 2006), 135–53.

26. D. Belyaev, "Stilyaga," *Krokodil*, March 10, 1949, in *Mass Culture in Soviet Russia*, ed. James von Geldern and Richard Stites (Bloomington: Indiana University Press, 1995), 450–53.

27. Harrison E. Salisbury, "Man, Dig That Stilyag!" *NYT*, January 11, 1953, SM 18; Edele, "Strange Young Men in Stalin's Moscow," 39, 41; "Russians Bare Wild Parties by 'Stylyagi,'" *Chi.Trib.*, January 20, 1953, 3; Jack Raymond, "Leningrad Curbs Zealots of Jazz," *NYT*, April 1, 1956, 15. There was extensive American press coverage of *stiliagi* as a version of the zoot suiter. See also Albert Parry, "The Zoot-Suit Youth Worries the Soviets," *Georgia Review* 7 (Winter 1953): 450–54; "Gorki St. 'Zoot Suiters,'" *Newsweek* 45 (January 3, 1955): 25–26; "Zoot-Suiters in Moscow," *Time*, November 3, 1958, 23–24.

28. Susan E. Reid, "Modernizing Socialist Realism in the Khrushchev Thaw," in *The Dilemmas of De-Stalinization*, ed. Jones, 215; Fürst, "Arrival of Spring?" 139. Mary Catherine French, "Chasing Postwar Soviet Youth: Soviet Styles and Sex Anxiety" (unpublished seminar paper, May 12, 2008, in author's possession).

29. James von Geldern, "Introduction," in *Mass Culture in Soviet Russia*, ed. von Geldern and Stites, xxv–xxvi. The social composition of *stiliagi* is a matter of debate among historians; Fürst, in "Arrival of Spring?" argues for a strong working-class presence. On Soviet youth and oppositional politics, see Juliane Fürst, "Prisoners of the Soviet Self? Political Youth Opposition in Late Stalinism," *Europe-Asia Studies* 54 (2002): 353–75, especially 368.

30. Salisbury, "Man, Dig That Stilyag!"; Fürst "Arrival of Spring?" 144; "Gently, Tovarishchi," *NYT*, October 6, 1958, 4; "Soviet Zoot-Suiter Apes Western Type," *NYT*, May 8, 1955, 14; Raymond, "Leningrad Curbs Zealots of Jazz." Miriam Dobson, "'Show the Bandit-Enemy No Mercy': Amnesty, Criminality and Public Response in 1953," in *Dilemmas of De-Stalinization*, ed. Jones, 21–40; Elena Zubkova, *Russia After the War: Hopes, Illusions and Disappointments, 1945–57*, trans. and ed. Hugh Ragsdale (Armonk, N.Y.: M. E. Sharpe, 1998), 192–93.

31. Ferenc Hammer, "Blue Jeans in Socialist Hungary," 7, paper for the Citizenship and Consumption: Agency, Norms, Mediations, and Spaces conference, Cambridge, 2006; see also "Sartorial Manoeuvres in the Dusk: Blue Jeans in Socialist

Hungary," in *Citizenship and Consumption*, ed. Kate Soper and Frank Trentmann (New York: Palgrave Macmillan, 2008), 51–68. Sándor Horváth, "Patchwork Identities and Folk Devils: Youth Subcultures and Gangs in Socialist Hungary," *Social History* 34 (2009): 163–83, doi: 10.1080/03071020902879598. Karl Brown, "Stalinization and Its Discontents: Subcultures and Opposition in Hungary, 1948–1956," Fulbright Student Conference Papers, I. Reports of U.S. Grantees. Fulbright Commission, Budapest 2004, 149–59, http://www.fulbright.hu/book1/karlbrown.pdf.

32. Potocki, "The Life and Times of Poland's 'Bikini Boys,'" offers an excellent analysis of the circulation of garments and their reinterpretation; quotation on 267. See also Maciej Chlopek, *Bikiniarze: Pierwsza Polska Subkultura* (Warsaw: Żak Akademickie, 2005); I am grateful to Matthew Kolasa for translating this text.

33. Thomas Harris, "Hatred of Russ Grows in Poland," *LAT*, January 4, 1953, 16. On Tyrmand, see Potocki, "Life and Times of Poland's 'Bikini Boys,'" 262. I am grateful to Jelena Milojković-Djurić for information about Yugoslavian youth, October 26, 2001 email; see also Milojković-Djurić, "Voice from the Darkness: Borislav Pekić's *The Years the Locusts Devoured*," *Serbian Studies: Journal of the North American Society for Serbian Studies* 15 (2001): 57.

34. "Barbaric Culture," *Time*, October 23, 1950, www.time.com/time/magazine/article/0,9171,813599,00.html. Karl Brown, "Stalinization and Its Discontents." See also George May, "Behind the Curtain in Hungary," *NYT*, March 15, 1953, SM10, 33, 35; Harris, "Hatred of Russ Grows in Poland"; "The 'Hooligan' Problem in Hungary," February 24, 1961, Report 182, Radio Free Europe Background Reports on Hungary, 1954–89, Open Society Archives, http://www.osaarchivum.org/files/holdings/300/8/3/text/31-2-182.shtml.

35. "Operator was podpatrzyl" ("The cameraman filmed while you were not looking"), Polska Kronika Filmowa, WFDiF (Wytwórnia Filmów Dokumentalnych i Fabularnych), http://www.youtube.com/watch?v = Ys7ywCbpZlY. My thanks to Matthew Kolasa for his translation of the Polish narration and information about the film.

36. John MacCormac, "Reds Crack Down on 'Hooliganism,'" *NYT*, April 18, 1954, 30. For an insightful analysis of Soviet media, see Roth-Ey, "Mass Media and the Remaking of Soviet Culture."

Aftermath

1. Dan Burley, "Back Door Stuff," *NYAN*, April 27, 1946, 19; "Manners and Morals: The Drapes," *Time*, January 30, 1950, http://www.time.com/time/magazine/article/0,9171,856482,00.html; "Zoot Suits Are Out for Men," *ADW*, September 29, 1950, 4.

2. William Graebner, *Coming of Age in Buffalo: Youth and Authority in the Postwar Era* (Philadelphia: Temple University Press, 1990), 42–45; Rudolph Elie, "High School Set's New High Style," *Life*, January 25, 1954, 133–40.

3. Brenda Jo Bright, "Remappings: Los Angeles Low Riders," in *Looking High and*

Low: Art and Cultural Identity, ed. Bright and Liza Bakemore (Tucson: University of Arizona Press, 1995), 103. George Carpenter Barker, *Pachuco: An American-Spanish Argot and Its Social Functions in Tucson, Arizona* (1950; Tucson: University of Arizona Press, 1974), 23–24, 28. George Lipsitz discusses these postwar cultural developments in "Cruising Around the Historical Bloc: Postmodernism and Popular Music in East Los Angeles," in *Time Passages: Collective Memory and American Popular Culture* (Minneapolis: University of Minnesota Press, 1990), 133–60. See also Lalo Guerrero and Sherilyn Meece Metes, *Lalo: My Life and Music* (Tucson: University of Arizona Press, 2002).

4. Bright, "Remappings," 111–12, 103. See also James Sterngold, "Making the Jalopy an Ethnic Banner: How the Lowrider Evolved from Chicano Revolt to Art Form," *NYT*, February 19, 2000, B9, 11.

5. Patrick Boyle, "'Lowriding'—Zoot-Suit Life of '70s," *LAT*, September 14, 1979, A6. Shifra M. Goldman, "The Iconography of Chicano Self-Determination: Race, Ethnicity, and Class," *Art Journal* 49 (Summer 1990): 167–73; Dorie S. Goldman, "'Down for La Raza': Barrio Art T-Shirts, Chicano Pride, and Cultural Resistance," *Journal of Folklore Research* 34 (May–August 1997): 123–38; Juan Flores and George Yudice, "Living Borders/Buscando America: Languages of Latino Self-Formation," *Social Text* 24 (1990): 57–84; Dan Luckenbill, *The Pachuco Era; Catalog of an Exhibit* (Department of Special Collections, University Research Library, UCLA, 1990). Michael Soldatenko, *Chicano Studies: The Genesis of a Discipline* (Tucson: University of Arizona Press, 2009).

6. Yolanda Broyles-Gonzalez, *El Teatro Campesino: Theater in the Chicano Movement* (Austin: University of Texas Press, 1994), 165–214; Luis Valdez, *Zoot Suit and Other Plays* (Houston: Arte Publico Press, 1992), 25; see also Jorge Huerta's introduction, 7–20.

7. Earl C. Gottschalk, Jr., "'Zoot Suit' and Pride Are Opening on Broadway," *WSJ*, March 23, 1979, 19. Dennis McLellan, "Manuel Reyes, 1925–2008," *LAT*, March 7, 2008, B8.

8. For Garcia's critique, see Gottschalk, "'Zoot Suit' and Pride"; Howard Reich, "'Zoot Suit': True Story of a Riot in a Unique Stage Play on Film," *Chi.Trib.*, January 24, 1982, E12. Richard Griswold del Castillo, Teresa McKenna, and Yvonne Yarbro-Bejarano, eds., *Chicano Art: Resistance and Affirmation, 1965–1985* (Los Angeles: Wight Art Gallery, University of California, 1991); for an excellent discussion of this exhibit, see Alicia Gaspar de Alba, *Chicano Art Inside/Outside the Master's House: Cultural Politics and the CARA Exhibition* (Austin: University of Texas Press, 1998), especially 62–68. For feminist perspectives, see Rose Linda Fregoso, "The Representation of Cultural Identity in 'Zoot Suit,'" *Theory and Society* 22 (October 1993): 659–74; Simon Webb, "Masculinities at the Margins: Representations of the Melandro and the Pachuco," in *Imagination Beyond Nation: Latin American Popular Culture*, ed. Eva P. Bueno and Terry Caesar (Pittsburgh: University of Pittsburgh Press, 1998), 227–64.

9. Anemona Hartocollis, "Showing Style with Black and Gold, Or Giving Cause for Arrest?" *NYT,* June 18, 2007, B1–2.

10. On Siegel's, see Heather Maddan, "Zooting Up: Brighten Prom Night with Flash, Dash–and Panache," *San Francisco Chronicle*, April 29, 2007, http://articles.sfgate .com/2007-04-29/living/17239922_1_first-zoot-prom-dress.

INDEX

Page numbers in italics indicate photographs and illustrations.

ACKNOWLEDGMENTS

When I was a faculty member at the University of Massachusetts, I had the opportunity to participate in a method of teaching called "Inductive Approaches to History," which explored vivid public controversies, used only primary sources, and taught students how to conduct historical research and analysis. The 1943 zoot suit riot seemed a fitting topic in a pedagogical tradition whose topics included the Salem witchcraft trials, the Lizzie Borden ax murders, the Beecher-Tilton affair, and the Black Sox scandal. While developing the course, I became a member of an innovative seminar intended to teach senior faculty how to use instructional technology. Developing a website allowed me the opportunity to explore a wide range of audiovisual material, and to ponder the relationship between aesthetics and politics on the home front. These pedagogical experiences stuck with me long after I taught the course, and indeed laid the groundwork for this project. I am grateful to the University of Massachusetts History Department, the Center for Teaching, and members of the Teachnology faculty seminar, led by Mei Shih, for their support and inspiration; thanks are also due James Kelly, Doris Peterson, Fred Zinn, the UMass Library's Interlibrary Loan staff, and the UMass Provost's Office.

I owe a special debt to Laura Abato-Paulus, who did extensive primary research for me in Los Angeles, and to the staffs of two libraries at UCLA, the Charles E. Young Research Library and the Chicano Studies

Research Library, for their assistance to her. At the University of Pennsylvania, I had excellent research assistance from Olga Gorodetsky and Aro Velmet; research librarian Nick Okrent and the Interlibrary Loan office have been unfailingly helpful. Thanks also go to Rita Barnard, Erin Park Cohn, Susan Delson, Mary Catherine French, Kim Gallon, Janine Giordano, David Glassberg, Rob Goldberg, Beth Hillman, Peter Holquist, Sarah Igo, Phoebe Kropp, Heather Murray, Elizabeth Pleck, Greg Robinson, Barbara Savage, Nick Spitzer, Kristen Stromberg-Childers, and Johnny Vardeman for references, information, and leads. Heather Murray and Matthew Kolasa translated several key texts. I have benefited from the responses and suggestions of faculty and students in presentations to the Montreal History Group, Texas A&M University Humanities Center, the University of Illinois Miller Com Lecture Series, Monmouth University, the University of Pennsylvania's Provost's Lecture Series, and in seminars at the University of Massachusetts and University of Pennsylvania. I especially appreciate the careful readings of the entire manuscript by Rob Goldberg, Daniel Horowitz, Bruce Kuklick, Heather Murray, and Susan Strasser; Carlo Rotella's review for the University of Pennsylvania Press provided excellent guidance as I completed revisions. Numerous conversations with Roger Abrahams, as well as his inspiring scholarship, shaped my thinking about extreme style. My editor, Robert Lockhart, offered an astute reading and advice that improved the final manuscript. I thank Mariellen Smith for securing permissions, and Mindy Brown, Noreen O'Connor-Abel, and Julia Rose Roberts for their superb work in the editing and production process. My husband, Peter Agree, encouraged me to write this work and has lived with drape shapes and reet pleats for many years now; he has pushed me to develop the larger argument and blue penciled every line. For this and everything else, I am grateful to him beyond measure.